"*Growing Women in Ministry* is a courageous analysis of the reality most female leaders face when developing their ministry leadership. With meticulous research and a deep understanding of organizational and cultural barriers, Anna Morgan offers an egalitarian perspective that is both practical and insightful regardless of one's ministry context. Through a beautifully articulated model, Morgan sheds light on the unique challenges faced by female leaders in ministry. From tackling the hot topic of single female leadership to navigating the complexities of sexual attraction between genders in leadership roles, this book takes a bold and comprehensive approach. Whether you're a seasoned leader or a leader just starting out, this book is a valuable resource for empowering the leadership potential in women throughout the kingdom."

—**Kadi Cole**, executive coach, leadership consultant, author of *Developing Female Leaders*, kadicole.com

"Morgan has written a masterful work that is both reflective and instructive. Drawing on her own life and leadership, Anna provides insightful scholarship, biblical teaching, and practical application for the development of women leaders. This book is a must-read for both men and women who care deeply about developing women as leaders."

—**Joy E. A. Qualls**, Biola University

"Morgan integrates the real-life insights of an experienced leader with the disciplined study of leadership development. Morgan's examination of critical issues identifies seven key areas for forming women as leaders. Building on the lifelong learning platform, Morgan skillfully develops a process based on extensive research on women leaders. *Growing Women in Ministry* is a book worthy of careful study by a leadership team and worthy of broad implementation."

—**Douglas McConnell**, Fuller Theological Seminary

"In the church, a systematic treatment of women's leadership formation is long overdue. Thankfully *Growing Women in Ministry* has closed that gap. Offering a holistic, seven-aspect model for development, one that takes seriously both internal and external factors, this book provides a comprehensive road map for helping women become all that God wants them to be. I can't wait to share copies of *Growing Women in Ministry* not only with the women in my networks but also with their male supervisors, mentors, and colleagues."

—**Rob Dixon**, InterVarsity Institute; author of *Together in Ministry*

"Morgan champions a holistic pathway for shaping women leaders. Based on solid research, *Growing Women in Ministry* provides female-specific training that is both practical and inspiring. Importantly, it envisions women as full partners with men in building the church and continuing the mission of Christ."

—**Jacqueline Grey**, Alphacrucis University College

"*Growing Women in Ministry* is a powerful resource for women called to serve, for men who work alongside them, and for the institutions that call and train them. Morgan offers practical guidance, tackles tough challenges, and celebrates the distinctive gifts women bring to ministry. This work also addresses the needs going unmet in leadership education, a system designed by men for men, and it does so without becoming polemical."

—**R. Robert Creech**, Baylor University (retired)

GROWING WOMEN
IN MINISTRY

GROWING WOMEN IN MINISTRY

SEVEN ASPECTS OF LEADERSHIP DEVELOPMENT

ANNA R. MORGAN

Baker Academic

a division of Baker Publishing Group
Grand Rapids, Michigan

Published by Baker Academic
a division of Baker Publishing Group
Grand Rapids, Michigan
BakerAcademic.com

Printed in the United States of America

Library of Congress Cataloging-in-Publication Data
Names: Morgan, Anna R., 1978– author.
Title: Growing women in ministry : seven aspects of leadership development / Anna R. Morgan.
Description: Grand Rapids, Michigan : Baker Academic, a division of Baker Publishing Group,
    [2024] | Includes bibliographical references and index.
Identifiers: LCCN 2024006111 | ISBN 9781540967190 (paperback) | ISBN 9781540967794
    (casebound) | ISBN 9781493446179 (ebook) | ISBN 9781493446186 (pdf)
Subjects: LCSH: Women in church work. | Leadership in women. | Christian leadership.
Classification: LCC BV4415 .M67 2024 | DDC 253.082—dc23/eng/20240408
LC record available at https://lccn.loc.gov/2024006111

Cover design by Laura Powell

Baker Publishing Group publications use paper produced from sustainable forestry practices and postconsumer waste whenever possible.

24 25 26 27 28 29 30   7 6 5 4 3 2 1

To my deeply loved partner in life and ministry,
my husband, John Morgan

CONTENTS

FIGURES

TABLES

ACKNOWLEDGMENTS

Thank you, Anna Gissing. You took a risk on me and made this book better. Thank you, Baker Academic editorial team, for your dedication and attention to detail.

Thank you, Bronwyn Lea, for a life-changing introduction.

Thank you, Betsy Glanville and Donna Downes, for mentoring me through this research. This book would not exist without your investment. Thank you to every woman who participated in this research, giving your time and your vulnerability so that other women can become the influential leaders God designed them to be. Thank you, Magnify Cohort, for walking the doctoral research journey with me and encouraging me.

Thank you, Wilmer Villacorta, for always advocating for women and particularly for your guidance and sponsorship of me. Thank you, Rob Rhoden, for dreaming with me about doing church in a way in which emerging women leaders thrive.

Thank you, Kent and Alli Munsey, for being dear friends and pastors and for giving me the opportunity for years of ministry leadership partnered with you. Thank you, Steve and Melodye Munsey, for being spiritual parents and being so present when I needed you most. Thank you for believing in me when I didn't believe in myself. Thank you, Scott and Jamie Gurulé and Stephen and Cindy Kenny, for guiding my earliest ministry formation.

Thank you to the ministry leadership teams at Word of Life Church, City Church Chicago, and Family Christian Center. It's been an honor to lead alongside you. Thank you, Word of Life Church and City Church Chicago, for your prayers and your love.

Thank you, Mom and Dad, for your steadfast love for Jesus, your faithfulness to his call in your lives, and for the immeasurable investment you have made in my life. Words fail to communicate the depth of my gratitude to you. Thank you to Sharayah, Chloé, Greg, Brooke, Marcus, Luca, and Kai. You have been patient through my years of study and writing and have cheered me on—I love you to the moon, family!

Thank you to John Morgan. From the very beginning, you viewed my ministry leadership calling as your responsibility to steward as much as your own. I am more emotionally healthy, wiser, more skilled, and have greater eternal rewards because of the enormity of what you have poured into me. I am so grateful, and I respect the man you are so deeply. It is a privilege to walk alongside you in life and ministry.

INTRODUCTION

For we are God's masterpiece. He has created us anew in Christ Jesus, so we can do the good things he planned for us long ago.

Ephesians 2:10 NLT

As a young girl, I did not dream about becoming a leader. Nonetheless, here I am today, a woman and a pastor. I don't see myself as a crusader for feminism, even though I agree with aspects of feminism. I'm more an advocate for women than an activist. I'm also not anti-men, and this book is not about blaming or shaming men because women have been oppressed—even though this should not have happened. My paradigm is that leadership is not a finite resource. It can be created, perhaps infinitely. This means that leadership is not a zero-sum game and that for women to gain power, men do not have to lose it. This idea is important for both men and women, because it means that the rising leadership of women is not a threat to men and that the rising leadership of men does not have to be a threat to women. This book is also not an egalitarian theological treatise defending women leaders in the church, even though egalitarian theology is vital and foundational to this book.

This book has a different purpose, purely focused on raising female ministry leaders. I aim to provide language and imagery to describe the development processes shaping women who lead in local church ministry and how their influence and authority are formed. This book looks beyond the debates that have mired the gender conversation and into places where women are welcomed into ministry leadership to explain just how female leaders have been gaining significant influence and authority in their ministry contexts.

I wish I had this book two decades ago, when I was a young female pastor. I became a leader by default, really. I never submitted a résumé to receive the leadership opportunities I've been given or had to campaign to make my voice heard. I wound up leading as a pastor in the church because God gifted me and called me to it, and I said yes, like so many other women leaders. I was deeply compelled to be obedient, and because I said yes, God sovereignly shaped my life.

I grew up in a loving, middle-class, Pentecostal Christian home. My parents wove the strength of our family's interconnection with faith. We were in church together at least twice a week, read Bible stories together before bed, prayed together before meals. Our family life was embedded in church life. By the time I was a teenager, I passionately loved Jesus, and I felt called to ministry. I was aware of the female founder of our Foursquare movement, Amy Semple McPherson, but few women were preaching. Some women were leading worship in our local church. I thought of myself as a quiet, behind-the-scenes person, but I deeply wanted God to use my life for his purposes. I was musical, and so I began to play the piano in church, as I saw women doing in my environment. My ideas about who I could become were influenced by what I saw women doing in my church.

When I was a teenager, I met Richard Bourke. He was charismatic, handsome, funny, and gifted—the center of every room he walked into. He shared my passion for Jesus and for local church ministry. Rich drew me out of my natural reserve, so we fit well together. We quickly fell in love and dreamed about what God would do in our future. At twenty-one, I married Rich, and a month later we moved to Chicago to be youth pastors at a nondenominational megachurch.

Things couldn't have gone better. Teenagers were coming in droves, encountering Jesus. Rich was preaching, and I was running the ministry from behind the scenes, supporting him. I believed this was how I would fulfill God's call on my life—by making Rich as fruitful as possible in ministry. And it was working. It wasn't long until the senior pastors of our church recognized my administrative and musical gifts. Eighteen months after we arrived, they invited me to lead the worship ministry of our church. This was not a small task, since it involved leading multiple music teams and choirs—hundreds of volunteers. I was concerned that taking on this role would hamper my ability to support my husband's call. I told them I would do it for six months until they could find someone else (twelve years later, I was still a worship pastor).

Our lives were going so well, but it didn't last. In 2001 we took a road trip East to celebrate two years of marriage. Returning home, we decided to drive through the night to make it to the youth meeting. Early in the morning, I awoke to our car rolling over. When the car came to a stop and I opened my eyes, Rich was gone. He had been thrown from the car and had died instantly.

In that moment, every plan and dream I had for my family, career, and ministry future also died. I was whisked off to the hospital, where they checked me over and found no serious injuries. My body healed in a few weeks, but my grief lasted much longer.

In the months that followed, I took stock of my circumstances. What next? I chose to keep going in ministry as a single, twenty-three-year-old woman, a worship pastor leading in a megachurch.

Everything was different. I had to set direction for the ministry and make hard decisions without Rich's leadership. I had to have challenging conversations to convince people about the right way forward that I had previously deferred to my husband. Earning the respect of men twice my age and women with twice my ability wasn't easy. I felt like I was in a fishbowl with everyone's eyes on me, and I had very little idea what I was doing. I was alone, and I didn't know any women, much less women my age, who were leading something on the scale that I was. The male pastors I met seemed very cautious to engage me. The ministry networks where I could find answers to my questions were essentially closed to me, and so I had to figure out most things by trial and error. I had women who were spiritual mentors to me but no woman who was a leadership coach to help me grow. I thank God for the handful of male pastors in my life (youth pastor, worship pastor, and senior pastor) who recognized potential in me and trained me in ministry leadership. But outside my local church, collegial relationships with male pastors seemed to be impossible.

Despite the difficulties I faced, my leadership skills grew, and as they did I encountered leadership opportunities. A few years later I was promoted to the executive leadership team of our church. It wasn't until a decade later that I recognized how God had used that season of singleness in widowhood to form my leadership.

As I healed, God brought another strong, funny, charismatic youth pastor into my life. Five years later, when I married my Aussie husband, John Morgan, we came to the relationship as leadership equals. We both had experience leading in an executive role. We led in different lanes, and neither of us was exclusively the support person for the other. We supported each other. When I had late rehearsals at church, he watched the kids. When he had late church meetings, I watched the kids.

I continued in ministry as an executive pastor and invested in emerging young women leaders in our egalitarian church. These women asked me thoughtful and sometimes tearful questions about their leadership that I struggled to answer. Why was this journey of ministry leadership so hard? Why were the challenges different for women compared to men? I realized that my experience as a young woman leader was not isolated. Other young women leaders had struggles similar to mine and different from male leaders' struggles. Leadership is hard work for men and women alike, but it seemed that men's experiences were not the same. Even in our environment, where a man and a woman co-pastored and we had equal numbers of women and men elders and more women than men on our executive leadership team, women leaders did not always thrive. I looked for books, articles, anything to help me understand these dynamics, but they just didn't exist. I recognized a significant gap in the leadership literature pertaining to women. The conversation seemed to be bogged down in theological debate. The literature couldn't even get past the starting gate to talk about the real issues that were impacting women in ministry.

I began a master's degree at Fuller Theological Seminary, and as I processed my own journey, I became convinced that we needed more research to understand female leadership development in local churches. I wanted to understand how female leaders were formed and how they became influential. How could women become the kinds of leaders they felt called by God to be? Just how different are men and women, and how do their differences impact their spiritual leadership formation? And the biggest question of all: How could I help women navigate their own development and emerge with the leadership influence they were called to? I wanted to help young women, to make it easier for them than it had been for me. My intense need to understand these issues drove me into a doctoral study of female leaders in egalitarian churches.

The easy answer that many have reached over the centuries is that it's hard for women to lead because they are less suited to leadership than men. Hundreds of studies have examined the differences between men and women, both biological (hardware) and sociological (software). Patriarchists and complementarians have used these studies as fuel for their arguments that men and women are suited for different roles and that women shouldn't lead.[1] In this line of thinking, leadership is considered *unfeminine* or even ungodly for women.[2]

Because complementarians and patriarchists have used gender differences to argue that women are innately not suited for leadership, egalitarian leaders and feminists typically minimize the social and biological differences between male and female leaders.[3] As a result, men and women typically receive identical leadership training and supports in egalitarian environments.

1. Van Leeuwen, "Opposite Sexes or Neighboring Sexes?," 184.
2. Lederleitner, *Women in God's Mission*, 166; Howell, *Buried Talents*, 45.
3. Eagly and Johannesen-Schmidt, "Leadership Styles of Women and Men," 782; Kay and Shipman, "Confidence Gap"; Tannen, *You Just Don't Understand*, 17.

This approach, however, has not resulted in equal outcomes for male and female leaders—in numbers or in influence or authority. Even though we have seen an increase in the number of ordained women over the past thirty years, fewer women than men are in Protestant vocational ministry, and fewer yet serve in non-mainline churches.[4] Within my own egalitarian environment, the Assemblies of God, less than 28 percent of ordained ministers are women. While this number is trending upward, only 6 percent of Assemblies of God churches in America are led by women.[5] Far fewer women are in a paid staff role than the number of women who are credentialed as ministers in the Assemblies of God.[6] This is a movement that fully endorses and values women preaching and leading in ministry. Something is creating an invisible barrier for women in church leadership. As a result, many of the gifted and most influential female ministry leaders of our generation—women like Christine Caine and Joyce Meyer—are not using their leadership gifts to pastor local churches. Instead, they are building parachurch ministries.

Even in egalitarian environments, emerging women leaders face a dearth of female leader role models, leadership mentors, and peers. They deal with social pressures that discourage leadership behaviors and practical and theological expectations for home life that can limit their availability. A female ministry leader's journey to developing power is unique, but even in the best environments she receives the same supports as her male counterparts, supports designed for men. In many more ministry environments, she receives fewer supports.

Scholar and linguist Deborah Tannen notes, "Pretending that women and men are the same hurts women, because the ways they are treated are based on the norms for men."[7] Because their egalitarian theological position welcomes women into leadership, egalitarian male leaders often do not recognize the problem revealed by a disparity in outcomes.[8] If approaching male and female leadership development identically has not produced identical results for each gender, then it stands to reason that we must reconsider how we develop women who are gifted and called to lead in the church. Before we begin to correct the inequity by creating training and supports designed for female ministry leaders, we need to understand how women leaders and their authority are formed. This book describes my research to discover the

4. Briggs, "Barna Study."
5. McClellan, "Assemblies of God Ordains Record Number of Women."
6. See Crabtree, "Women Ministers in the Assemblies of God" and Roncone et al., *Female Lead Pastors*.
7. Tannen, *You Just Don't Understand*, 16.
8. Catford, "Women's Experiences," loc. 689 of 8092, Kindle.

development processes and factors that support the emergence of female ministry leaders in theologically egalitarian environments. It presents a holistic model for understanding women's leadership development in local churches. I view leadership development as a lifelong process and build on the work of leadership scholar J. Robert Clinton and his leadership emergence theory. Women face unique obstacles to developing leadership authority, and so developing women for leadership requires awareness of these challenges and strategies for moving beyond them.

Chapter 1 introduces leadership development for women in ministry and egalitarian theology. Cultural changes in the past century have changed the missional landscape in the West, making women leaders essential coparticipants in mission for effective contextualization of the gospel. Chapter 2 presents a holistic model of female leadership development called the Seven Processes of Female Leadership Development.

The following chapters examine each aspect of development in detail. Chapter 3 describes how female leaders process their calling and the journey of spiritual formation. Chapter 4 examines the identity work that women leaders undertake and barriers to developing patterns of leadership thinking. Chapter 5 explores the emotional work involved in female leadership development as women develop self-awareness, process criticism, learn self-regulation, develop inner motivation, embrace authenticity, and develop empathy. Chapter 6 describes the impact of domestic life on female ministry leaders and how the responsibilities a woman faces at home—whether a wife, single, or a mother—shape her ministry leadership. Chapter 7 presents the hindrances a woman deals with in her ministry leadership environment, the kind of culture that allows women leaders to thrive, and the importance of opportunities and sponsorship for women leaders. Chapter 8 shows how women leaders form influence through developing various types of relationships. Chapter 9 continues the discussion by explaining the difficulties women face when navigating mixed-gender ministry partnerships. Chapter 10 describes how women leaders form influence through communication. A woman often faces unrecognized societal expectations that govern how she speaks and engages others, creating an impediment to successfully moving people forward.

Chapter 11 provides a long-term perspective on female leadership development by explaining three distinct phases of influence development for women. Chapter 12 provides recommendations to individuals and institutions for supporting female leadership development. The appendixes include group discussion questions, the study's data collection instruments, demographic data about study participants, and further detail of the study's methodology.

This book considers the leadership development of Christian women, but space precludes an examination of how leadership development varies based on the race or ethnicity of the woman leader. It also does not examine issues of sexual orientation or the experiences of trans women in ministry leadership. I come to this research as a female Pentecostal and evangelical scholar and pastor ordained in the Australian Christian Churches.

I was compelled to write this book because of my experiences as a female pastor. Despite the Western church's slow pace developing women leaders, Western culture is increasingly producing women leaders in business, the academy, entertainment, medicine, and government. If we do not provide leadership development opportunities for gifted young Christian women inside our local churches, then they may well pursue leadership opportunities outside the church, thus weakening it.[9] The kingdom of God will suffer from these God-given gifts for leadership being redirected into secular endeavors. Contextualizing the gospel for the emerging generation of female leaders in the West means helping women identify their leadership calling, supporting the formation of their God-given leadership gifts, and pointing that leadership toward kingdom causes. My prayer is that this book contributes to the full flourishing of women called into ministry leadership so that they can obey God and fully realize what he has planned for them.

9. Glanville, "Leadership Development for Women," 262.

1

LEADERSHIP DEVELOPMENT FOR WOMEN IN MINISTRY

Several years ago my friend and colleague Laura called me for advice. "Hey! Do you have a minute to talk?" She paused and chuckled awkwardly. Laura was a creative pastor at a large local church. She managed a team of three young women and three young men leading various departments of the church. She explained that while the men on her team rarely asked for her help to resolve interpersonal or emotional issues, the young women leaders on her team were struggling and leaning heavily on her for support. They were encumbered with insecurities that bled into their conversations, heightened emotions and fragility, and led to unresolved tensions that hindered their leadership. These women loved Jesus passionately and were very gifted, capable, and technically skilled in their work, but leading them into the kind of influence they needed was an ongoing challenge. Laura asked me, "Why is it that the guys on the team need little help but the women continually seem to struggle in their leadership?" She wanted guidance. What was she doing wrong as their leader? How could she help these young women leaders thrive?

Laura is an all-star leader. She is remarkably capable, great with people, effective, articulate, easy to respect, and intelligent. Most of the other executive staff members in her church are women, as are half of the board members. Women regularly preach on Sundays at this church, both female pastors from within the church and female guest speakers from other places. And yet the young women on her team were not thriving, creating a weight for Laura and a reason to doubt her own leadership. As we chatted that day, I wondered, *Why does some women's leadership development seem stunted while other women leaders flourish in the same empowering environment? And why do women leaders deal with challenges that don't seem to impact male leaders in the same way?* The answer to these questions is not simple.

These young women were as skilled in leadership as their male peers, but they were facing dynamics that their male teammates simply did not have to deal with. This church's organizational culture placed great value on successful outcomes and exceptional performance. The slim financial margins meant that staffing dollars had to be maximized, so staff members who could multiply their work by motivating volunteers were highly prized. Attracting and keeping volunteers required more than a position or a title, however. What often was overlooked was the slow work of building leadership trust with people. This is where influence begins. Skills and experience come slowly, and this slow pace is compounded by a distrust for leadership that pervades Western culture. Leadership influence cannot be microwaved or demanded. The young women on Laura's team were also single in a church culture that valued and promoted married women, like Laura. This created an unrecognized second-class tier of leaders where talented single women leaders got stuck and disheartened. These women faced a lack of respect from others because they were unmarried, and they underperformed in leadership because they could not attract and keep volunteers due to their second-class status. In an environment that emphasized immediate results, these women struggled with insecurity, frustration, and anxiety.

A few exceptional churches are effectively developing female leaders for local church ministry roles—even if imperfectly. Many female leaders in these churches are thriving, and leadership pipelines are moving influential women into formal, significant leadership roles. These women are not just in behind-the-scenes roles. They are writing, preaching, managing, and leading executive teams. By taking a step back to see the big picture of what is happening in and around the emergence of these successful women leaders, we can begin to understand what is happening in teams like Laura's. The way forward doesn't presume that a lack of talent or calling must be the cause for the languishing of women leaders in ministry contexts. We must look deeper at the unrecognized dynamics within teams and the unmet needs of their women leaders.

If I could sit down with Laura and pick up that conversation from so many years ago, I would respond with more than sympathy. To provide the right kind of support for young female leaders, we must first understand the complexities of a woman's leadership formation and the ideal growing conditions for women leaders. Growing in leadership influence and authority is difficult for both men and women. But women face unique hurdles that often go unnoticed, and they require unique supports to climb over them. To successfully grow women leaders, we need a holistic understanding of how women are formed for ministry leadership.

DEFINING LEADERSHIP

To begin, we need a common lexicon so we can unpack the nuances of leadership development. A leader is a person who causes others to go with them in pursuit of a common goal. J. Robert Clinton defines a Christian leader as someone "with God-given capacity and with a God-given responsibility to influence a specific group of God's people toward God's purposes for the group."[1] Simply put, a Christian leader's primary work is influencing others to be like Jesus and to carry out his mission.

A leader practices leadership. Leadership is the interactive process that occurs inside the exchanges between leaders and followers.[2] A leader may or may not be exercising leadership at any given time. A leader's title or position alone does not initiate leadership; a leader's interactions with and ability to influence people do. Leadership is found in relationships and in the communication that shapes those relationships.

Influence is the permission granted to a leader by a person or a group to convince that individual or group to pursue a specific course of action. Influence is based on respect for a leader's character, knowledge, skills, or reasoning. It is earned. Someone does not have to have power over someone else to influence them. For example, every time I go to a restaurant and ask for my server's opinion about what food to order, I'm being influenced by them. The server cannot dictate what meal I order, so they do not have power over me. But they can influence my decision about what meal to order. In a similar way, women leaders often have influence in church environments. People will listen to these women and be influenced by them, but these women cannot make decisions for the group or initiate change. To do this, a woman needs power.

Power enables a person to make a decision for a person or group or direct another person's actions. Power has to do with control or dominance. Power

1. Clinton, *Leadership Training Models*, 18.
2. Northouse, *Leadership*, 6.

often has a negative connotation, but it is built into our human interactions. As Wilmer G. Villacorta observes, power is not inherently good or bad. It is neutral. We all depend on power.[3] Parents have power over their children because they are physically stronger and have the survival skills, knowledge, and resources their children need to survive. Parents must control their child's behavior when the child wants to do something dangerous, like grabbing a sharp knife, to prevent the child from self-harm. This power is not a negative force in the child's life but is necessary for their very survival. Power can be life-giving.

When an institution, a powerful person, or a group of people gives power to a leader, that power becomes authority. While influence is earned, authority is granted. Authority allows the leader, empowered by a greater authority, to make commands. God has ultimate authority, so when he grants us authority, we have the power of God backing us. When a church gives a person a position as an executive pastor of operations, this person has been granted institutional power to make decisions about the finances and physical resources of the church, within the limits of the job description.

LEADERSHIP DEVELOPMENT FOR WOMEN

Gender is highly complex. Leadership consultant Karin Klenke describes gender well, calling it "a knot that consists of pieces of biology, psychology, sociology, and culture—the complex interplay of which is difficult to unravel."[4] The extent of male and female differences has been hotly debated for decades and leads to questions: Do women lead differently than men? And if they do, does that mean women are less able to lead?

Some egalitarian local churches in my context are effectively developing female leaders for local church ministry roles, and these women leaders are thriving. My study looks at what these churches are doing and how these successful women leaders developed and emerged so that we can understand best practices for developing female church leaders in local churches that embrace egalitarian theology.

Analysis of the experiences of female and male leaders in these egalitarian environments reveals a new way of understanding female leadership development. Seven development processes are at work in forming a female leader. Three aspects of development are internal, two are external, and two form

3. Villacorta, *Tug of War*, 3.
4. Klenke, *Women and Leadership*, 139.

her leadership influence. This model provides a framework for understanding female leadership training and support needs.

LIFELONG LEADERSHIP DEVELOPMENT CASE STUDY: DONNA CROUCH

God forms leaders over their entire lives. God takes a long view of our lives and forms us today for the roles we will fill years, even decades, from now. For as long as we are responsive to the Lord's shaping, God will continue to refine us and shape our leadership. By listening to the life stories of mature women leaders, we can trace this slow, steady developmental work of God's own hand.

Donna Crouch is a seasoned pastor and respected leader. She grew up in an Australian Catholic working-class home. She came to Hills Christian Life Centre in Sydney, Australia, in 1983 as a twenty-one-year-old new believer. The church plant was just weeks old and started with forty people. The church's pastor hired her as the assistant youth leader in 1985, the church's third hire. She was single and immersed herself in the ministry of the church. No other woman was doing what she was doing, and so Donna felt like an anomaly. She was focused, single, and loved working in church ministry. As a result, she felt very different from the women who served as pastors' wives, a common female ministry role in the 1980s. She loved participating in discussions about ministry leadership, but in those conversations she was often the only woman among male peers. When Donna started preaching, she had never seen another woman preach, and she wouldn't see another woman preach for a decade.

Donna's pastor, Brian, invited her into a pastoral mentoring group that consisted entirely of married men. Brian made it clear to the group that Donna was part of the pastoral team and belonged. When she attended her first pastors' retreat, she had to bring a little one-person tent, while the guys shared a big tent. She felt awkward and asked to be excused, but Brian insisted that it was important for her to come. If she was on the team, then participation with the group was essential. On one occasion, a visiting minister pulled her aside and told her that Brian was taking a terrible risk hiring a single woman. Donna felt ashamed and embarrassed that she could be perceived as morally or emotionally untrustworthy due to her being a single woman. Brian encouraged her to not allow the encounter to discourage her and he assured her that she didn't need to feel pressure to get married to be on the team. She had never doubted her ministry ability and calling simply because of her gender, although at times she wondered if others would have been more comfortable if she were a man.

After setting boundaries around her personal life, Donna eventually met a great man who held a similar sense of calling and passion to serve God. They married in 1992. Steven works in business and executive leadership, and Steven's and Donna's gifts complement each other. Steven provided continual encouragement and affirmation to Donna through many seasons.

In 1996, a leadership crisis in the church required Donna to transition out of youth ministry and into leading the worship and creative ministries department. Also that year, her church released a worship album that began to take off around the world. In this busy season of expansion, Donna also had children and could take only a few weeks of maternity leave as she had to manage the demands of a growing church. Donna described her pastor to me as "a hard-working, visionary leader with high standards who required his team to do the same. He saw potential in people, expected innovation and creativity, and cheered the team on, celebrating their wins."[5] Donna viewed her opportunities to succeed and grow as unlimited, with no ceiling to her success.

In 1998, with a newborn and a two-year-old, Donna became the executive pastor at Hills Christian Life Centre and was responsible for the day-to-day operations of the church. She organized her own childcare at church and soon other women on the team followed suit rather than resign once they had children. During that season, she had no mentors to tell her how to make this work, as the team pioneered a fast-growing, multisite church model. No other women she knew were in these kinds of executive roles and yet she felt a responsibility to younger women coming behind her to make it work. At this time the multisite campus model was a new concept, and similarly there were no mentors or methodologies to follow.

God had been speaking to Donna for several years about leading within her denomination, the Australian Christian Churches (Assemblies of God Australia). She waited, recognizing the barriers. Not only had no women been involved in denominational leadership at a national level, but every other national executive member was a senior pastor, while she was merely a campus pastor. When a seat on the national executive team opened in 2009, her husband encouraged her to put her name forward, knowing that God had been speaking to her about this. After getting Brian's blessing, Donna stepped forward, the first woman to ever run for a national executive team

---

5. Quotations without a citation, such as this one, represent comments shared with me during the interview portion of my study.

seat. She was elected by a 90 percent majority. During this ten-year period of denominational executive leadership, Donna ran the church's charity and represented the church nationally, building strategic relationships and partnerships.

There have been long seasons of great sacrifice for Donna and her family. As a campus pastor, she worked long hours, including weekends. This meant she and her husband did not have a whole day off together. She had to leave early for church on Saturday afternoon and Sunday mornings, leaving Steven on his own to get their kids ready and off to church. He was in graduate school studying for his (self-funded) PhD as well as running his own financial practice. The entirety of Donna's salary went to childcare and giving to the church. They made tremendous financial sacrifices. During one eighteen-month stretch, they could afford to buy only one set of work clothes each. Once on a family vacation, her youngest toddler kept crying for their babysitter. Subsequently, Donna struggled with depression for a short period. Was she doing the right thing? She felt terrible mom-guilt and eventually requested some slight adjustments to her work schedule. This ultimately led to a change in roles. Donna's children later told her they were proud to have a mom making an impact in ministry leadership. Balancing the intensity and focus required for ministry leadership and marriage/family life continued to be a high priority for her.

In 2007 Donna left her role as campus pastor and moved into a new role, overseeing CityCare, her church's community service program that served local neighborhoods and the vulnerable. In 2011 Donna saw a need for the church to engage with government, interfaith, and charitable sectors at a national level in Australia. Donna's ministry continues to be fruitful. She recognizes that the call of God and a love for the local church have kept her going—this fire in her bones has not been extinguished, even through great difficulty, isolation, and exclusion. To survive the demands of ministry leadership, Donna said, "You really have to figure out what's most important for the stage of life you are in." This sense of calling has sustained Donna in her ministry role, especially through recent crises surrounding a pastoral transition at her church.

God grew Donna's influence and authority as the influence of her church grew. These two elements were interwoven and cannot be separated. As God shapes environments over time, those environments shape people as leaders. Then their leadership shapes the ministry and the people entrusted to their care. Donna's story is still in the making, but her leadership has been developing for almost forty years now. God forms leaders slowly, growing them carefully and intentionally. Donna has become an influential leader through

God's shaping. Donna's emergence as an influential pastor has been possible only because her church and her husband embraced and practiced egalitarian theology.[6]

EGALITARIAN THEOLOGY BASICS

It would be impossible for us to understand how women become church leaders without a working knowledge of the theology that supports women's leadership.

Egalitarianism in its broadest sense refers to social equity, but the word *egalitarian* has a more nuanced meaning in relationship to theology. Egalitarian theology holds that while gifts are unique to an individual, the ministry gifts of the Holy Spirit are distributed equally to men and women and that men and women are called to exercise the gifts they have received. Gifts of apostleship, pastoring, teaching, and leading are not limited to men.

Egalitarian theology is not merely modern feminist ideas revising the Bible. Feminist theology, as a branch of liberation theology, typically uses a hermeneutic of suspicion to challenge the biblical text, believing that the text's views are tainted by its patriarchal human writers. Egalitarian theology, on the other hand, uses a hermeneutic of trust and careful exegesis for Bible interpretation. It assumes that the Bible is an inspired, authoritative guide, and that we can learn God's plan for women through careful Bible study. These two theological approaches often have the same goal—female flourishing—but different assumptions.

Egalitarian theology recognizes the many ways Scripture liberates and empowers women. Galatians 3:28 provides a jumping-off point: "There is neither Jew nor Gentile, neither slave nor free, nor is there male and female, for you are all one in Christ Jesus." An egalitarian approach centers the Bible's descriptions of women and the leadership roles they fill and interprets what the Bible says about women in view of these passages.

Egalitarian theology is practical theology. As Scott Cormode describes, practical theology works "to integrate the many voices in Scripture so that we know how to live in the world."[7] Scripture presents many different ideas about women and leadership, and we must integrate them in a way that makes sense spiritually for women with God-given leadership gifts and a calling to ministry.

---

6. Donna's experience is her own, and this description of the Hillsong environment is not representative of every female leader's experience at Hillsong Church. Sadly, Hillsong Church spent several recent years mired in the scandals of multiple leaders. Donna's story reveals the aspects of the church culture that contributed to her emergence as an influential leader.

7. Cormode, *Innovative Church*, 119–20.

Lucy Peppiatt states, "The Bible tells a story of God releasing women alongside men into all forms of ministry, leadership, work, and service on the basis of character and gifting rather than on the basis of biological sex."[8] Egalitarians believe that to differentiate the functions of men and women is to create an inequality.

From the very beginning of the Bible, God's plan for gender equality is revealed. God names woman *ezer* (Gen. 2:18), meaning "warrior," "helper," or "aid." God himself is described as *ezer* (Ps. 46:1), which connotes not weakness or subservience but strength and companionship. Women reflect God as female image bearers and are designed to stand alongside men in kingdom building.[9] The fall disrupted God's original design for gender equality, but Jesus redeemed that curse, restoring equality.[10] The spiritual gifts and church functions described in Romans 12:6–8, 1 Corinthians 12:8–10, and Ephesians 4:11 are never assigned by gender.[11]

As Scot McKnight points out, understanding God's design for women in ministry requires not just asking what the Bible says about what women are permitted to do in the church but also looking at how God uses women to minister, speak, and lead in the Bible.[12] Women have been proclaiming the kingdom of God and leading since Jesus was alive. Mary Magdalene proclaims Jesus's resurrection in John 20:17–18. Other women who proclaim the kingdom of God include the Samaritan woman (John 4:39), Priscilla (Acts 18:26), Junia (Rom. 16:7), Lydia (Acts 16:13–15), and Tryphena and Tryphosa (Rom. 16:12). Jesus's final commission is for his followers, not just men, to go into the world and teach people about him (Matt. 28:18–20). Egalitarians believe women are called to speak up about the good news of Jesus and to tell it from their unique, contextualized experience.[13]

Egalitarian may be an insufficient term because of its focus on social equity. *Mutuality* is a similar term with a greater focus on praxis. Mutuality recognizes not just equal value or status but a partnership between men and women, implying support and empathy for one another in leadership. This is about a harmonious, balanced alignment rather than jostling for status.[14]

God's design for church leadership is like God's design for family. Children need the leadership of both parents, and likewise, congregations need both a

8. Peppiatt, *Rediscovering Scripture's Vision for Women*, 1.
9. James, *Half the Church*, 100, 114–15.
10. Scott, *Dare Mighty Things*, 26–27.
11. Stackhouse, *Partners in Christ*, 48.
12. McKnight, "Women Ministering," 5–6.
13. Turner and Hudson, *Saved from Silence*, 55.
14. The terms *egalitarian* and *mutualist* are synonymous, as are *complementarian* and *hierarchist*.

mother and a father leader to be healthy and strong. Holly Wagner explained it to me this way: "If you're raising a healthy home, it has a mother and father present. The church is the same. If you have a healthy mother and father present in church, it creates a healthy environment. Having both male and female voices present is hugely important because we bring different things to the table." When the weight of leadership rests on both men and women equally, then men are not burdened too heavily. Perhaps one of the reasons for the many failures of men in pastoral ministry is that they are carrying far more than they should. When women carry the load of leadership in partnership with men, the burden on men becomes lighter.

Egalitarian local churches embrace a theology of mutuality that values men and women as equal partners in the sight of God. According to an egalitarian interpretation of Scripture, the qualifications for leadership roles are not gender based, and women are not limited to specific roles. In these churches, women are ordained as pastors and elders, and they preach, teach, and have executive leadership functions.

Egalitarian Theological Environments

A female leader's theological environment is the soil in which she grows. The condition of this soil impacts her ministry leadership development, either limiting or expanding her view of acceptable gender roles in her early years. An unfavorable theological environment may cause a delay in a female ministry leader's development.[15] Even when a denomination has adopted an egalitarian position, churches within that denomination vary in how they interpret and practice egalitarian theology. Furthermore, local churches are not theologically homogenous within themselves. Many people who belong to egalitarian church environments did not receive their theological training in egalitarian environments. As a result, women leaders in churches that formally embrace egalitarian theology are likely to encounter church attenders who hold theological views that limit the role of women.

Elizabeth Loutrel Glanville offers a continuum of theological perspectives regarding women in ministry (see table 1). Traditional theology, at one end of the spectrum, gives women a lower status than men. Complementarians view men and woman as equally valuable but designed by God for separate and unique gender-based roles, with men occupying God-ordained leadership roles. A nuanced complementarian perspective occasionally allows that God may use a woman for a male role. A modified egalitarian perspective sees men

15. Glanville, "Leadership Development for Women," 145, 160–61.

and women as having equal status and rejects predetermined gender-based roles, but in praxis women are rarely selected for leadership opportunities. An egalitarian theological position supports women leading at every level of ministry without any gender-based barriers.

TABLE 1. The Continuum of Male-Female Theological Positions*

Traditional	Men are created to have leadership and authority and to teach. Women are to follow and can have leadership over other women or children.
Complementarian	Men and women are equal in the eyes of God but created for different roles. Women can lead in some but not all areas of the church.
Complementarian but . . .	The official position is complementarian, but on occasion God will use a woman in a man's role.
Egalitarian but . . .	The official position is that men and women are completely equal. (But men are more equal!) Women find it difficult to move into top leadership roles.
Egalitarian	Men and women are completely equal. Women may do anything a man does in leadership.

*Based on Glanville, "Leadership Development for Women," 99.

In pragmatic, Pentecostal environments, egalitarian theology may not be adequately taught because of a lack of clarity at a denominational level or because the individual church lacks a clearly articulated egalitarian theological position. Pentecostal women are sometimes clearly empowered to preach and teach but not given leadership roles. This is an example of Glanville's "egalitarian but . . ." theological position.

Egalitarian Theology in Marriage

Egalitarian theology guides ministry praxis in the church but also has application in the home. An egalitarian marriage is one in which husband and wife have equal power and value, function in a partnership under the headship of Christ, and make decisions jointly.[16] In an egalitarian marriage, roles and responsibilities are not necessarily gender based. They are mutually agreed on based on giftedness and responsibilities outside the home. Mutual submission is not about power over but rather selfless giving.[17] Ruth Haley Barton describes this kind of marriage as a team: "God's original and best plan for the marriage relationship was a partnership model in which a man

16. Peppiatt, *Rediscovering Scripture's Vision for Women*, 110.
17. James, *Half the Church*, 121.

and a woman function together as a team of equals."[18] Egalitarian marriage is a relationship in which both individuals are loved and served, and they flourish as they grow into their full selves. Wives increasingly become a blessing to their husbands and children as they grow into the full strength of their giftedness at home and in the church.[19] This differs from a complementarian theological position, which undergirds male headship and a patriarchal hierarchy in the home.

John G. Stackhouse Jr., a conservative (converted) egalitarian, cautions men not to move too fast toward empowering women lest it destroy a marriage or a church, which he claims would not be God's will.[20] This caution may initially seem reasonable. However, putting women's empowerment on hold indefinitely devalues the female contribution to the *missio Dei*. Embracing delay implies that women being faithful and obedient to their leadership calling is somehow not essential to God's plan.

Pentecostals have historically empowered women for ministry roles but have publicly aligned with the wider evangelical position of male headship and wifely submission. Patterns of male headship are noted throughout evangelical and Pentecostal discourses.[21] Nevertheless, often in practice Pentecostal marriages don't reflect this complementarian ideal. Numerous studies have found that most Pentecostal marriages are between equals who make decisions jointly or are "pragmatically egalitarian."[22] This theological ambiguity creates difficulties and confusion for wives with leadership gifts. Cheryl Catford observes, "Pentecostals easily dismiss the concerns of evangelicals over biblical passages that prohibit women from preaching, but many are unable as easily to dismiss those passages dealing with women having authority over men. Consequently there is an entrenched theological conviction among many Pentecostals that women require the spiritual 'covering' of a male, both in the home and the church, thereby denying women ultimate authority over men."[23] This creates what Bernice Martin termed the "Pentecostal gender paradox," a self-contradicting theology.[24]

True egalitarian mutuality does not demand that a male leader set aside his ministry leadership calling in deference to his wife's leadership calling. Instead, husbands and wives serve together in leadership, jointly pursuing

18. Barton, *Equal to the Task*, loc. 2011 of 2871, Kindle.
19. Barton, *Equal to the Task*, loc. 2052 of 2871, Kindle.
20. Stackhouse, *Partners in Christ*, 129.
21. Maddox, "Rise Up Warrior Princess Daughters," 14.
22. Catford, "Women's Experiences," locs. 557, 561 of 8092, Kindle.
23. Catford, "Women's Experiences," locs. 511, 526 of 8092, Kindle.
24. Martin, "Pentecostal Gender Paradox," 52.

their kingdom callings. William and Catherine Booth modeled this kind of partnership when they founded the Salvation Army. Catherine preached and led alongside her husband, and each partner took turns at home with their children.[25] Pentecostals also encourage partnership between husbands and wives in ministry but often emphasize complementary roles and experiences.[26] In Pentecostal churches, a pastor's wife has authority that a pastor's wife in a fundamentalist church does not have. This stems from her ability to publicly pray, preach, teach, and prophesy. She has organizational power (with or without a formal church role) purely based on her marital connection.[27] Egalitarian theology provides the basis for husbands and wives to lead together as ministry partners.

EGALITARIAN MISSIOLOGY

Egalitarian theology is a practical theology. It explains how we should practice leadership in the church and at home. Egalitarian theology is also a contextual theology. Egalitarian missiology is the intersection of egalitarian theology and engagement in God's mission through the local church. It brings egalitarian theology beyond theological reflection and into church praxis and mission. The West is becoming culturally less Christian and increasingly more egalitarian. To contextualize the gospel for emerging generations in the West, young women with leadership gifts must recognize their place in God's kingdom. Egalitarian missiology empowers women for ministry, allowing them to bring the gospel to Western cultures that embrace gender equality. Egalitarian theology undergirds egalitarian missiology, in which women are full partners with men in God's mission to redeem and bring healing to the world.

To effectively reach Western, egalitarian societies in the wake of the feminist movement's undeniable transformation of culture and where Christianity is losing ground,[28] we need a different kind of mission approach: mission as inculturation, or contextualization.[29] This kind of mission approach frames the gospel inside the receiving culture, attaching it to recognizable cultural reference points. The apostle Paul contextualized the gospel for the Athenians, using their own cultural monuments and poetry to reveal the truth of Jesus the Lord (Acts 17:22–31). American evangelicalism has been

25. Grenz and Kjesbo, *Women in the Church*, locs. 471, 538, 558, 628 of 3642, Kindle.
26. E. Miller, "Women in Australian Pentecostalism," 65.
27. Catford, "Women's Experiences," loc. 728 of 8092, Kindle.
28. Yeh, "Future of Mission."
29. Bosch, *Transforming Mission*, 445.

caught in a kind of syncretism with politically conservative culture that began in the 1940s and 1950s.[30] This has led evangelicals to view feminism as a threat to a politically conservative identity, and it has meant that evangelicals have not always accepted an egalitarian theology regarding women's roles. Embracing political conservatism is not working to strengthen the Western church. We are losing ground with each new generation. Political affiliation cannot form a strong foundation for the church; Jesus must be the foundation.

Embedded Cultural Renovation

The challenge for contextualization is that our approach must straddle the razor edge between being embedded in culture enough that people are able to express their faith in a culturally appropriate and relevant way and, at the same time, renovating the parts of culture that are broken and need to be redeemed by the gospel. This requires continually looking for the places in culture that we can align with and embrace while continually realigning broken places with the gospel. This is a dynamic, fluid process that must take place at the same rate that Western culture is changing. Change happens quickly, as information and technological advances shape society. We have no time to lose, for we are already behind. We must avoid uniting the gospel with political agendas on either side of the ideological aisle and point out where biblical truth aligns and misaligns with the cultural trends and power structures of our society.

Contextualization involves adopting an egalitarian missiological approach that puts women into partnership with men in mission. This approach understands that men and women are equal in ministry and in marriage.[31] It recognizes that the gospel provides good news for women with leadership gifts: God gave them those gifts for the purpose of building his kingdom. For men and women in Western culture who are looking for strong, healthy spiritual leadership by mothers and fathers, the good news is that God has designed this kind of spiritual family for them in the church. We must not resist this change because of our cultural biases and discomfort with change. As David J. Bosch notes, "Missiology acts as a gadfly in the house of theology, creating unrest and resisting complacency, opposing every ecclesiastical impulse to self-preservation, every desire to stay what we are, every inclination toward provincialism and parochialism, every fragmentation of humanity into regional or ideological blocs. . . . Missiology's task,

30. Du Mez, *Jesus and John Wayne*, 8–10.
31. Bosch, *Transforming Mission*, 413.

furthermore, is critically to accompany the missionary enterprise, to scrutinize its foundations, its aims, attitude, message, and methods—not from the safe distance of an onlooker, but in a spirit of co-responsibility and of service to the church of Christ."[32] Contextualization requires wrestling with feminism.

Feminism and #MeToo

Despite the influence of the feminist movement on Western society, the relationship between Christianity and feminism is still tense. The women leaders in this study had a predominantly negative view of feminism, perhaps surprisingly. This attitude is likely influenced by evangelical Christianity's rejection of feminism. An evangelical woman leader who assumes a feminist identity runs the risk of marginalization in the church. Perhaps these women's views are also influenced by social conditioning that aggression is unfeminine. However, these women leaders had concrete criticisms of feminism. Feminism, as they understand it, involves more than advocating for political power, economic power, or equal social status with men. For them, feminism is often associated with pro-choice and pro-abortion movements, and many find these views not in line with their theology. Feminism, they say, is also associated with aggression against oppression (distinct from assertiveness) and self-promotion, qualities that run counter to Jesus's call to selflessness.

Some women leaders in this study said they dislike the activist culture of feminism. One said, "It can come across wrong, and it's unattractive and it's unconvincing." Activism, they believe, is perceived as a form of distasteful self-promotion and so not appropriate for Christians. Many of these women struggle with radical feminism, which views men as oppressors whose power must be eliminated so that women can rise. Mutual respect between men and women leading side by side is incompatible with the radical feminist view, and these women leaders highly value working alongside men. They find "toxic masculinity" to be a vague and unhelpful term that alienates men, even the good ones. According to Pew Research, half of American men feel punished by society just for being male.[33] Women in this study are not advocating for men to repent, step down, and humbly surrender their positions to women. They want men to use their power to give them a hand up.

Surprisingly, while many of the female study participants view the #Me Too movement as having done important and necessary work, several view

32. Bosch, *Transforming Mission*, 489.
33. Reeves, "Toxic Masculinity Is a Harmful Myth."

#MeToo negatively, believing that #MeToo and the larger feminist movement devalue men.[34] They disagree with this devaluing of men, believing that men do not have to lose value and power for women to gain value and power. They do not see power as a zero-sum game. While these women unabashedly and actively work to empower, honor, and value women, they find feminism to be an uncomfortable label because of their desire to honor and partner with men in their leadership.

The male leaders in this study describe a hesitancy to engage women leaders who take an activist stance about women's issues. "As a senior pastor, if I have women on the team who are seeing sexism everywhere and saying we need to break through sexism in the church, that's going to become a problem for me. I don't want crusaders on our team," one leader said. These male leaders are concerned that they will be judged by accusation rather than by facts. They believe that public opinion is stacked against them, as women gained power through #MeToo and are now believed first more often. A male pastor is more likely to develop female leaders if he feels honored, valued, and respected. But if a woman comes with an attitude that feels like activism or victimhood, the male pastor will likely pull back because he fears that eventually he will be accused of misconduct or that he will somehow become the bad guy. This creates a polarized environment. As long as everything is great, women have all the opportunity they want. But if women challenge something in the makeup of the environment, they will find themselves shut down rapidly—not necessarily as a power play but because the male leader is now self-protecting.

The male pastors in this study come from churches that are successfully empowering women at all levels of leadership, even though they have distanced themselves from feminism. Women leaders in their churches are thriving in entry-level positions and as preachers and pastors. This means that a church does not have to align with every ideal of feminism to see women leaders thrive. Feminism and egalitarian praxis have points of overlap, but the two are not the same. An egalitarian theology places men and women in equal partnership with mutual power sharing, respect, and honor. Both feminism and egalitarian theology seek to elevate the status of women, but feminism in many instances takes a negative view of men as oppressors that egalitarian theology does not.

34. The #MeToo movement, which began in the early 2000s but gained widespread attention with the use of the hashtag #MeToo around 2017, is a social campaign in which women have spoken publicly about their experiences with sexual abuse and harassment. In some cases, women have named men who perpetrated these behaviors, catalyzing legal and social consequences.

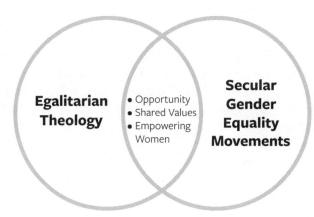

Fig. 1.1. Contextual Overlap

Contextual Overlap

Egalitarian theology is not identical to secular movements promoting gender equality, but they do share overlapping practices (see fig. 1.1). Western culture is trending toward gender egalitarian values that influence many dimensions of society.[35] Effective ministry to the West includes locating our praxis and theological reflections inside this cultural trend. As missiologist Sherwood G. Lingenfelter notes, "The idea of contextualization is to frame the gospel message in language and communication forms appropriate and meaningful to the local culture and to focus the message upon crucial issues in the lives of the people."[36] Lingenfelter encourages us to adopt what might be an uncomfortable perspective in order to apply the gospel's transformative power to the brokenness within a culture through kingdom principles.[37] Contextualization of the gospel in the West requires understanding and valuing gender equality.

If we recognize this trend toward gender equality as an opportunity rather than as a threat to traditional family values, then we can identify where this cultural trend and the good news of Jesus intersect. Stackhouse credits the Christianization of Western culture for this egalitarian cultural trend and celebrates it as an outcome of mission. Ironically, however, the church lags behind culture in issues of women's equality.[38]

If we do not embrace contextualization, we lose the opportunity it represents. Halee Gray Scott writes, "The church has failed Christian women

35. Equal Measures 2030, *Harnessing the Power of Data*, 8, 27.
36. Lingenfelter, *Transforming Culture*, 12.
37. Lingenfelter, *Transforming Culture*, 21.
38. Stackhouse, *Partners in Christ*, 92.

because it has failed to cast a comprehensive vision of what God can accomplish in and through the life of a woman. So in the midst of all our doing and dreaming, our strength is blunted."[39] Without this vision, the women whose leadership potential goes unfulfilled as they miss their divine call for ministry are not the only ones who lose. We all lose. Carolyn Custis James warns of the dire results for Christianity if the church continues to avoid the issue of women in ministry leadership. We will lose the resources of feminine gifts, ideas, and theological work that can emerge only from a woman's experience. Furthermore, James cautions that by not mobilizing daughters, we send a message to the world that we devalue women.[40] Women have important ministry not only to other women but also to men. If the Western church releases its feminine leadership voice, it can address cultural problems like abuse, fragmented communities, violence, sexual immorality, pornography, poor mental health, and sex slavery.

SUMMARY

A woman leader's experience is unique. God shapes each woman for ministry leadership different from her male colleagues. This formation occurs over her entire life, and we can trace that development. As God forms a leader, that leader forms leadership influence. Women leaders can become influential in any kind of ministry environment, but they form authority only in theologically egalitarian environments. Egalitarian theology provides a spiritual empowerment based on how the Bible describes God's work in gifting and empowering women for his kingdom work. It puts men and women into an equal partnership, both partners carrying the load of leadership and responsibility together. As men and women do this, they contextualize the gospel for a new generation that has grown up in the wake of feminism's transformation of Western society.

---

39. Scott, *Dare Mighty Things*, 12.
40. James, *Half the Church*, 41, 81. See also Edwards, Matthews, and Rogers, *Mixed Ministry*, loc. 175 of 2590, Kindle.

A MODEL OF FEMALE
LEADERSHIP DEVELOPMENT

A fter twenty years of processing my own leadership development and with unanswered questions from the women leaders in my care rattling around in my head, I was compelled to discover answers. I had no ambition to pursue doctoral studies, and so it was a tremendous surprise to me when, after much prayer (I can't emphasize enough the amount of convincing God had to do), God began to point me to doctoral research as the pathway to answers. I am a local church pastor and an uneasy academic at best. So it was a point of calling and obedience to God for me to spend five years engaged in a study of female leaders in local churches.

The findings in this book emerged from my doctoral research at Fuller Theological Seminary. The purpose of the study was to understand the development processes and factors that influence the emergence of female ministry leaders in theologically egalitarian environments. I wanted to develop a new model for female leadership development that informs best practices for supporting such development in churches practicing egalitarian theology.

These core questions guided the study:

- How does egalitarian theology shape female ministry leaders?
- What are core processes of development for female ministry leaders within egalitarian contexts?

- How do female leaders increase in influence and authority in egalitarian contexts?
- What are best practices for supporting the leadership development of women leaders in egalitarian churches?

The findings from this study support the work of Christian leaders, ministry training institutions, and churches looking to prioritize the development of women leaders for lay and professional ministry in local churches.

THE RESEARCH

The study focuses on women leaders with significant influence and authority in churches, denominations, and social media. To find these women, I selected twenty-four egalitarian churches in the United States, Canada, and Australia. In these churches, women are senior pastors, lead on executive teams, serve on boards, preach, and teach. Many of these churches are large churches, predominantly multisite, the largest of which has thirty-seven campuses. These churches represent eleven Pentecostal movements, and many are nondenominational.[1] Eleven of the churches spearhead large church leadership networks or are key churches within their denomination. In this study I wanted to examine the growing conditions that produced these remarkably powerful women and how they grew in authority and influence. I explore what was happening in and around the emerging women leaders in these environments, and how male senior pastors cultivated female leaders.

To get answers to my research questions, I used interview, focus group, and survey methodologies to gather data from three groups of church leaders. Mature, influential female pastors comprised one group; younger, emerging female ministry leaders comprised the second; and male senior pastors comprised the third. Snowball sampling led to a fourth group of female ministry leaders for a survey.[2] (See appendix B for all data collection instruments.) In all, the sample group was made up of eighty-four female and male local church

---

1. The Pentecostal/charismatic movements represented in this study are the International Networks of Churches, Hillsong Church and Hillsong Family of Churches, Christian City Churches (C3), Team Church Network, Integrity Leadership Ministries, Praise Chapel Fellowship, Australian Christian Churches, Assemblies of God USA, and Association of Related Churches.

2. *Snowball sampling* is a sampling methodology that begins by locating one or two key members of a (difficult to locate) population, then asking for referrals to other similar representatives of the population. The researcher moves from representative to representative until there are no more potential research participants.

leaders, including married leaders, single female leaders, and mothers.[3] (See appendixes C and D for participant descriptors.)

Interviews and Focus Groups

I conducted in-depth interviews with thirteen mature and influential female pastors, ages thirty-two to sixty, using an active, semi-structured interview style. I used an interview guide but did not always follow the guide perfectly. My goal was to help the interviewee articulate their story. These women are in executive leadership roles in large egalitarian churches that carry significant influence. They all preach or teach in their churches and have executive leadership responsibilities in accordance with their gifting. They are participants in making major decisions about the vision, budgets, and staffing within their organizations. Eleven of the women lead alongside their husbands in ministry. Nine women are co-senior or lead pastors, two are executive pastors, and two are campus pastors. I gained a comprehensive understanding of their leadership development journeys and the issues that played a significant role in their development and in the women they lead. My questions and prompts guided a process of making meaning of their stories together. I asked them to shift positions and answer the questions as a leader, a wife, a mother, and a mentor.[4]

I interviewed six male senior pastors, ages thirty-two to sixty. These men were selected from the twenty-four churches, have hired female leaders for executive leadership roles in their churches, and are actively working to support their development. All six men are married, and one was divorced and remarried. I asked for their observations about issues that influence the development of female leaders and about their relationships with female leaders in their contexts.

I divided an additional eighteen women church leaders, ages twenty-nine to fifty-two, into four focus groups as a second research method. These women are paid church staff and have leadership and pastoral responsibilities within their local church. Some are not yet teaching or preaching publicly. One is a senior pastor, five are campus pastors, seven are executive pastors, three are in student ministry, and two are assistants. In the focus groups, rather than focusing on problems, I guided the conversation toward what is working in churches to develop female leaders. This meant discovering what each female leader has experienced and is doing for her own development; what other

---

3. Some of the participants were divorced and remarried, but this is not specified in the tables in appendixes C and D.

4. Holstein and Gubrium, *Active Interview*, 32, 37, 39.

leaders have done that made a difference in her development; and what systems, organizational culture, or policies supported her development.[5]

Data Analysis: The Theory-Making Process

I used an inductive approach for data analysis to develop new theory in female leadership development.[6] Rather than merely considering what is *not* working to develop women as leaders, the study focuses on what *is* working where women have developed significant ministry influence and authority so that we can appreciate these unique successes and continue to build on them in other environments.[7] Analysis of the data from interviews and focus groups produced the theories presented in this chapter.

Surveys: Testing the Model

After completing this analysis, I tested the theory against a new group of female leaders from outside the original twenty-four churches. I hoped to discover whether the findings held up in additional groups of female leaders in egalitarian churches. I used an anonymous survey distributed to the various ministry and relational networks of which I am a part. Forty-seven female leaders in egalitarian churches with various levels of leadership influence and authority participated. (See appendix E for an analysis of study participants' leadership influence.) Nine participants had never married, two women were divorced, and thirty-six were married. Thirty-one women considered their marriages to be egalitarian, and five considered their marriages to be mostly egalitarian. Survey participants included women leaders from the following generations: baby boomer, Gen X, xennial, millennial, and Gen Z.[8]

Encouragingly, the findings from my first stage of research were indeed applicable to the survey group of female leaders, which means that the study has useful broader application. The primary theory based on this study is that

5. Hammond, *Thin Book of Appreciative Inquiry*, 1, 25–26.
6. Strauss and Corbin, *Basics of Qualitative Research*, 23. Specifically, I employed grounded theory. Analysis involved several phases of coding, beginning with line-by-line or open coding, and moving into increasingly generalized codes as concepts were connected in axial coding.
7. Hammond, *Thin Book of Appreciative Inquiry*, 50.
8. For my analysis, I divided the generations into ten-year increments, shorter than the typical twenty, because the impact of rapid social changes spurred on by the feminism of the late twentieth century and early twenty-first century required that I use shorter time periods to accurately account for the different ways of thinking and the different experiences of participants of various ages. I grouped generations as baby boomer: 1955–64; Gen X: 1965–74; xennial: 1975–84; millennial: 1985–94; and Gen Z: 1995–2002. No study participants were younger than eighteen or older than sixty-four. Women older than sixty-four were not intentionally excluded from the study; no women older than sixty-four chose to participate.

there are seven processes of female leadership development. The rest of this chapter provides an overview of the theory, and the rest of this book unpacks each of the seven aspects of female leadership development.

A NEW MODEL: THE SEVEN PROCESSES OF FEMALE LEADERSHIP DEVELOPMENT

A woman's leadership development involves more than being granted a position or an opportunity to lead, even though this is important. A woman is not simply born to lead because she has a charismatic personality. Leadership doesn't come from completing a training program or learning information. Even a Damascus-road experience alone cannot create a woman leader. A woman leader is formed gradually over a lifetime by forces shaping her thinking and actions and through relationships with other leaders. Christian women leaders build credibility, oh so slowly, to guide others toward a kingdom vision God put in their hearts. A woman leader is formed gradually over a lifetime, by a series of thoughts, patterns of responses, and a sequence of actions. Developing leadership influence and authority happens through a process. A woman's leadership development can be divided into seven distinct but interwoven processes that work together, over her lifetime, to shape her as a leader and form her leadership influence. Three of these processes are internal, two are external, and two create her leadership influence.[9] Many potential hindrances, from gender discrimination to abuse to an insecure husband, can delay or derail a woman's leadership development. Women in ministry leadership are rare because aligning all these developmental factors in the ideal growing conditions is difficult.

Despite the odds, however, God is the master artisan in the divine shaping of a woman leader, and his good purposes guide all aspects of the process. He creates his masterpiece as he orchestrates events and puts people into place around her, gives her the spiritual gift of leadership, and guides her forward. God has purposed her for a specific role, and his creative shaping directs that purpose. She is created by God in his image to participate in his mission to reconcile with and restore the world by leading in Jesus's church (Gen. 1:27; Matt. 28:19–20; Rom. 12:8). Her surrendered responses to God's shaping experiences form her ministry and lead her toward her purpose.

To understand the seven developmental aspects and how they work together, we will begin by exploring the internal formation of a female ministry leader (see fig. 2.1). Three unique processes work together to shape a woman

9. Morgan, "Female Leaders in Egalitarian Churches," 198.

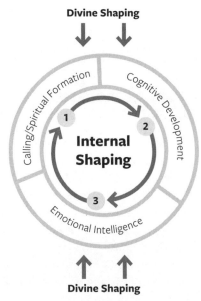

Fig. 2.1. Three Internal Aspects of Female Leadership Development

leader's inner life, each process affecting and being affected by the others. They are so tightly interwoven that if one process is absent, her leadership development will unravel. Her inner life is continually being formed, often in response to her environment and opportunities. Opportunity and support alone will not grow her influence, however. She must navigate the spiritual, cognitive, and emotional demands of this processing to emerge as an influential leader. Spiritual development is the fuel for her progress. Without it, she will lack the motivation to push past the difficulties to come. Cognitive leadership development is the foundation for her leadership. Without it, she will not learn to trust her own leadership and so will not step out and lead. Emotional development builds resilience. Without it, she cannot grow. This internal processing takes place in response to God's sovereign shaping, her environment, and her experiences.

Let's unpack each of these three internal processes.

Three Internal Aspects of Female Leader Development

The first of these internal processes forms a woman leader spiritually. Most women don't begin their lives thinking they will pursue vocational ministry. Very few have seen a woman leader working in their ministry context to inspire them. In fact, the older a woman is, the less likely she is to have had a female leader role model. Without a role model, women lack imagination for what might be. If women don't see other women leading, they are less likely to imagine that they might also become women who lead. This does not stop God from activating women for leadership, however.

After a season of pursuing other things, future female ministry leaders typically experience powerful moments of being called into God's mission. Their decision to respond to God with a "yes" comes with many questions and concerns. When this calling to leadership seems out of sync with normal or common female church roles, egalitarian theology provides a conceptual framework for processing a spiritual vocation. It frees a woman to say yes and accept that God wants to use the gifts within her for his kingdom purposes. When a woman hears and accepts her leadership calling and chooses to be obedient to the leadership of the Holy Spirit, she begins her journey of spiritual formation. As she walks in her leadership calling, she learns how to discern and follow the Holy Spirit's guidance for her leadership. She must discover her unique spiritual gifts and then develop those gifts. This process is interwoven with her emotional development as she gains self-awareness. This is not simply self-discovery but a process of becoming more like Jesus as her gifts grow.[10] She gains spiritual authority as she surrenders to God's leadership in her life.

A second internal process forms a woman leader's cognition, beginning by shaping her self-concept. For women to become leaders, they must learn leadership skills, as men do, but they must also learn a new identity that may seem incongruent with femininity. A woman may be a daughter, a mother, a wife, a friend, and a skilled professional, but she must learn to view herself as a leader and recognize her influence as it develops. She must internalize a leader identity and accept leadership as part of her personhood. To do so, she must move past cultural or social messages she may have received throughout her life that associate authority with masculinity, or the idea that to be a leader is to be unfeminine.[11] Her new identity flows from an awareness of her position and authority as a daughter of the King. Women leaders face unique inner battles with insecurity, risk aversion, and comparison that must be fought in every season of their development. A woman's spiritual development helps form her thinking. She develops confidence that comes from an inner certainty of her divine calling when she lacks confidence in herself.

A third internal process works with the first two, shaping a woman leader through the formation of emotional intelligence that helps her to process her

10. Scott, *Dare Mighty Things*, 77, 155.
11. Adeney, *Women and Christian Mission*, 111, 113–14; Howell, *Buried Talents*, 45.

feelings as a leader. Successful female leaders develop emotional intelligence and can skillfully guide their own emotions.[12] Emotional intelligence consists of four domains: self-awareness, self-management, social awareness, and relationship management. To emerge as an influential leader, a woman must grow her emotional intelligence because "great leadership works through the emotions."[13] The mood and tone of a female leader directly impact the motivation, commitment, and morale of those who follow her. Leaders who are optimistic and enthusiastic retain their people.[14]

Women leaders often face lose-lose scenarios. For example, they are typically perceived as either too tough or too soft on others instead of an appropriate balance of the two.[15] These double-bind tensions and challenges produce emotional pain. Despite the resultant sensitivities and struggles with low self-confidence, successful women leaders have learned to process negative feedback, resulting in self-awareness, which is essential for personal growth. Emotional development helps women leaders push through their pain and purifies their motives. They learn empathy, which helps them connect with and influence those they lead and those they follow. Through this process of developing emotional intelligence, women leaders learn to lead authentically and openly with their whole, genuine selves.

Two External Aspects of Female Leader Development

While a woman's spirituality, cognition, and emotional intelligence are being formed internally, two external processes are also shaping her as she interacts with her environment. Both her ministry environment and her home life have an impact on her leadership development. These two contexts either limit her ability to lead or help her leadership by the support or lack of support they offer her. Figure 2.2 shows how the internal and external processes work together to form a woman leader.

A woman's ministry environment shapes her through its leadership culture and the training and opportunities it provides. Women, particularly mothers, tend to prefer (and need) flexible work environments. Often flexibility becomes an important point of negotiation in a woman leader's role. A woman will often accept a less-prestigious role or less money to gain flexibility in her work schedule. However, churches show the value in developing women

---

12. Tarr-Whelan, *Women Lead the Way*, loc. 1498 of 4551, Kindle; Cole, *Developing Female Leaders*, 69; Eagly and Carli, *Through the Labyrinth*, 75; Bradberry and Greaves, *Emotional Intelligence 2.0*, 43.
13. Goleman, Boyatzis, and McKee, *Primal Leadership*, 21.
14. Goleman, Boyatzis, and McKee, *Primal Leadership*, 23.
15. Catalyst, "Double-Bind Dilemma for Women in Leadership."

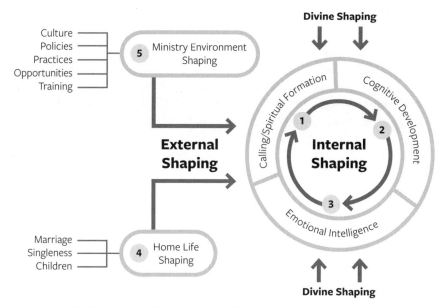

Fig. 2.2. Internal and External Aspects of Female Leadership Development

leaders by providing this flexibility without diminishing a woman's authority or giving her lower-quality opportunities.[16] The flexibility she needs may
look like a workday with a break in the afternoon for after-school pickups,
or it may look like taking a break from a leadership role for a season to meet
the demands of family and returning to leadership later. In a supportive
ministry environment, policies grant women this kind of flexibility because
their leadership and their families are valued. In these fertile environments,
women are given high-quality, clearly defined opportunities to lead. Women
are valued for their potential, not merely their proven expertise and experience. In a supportive ministry context, calling and gifting matter more than
gender. Men and women are provided clearly defined pathways for healthy
ministry partnerships, whether they are married or unmarried. These ministry
opportunities produce organizational authority for women.

A female leader's home life also shapes her through the kinds of support
she receives from her husband and others. Even when both spouses are working, most wives still carry the burden of childcare and household management.[17] Mothers need help with their children to be able to continue leading.
This may come from a father who takes equal responsibility for parenting

16. Lederleitner, *Women in God's Mission*, 187; Beach, *Gifted to Lead*, 91.
17. Vinnicombe and Singh, "Women-Only Management Training," 298.

and childcare, or it may come from other types of paid or unpaid support. Both married and unmarried female leaders need help managing their households. In successful ministry partnerships, the husband and wife have clearly defined how they relate to each other, not just as husband and wife but also as leaders. To navigate the relational dynamics of ministry partnership in a healthy way, their roles must be clear. An egalitarian marriage marked by mutual respect and mutual responsibility is vital to the development of a female leader.

Two Aspects of the Formation of Female Leadership Influence

The last two of the seven development processes create a woman leader's influence. While men often receive organizational power before they have earned personal influence, women typically must build personal influence before they are granted roles with organizational power. Even when the power of a ministry organization backs a woman leader, people can opt in or opt out of following her at any time because most likely they are volunteers and money is not incentivizing compliance. If a volunteer disagrees with a church leader, they can simply leave the team for another group inside the church or leave the church entirely. As a result, women leaders in churches must be very adept at developing personal influence, with or without a powerful role validating their leadership. This personal influence is formed through the development of leadership relationships and communication skills. The more types of leadership relationships a woman leader cultivates, the more her influence expands. The better and broader her communication, the more significant her influence becomes.

Women leaders tend to be unconcerned about accumulating power, however. They are not socially driven to dominate others or to climb a hierarchy ladder. Several women leaders I studied opted to move into leadership roles with less power and responsibility than their current roles when those roles better fit their giftedness or need for flexibility or their interests shifted.

A female leader develops many types of leadership relationships. A leadership relationship has a goal beyond personal connection and support. A woman leader needs key relationships with other leaders who will invest in her and validate her leadership. She needs female role models who expand her thinking about what a leader looks like. Role models help a woman see her gifts and abilities for what they can be. A woman leader needs spiritual mentors, leadership coaches, and especially sponsors who open doors of leadership opportunity by vouching for her capability. These leaders share their credibility with her as she establishes her own. Her leadership expands as she

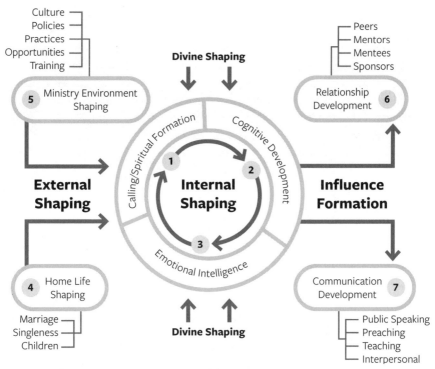

Fig. 2.3. The Seven Processes of Female Leadership Development

coaches her own mentees and gives opportunities and trust to new leaders. She also needs a network of peers to grow her influence. Building relationships with peers leading in similar roles in similar contexts can bring fresh ideas for meeting shared challenges and expand a woman leader's influence into new contexts as her ideas are used by others. These relational dynamics are complicated as they cross gender lines. Male and female leaders need a framework for navigating mixed-gender relationships in a healthy way. As a woman leader develops a relational approach that supports healthy partnerships with men, her influence expands.

A female leader's influence also expands as she develops various kinds of communication skills. These skills prepare her for both public platforms and interpersonal conversations in which she negotiates with people and works through challenges. She develops her own unique leadership Voice[18] as she learns to communicate her perspectives, ideas, and vision with persuasive

18. *Voice* is capitalized in reference to free self-expression, and it is lowercased in reference to physical speech.

effectiveness in her own authentic style. Influential women also learn to control the physical aspects of speech and body language in ways unique to women leaders. For women in ministry, skillful public speaking is essential to leading large meetings, teaching, and preaching. They must learn to craft a message that can be communicated through speech or writing. Social media has become an important platform for ministry communication, and influential female leaders establish their leadership Voices online in strategic ways.

Both developing relationships and developing communication provide an output of expanding leadership influence (see fig. 2.3).

THE MODEL AT WORK

I wish I could animate figure 2.3 to show movement in the model represented by the arrows. Unfortunately, the limitations of print prevent us from seeing these seven processes in motion. If I could put the figure in motion, we would see movement above and below as God's divine shaping guides and fuels these development processes. God's work to prepare a woman for leadership starts within as she responds to a spiritual process. We would also see movement within the center of this model as her spirit, mind, and emotions work to influence one another. Movement flows from the left toward the center as she continually processes the impact of her ministry environment and home life on her leadership. Movement also flows from the center to the right as she develops relationships and communication skills, creating leadership influence output.

But this is a far more organic process. In each season and in each woman leader, God works uniquely. God may focus on one process to speed up development in a certain area while he slows down development in another area for a time. Regardless of the pace, these seven processes work together and depend on one another to produce authority and influence.

MEASURING AUTHORITY

We can measure a person's authority within a church based on position, organizational power, and reach, such as social media audience.[19] A leader's authority increases as they move from one level of leadership to another. Five particular levels of leadership include the following:

19. In 1980 Lois McKinney identified five levels of leadership to categorize a church leader's authority. See McKinney, "Leadership," 179. My study updates McKinney's model with current local church leadership opportunities.

- *Level 1*: Lay leader in a local church
- *Level 2*: Support staff in a large or multisite church, or executive staff in a small to midsized church
- *Level 3*: Executive staff or campus pastor in a large or multisite church, or senior pastor in a midsized church
- *Level 4*: Senior pastor in a multisite or large church, or denominational leader of a large conference or a network of pastors
- *Level 5*: International leader speaking in churches and conferences internationally, consulting with churches, training leaders, leading international networks or denominations, having significant social media influence[20]

This study categorized the leadership influence of participants using this list. Detailed analysis can be found in appendixes C and D. Chapter 8 delves into this in more detail.

FEMALE MINISTRY LEADER SELF-ASSESSMENT

When women leaders find themselves stuck, assessing their development in relation to each of the seven processes may offer clues for a way forward. Below are links to a two-part self-assessment. Part 1 of the assessment is for all women leaders in local church ministry. Part 2 comes in two versions, one for married women and one for single women. Completing the assessment will generate a female leader profile offering feedback about a leader's development.

- Part 1: https://www.onlineassessmenttool.com/female-leader-profile -builder/assessment-113589
- Part 2 for married women leaders: https://www.onlineassessmenttool .com/married-female-leader-home-profile/assessment-113864
- Part 2 for single women leaders: https://www.onlineassessmenttool.com /single-female-leader-home-profile/assessment-11386

If you are a female leader about to dive into this assessment, please know this: you will probably score yourself lower than what is true, so don't think you are a failure as a leader or that you shouldn't continue down this leadership path. The assessment is designed to show you what parts of your

20. McKinney, "Leadership," 179.

development you have paid attention to and what parts might benefit from your focus. What we are unaware of will slow down our progress. Please (I'm begging you), do not beat yourself up with the results. They merely reflect what you already think of yourself. Use the results as a road map for where to start growing.

The chapters that follow delve deeper into each of the seven processes, exploring their implications for the women ministry leaders who are growing in influence and those around them supporting their development.

SUMMARY

Despite the best of intentions, even in church environments where women leaders are theologically and culturally supported, male leaders often outnumber female leaders. Leadership development efforts are not effectively forming female ministry leaders. There is a need for female-specific leadership development, but to equip and support women ministry leaders, we must first understand how women leaders are formed.

A woman's leadership development can be divided into seven distinct but intertwined processes. Three of these processes are internal: spiritual development, cognitive development, and emotional intelligence development. These three aspects deal with the spirit, the mind, and the soul of a female leader. Two of these processes are external and involve a woman's ministry environment and home life. The last two processes help form a female leader's influence: building leadership relationships and developing effective public and private communication. These processes are made possible by key leadership opportunities and accelerated by validation. All the processes work together to form a female leader who has influence.

GOD CALLING AND FORMING FEMALE LEADERS SPIRITUALLY

ASPECT 1

The development of a woman in Christian ministry leadership is first profoundly and fundamentally spiritual. Believers first receive a call into God's family, then a call into ministry to flourish in their giftedness.[1] Women on mission experience transformational moments when they sense an undeniable urge to follow God's calling.[2] They move beyond saying yes to the call to salvation to saying yes to the call to participate in the mission of Christ. Jennifer Moe identifies a sense of calling as an essential component of female ministry leadership development.[3] A sense of purpose creates longevity and deep satisfaction for female leaders.[4] The subsequent spiritual journey of a woman whose primary gifts are in leadership or teaching God's Word is unique.

When I sensed God calling me to ministry as a teenager, I wasn't alone. My youth pastors, a married couple, took me and a group of my friends under their wing. They encouraged us to obey God's call to make his mission our

1. Scott, *Dare Mighty Things*, 74–75, 85–87.
2. Adeney, *Women and Christian Mission*, 20–22.
3. Moe, "Discerning an Uphill Calling," 55–56.
4. Barsh and Lee, "Unlocking the Full Potential of Women."

mission. Some of my friends felt called as missionaries, others as pastors, and others as local church volunteers. I began to pray and journal about pastoral ministry. I felt drawn to leadership, sensing that God wanted me to influence others to serve Jesus. I was quiet and reserved, and I had no idea how this might happen. Did God even call women into leadership? Anxiety pushed me into deep Bible study to discover what God says about women in ministry. What did God want from me? What had he designed me for?

My male friends who felt called to pastoral ministry weren't asking the same questions. They knew not only that the path to ministry leadership was open to them but also that they would be cheered on every step of the way. My female friends who felt called to be administrative assistants or to teach children on the mission field weren't wrestling with the spiritual and biblical implications of what they were sensing. As I struggled to understand my calling, I began the long journey of my spiritual development.

SPIRITUALITY AND CALLING

The very first process of a female leader's developmental journey is spiritual. God shapes her and calls her to leadership. My study reveals three major aspects of spiritual formation over time in a female leader: accepting and obeying her divine calling to ministry, learning egalitarian theology, and learning to follow the Holy Spirit. The women in this study recognized their divine calling as an important part of their early leadership development. Just sensing this call isn't enough, however. Over 80 percent of the women recognized that responding to the call with obedience was the essential first step in their leadership development.

Often the call comes in an invitation from someone else—a pastor, a church friend, or a husband—who says something like this: "I see something in you. Will you help?" In this simple ask, God invites women into kingdom service.

Several women in this study are married to pastors. Recognizing their own calling as distinct from their husband's calling was very important. One of the women told me, "Even though I came into ministry to be a support to my husband, I found more of my call and solidified who I was as a woman of God along the way." As she said yes and responded to God's calling, he called her into more over time.

Many of the women experienced a powerful spiritual moment when they recognized God's voice directing them into ministry. Andi Andrews recalled it as a transformational moment: "I was standing at the front of the church when I prayed, 'All I want to do is build your church.' I felt this overwhelming love for Jesus, and I just knew what I was made for." Leanne Matthesius recognized it as a watershed spiritual moment that changed the trajectory of her life: "It was one of those definitely life-changing moments for me. I'll never forget it. It was a mile-marker moment in my life."

Katie Ellis stayed home with her children while they were young, but when her children were old enough to go to school, she felt restless. She went back to school for a master's degree in education, but after teaching middle school for a year and a half, things just felt off. After spending so much time and money, Katie was frustrated. She knew she wasn't in the right place but didn't know where she was supposed to be. Her senior pastor approached her and asked her to occupy a vacant church staff role as the next-generations pastor. In that moment, it was like a light bulb switched on in Katie's heart and mind, and she had a revelation. The confusion and frustration were gone, replaced by clarity. She realized that this was the opportunity God had been preparing her for and the reason she didn't feel passionate about teaching school. She knew immediately that God wanted her to say yes. This began a journey of ministry development, leading to her becoming her church's executive pastor.

God Remaking Women's Life Plans

Nearly every female church leader in this study had a different plan for her life, either another career or motherhood. Many didn't consider Christian ministry until well into their adult years after they were already well established in another career. They needed God to change their minds about their vocation. They saw this change as a process that took place through a series of revelations.

Nicole Barker was happily pursuing a successful career in television while her husband worked as a young adults pastor in their church. Great opportunities were opening before her, and her dreams were on a fast track. Nicole loved God and her church. So when her pastor decided to launch a women's conference and asked for help, Nicole said, "Of course!" But what now? She realized she would need to experience a great women's conference to know what to do.

Nicole made arrangements to attend a popular women's conference. As she experienced the event, she was awed by the excellence, detail, and care that had gone into designing it. It placed value on womanhood and was incredibly impactful. In that atmosphere, Nicole's heart was open; surrounded by thousands of women, she sensed God speaking to her. In that moment, God brought Nicole's attention to her husband's ministry. She understood that if she said yes to God's invitation to join her husband in ministry, they would see God move in a powerful way through their partnership.

Nicole went home excited and shared with her husband what she had heard. To her surprise, tears began to flow down his cheeks. He told her that he would never want her to give up her career and dreams for him but that having her as a full partner in ministry would be so much better. Nicole left her job and began working full time in ministry. What began as God's invitation to support her husband grew as she discovered her own giftedness and passion. This was just the beginning of an expanding revelation of her call. Today she is the co-lead pastor of their church, leading the ministry operations of the church and creative ministries. God intended her to use the skills she had honed in television to build her local church.

Nicole's story parallels many women's experiences of God's call. That first invitation into ministry is a spark that becomes an unquenchable flame over time. For women, calling is often an expanding revelation. It starts with God opening a small window for them to see what kinds of roles he has in mind for them, and then as they grow, he shows them more.

Affirmation of the Call

Some of the women in this study had to wrestle with the theology they were taught from childhood that limits women's ministry leadership. We process what we perceive God is saying to us through our mental maps, which have been formed by cultural models.[5] So if a woman who has never seen a woman preaching or pastoring hears God speaking to her about pursuing ministry leadership, she is far more likely to dismiss this message as not from God unless that calling is affirmed by another leader.

Women become motivated to accept their leadership calling when their church leaders affirm it. Missiologist Mary Lederleitner recognizes that this affirmation is so important that without it a calling experience is incomplete. She describes a calling experience as having three parts: feeling strongly called by God to leadership, that calling being affirmed by leaders in the church, and accepting the leadership call.[6] Once a woman recognizes her leadership call, she must grapple with the theological implications of what she is hearing. This requires personally engaging with what Scripture says about women in ministry leadership. Receiving a scriptural confirmation of her calling is especially essential if her church environment does not affirm the call.[7]

In every story shared with me, saying yes to a ministry leadership calling required someone else—often a man—affirming that calling and inviting her

5. Maros, *Calling in Context*, 23.
6. Lederleitner, *Women in God's Mission*, 38.
7. Adeney, *Women and Christian Mission*, 39–40.

into a ministry role. Men have a powerful role to play in birthing a female leader's call. When a male leader recognizes potential in a woman and tells her that God wants to use her life, a window opens. As he helps her see her own giftedness and expresses his confidence in her future fruitfulness, something begins to transform in her mind. A pathway opens before her that she had never recognized as a possible future. While women can certainly encourage other women in this way, in environments where women leaders are scarce or don't have much authority, male affirmation of calling is even more powerful.

Step by Step

A woman's leadership journey begins with recognizing God's invitation. Most of the time God doesn't call us as obviously as he did Mary, with the archangel Gabriel appearing dramatically with a divine message. If I had known what God would ask of me, I probably would never have begun the journey of ministry. I would have been intimidated and asked a question like Mary's: "How will this be?" (Luke 1:34).

Jesus just asks for our "yes," the response that says, "I am the Lord's servant" (Luke 1:38). Then he shows us the next faithful step of obedience. If Mary had known at that moment about all the terrifying, painful moments to come, would she have accepted the call? As a good gardener, God gently and slowly cultivates us into fruitfulness, sharing with us only as much as we need to know.

A sense of calling is important not just early on. The women in this study explained that being convinced of God's calling into leadership propelled them forward through difficult seasons of ministry, insecurity, and resistance from others. It kept them committed and created ministry longevity.

GIFTEDNESS DISCOVERY AND DEVELOPMENT

Following the Holy Spirit into his work requires a female ministry leader to both recognize her spiritual gifts and be given opportunities to exercise her strongest gifts.[8] Once a woman realizes she has been called to local church ministry, she must engage the process of discovering her gifts and then develop those gifts. This is not simply self-discovery but a process of becoming more like Jesus as the gifts grow.[9]

The Holy Spirit gives the same spiritual gifts to women and men—without limitations—and women are just as likely as men to be gifted in preaching,

8. Cole, *Developing Female Leaders*, 63–64.
9. Scott, *Dare Mighty Things*, 77, 155.

teaching, and leadership. Therefore, women have an equal responsibility to develop, steward, and use those gifts. Female leaders can easily get caught up in meeting the needs of their churches or ministries rather than faithfully developing their gifts. Taking time for regular reflection about how their gifts intersect with ministry needs can help keep these tensions in balance.[10]

A leader has three types of giftedness: natural abilities (innate capacities, skills, talents, or aptitudes), acquired skills (learned capacities, skills, talents, or aptitudes), and spiritual gifts.[11] J. Robert Clinton and Richard W. Clinton define a spiritual gift as "a God-given unique capacity which is given to each believer for the purpose of releasing a Holy Spirit empowered ministry."[12] While a leader will have multiple gifts, one gift will dominate and be central to their ministry. This gift will develop over the lifetime of a leader's ministry. Clinton and Clinton explain how the three types of giftedness develop over the course of a lifetime, for both men and women. A woman begins with natural abilities and then learns basic skills. As she recognizes her spiritual gifts, she learns more skills. Her giftedness continues to grow throughout her ministry as her roles shift. As a woman leader matures, her spiritual gifts, natural abilities, and acquired skills converge in the ideal ministry opportunity that maximizes her giftedness and produces the season of her greatest fruitfulness.[13]

Emerging leaders are often attracted to established leaders with similar gift mixes, or they are attracted to leaders with weaknesses complementing their own strengths. Those weaknesses create gaps of opportunity that an emerging leader can fill. Most often, an emerging leader will respond to ministry assignments that align with their gift mix, but when the assignment requires undeveloped giftedness, the Holy Spirit gives the leader new gifts they need to complete the assignment.[14] The discovery of gifts is a spiritual process that requires both discerning God's Spirit and self-awareness. As a woman becomes aware of her unique giftedness for leadership, she can respond to the Spirit's tug for her to use her gifts to serve the kingdom of God.[15]

Female Leader Spiritual Formation

Spiritual formation is vital for female ministry leaders. We have all been formed by a broken world and must be transformed. Christian philosopher

10. Scott, *Dare Mighty Things*, 83–84.
11. Clinton and Clinton, *Unlocking Your Giftedness*, 5.
12. Clinton and Clinton, *Unlocking Your Giftedness*, 40.
13. Clinton and Clinton, *Unlocking Your Giftedness*, 51–55.
14. Clinton and Clinton, *Unlocking Your Giftedness*, 60–62.
15. Moe, "Discerning an Uphill Calling," 55–56.

Dallas Willard states, "The greatest need you and I have . . . is renovation of our heart."[16] He describes this as "a Spirit-driven process of forming the inner world of the human self in such a way that it becomes like the inner being of Christ himself."[17]

This process of transformation is wholly dependent on our willingness to put self to death, as the apostle Paul describes, moving further away from self-worship (Gal. 2:20).[18] We cultivate this willingness through spiritual disciplines.[19] As we learn selflessness, we imitate Christ in his humble emptying of himself of divine power as a human infant bedded in an animal shelter and again as he is nailed to the cross. Selflessness also reflects Christ's humble act of washing the feet of his followers (Luke 2:7; John 13:1–17; Phil. 2:1–8).

All Christian men and women are called to this kind of spiritual formation, but women leaders note several key features of their process of spiritual development. The women leaders of this study learned to steward the church well, not because they chose the career of a clergy member but because they learned the heart of Jesus toward the church. Jesus loves the church so much that he gave himself up for it (Eph. 5:25). Jesus entrusts the church to our care, and so as we learn to steward it well, we become increasingly Christlike. The women went beyond simply loving Jesus to embodying his mission through the work of the local church. They came to understand their responsibility to shepherd their local church as part of their spirituality. Loving Jesus means loving and serving the church, the people he loves.

As we are spiritually transformed, we become increasingly aware of the Holy Spirit's work around us and learn to follow him. Both men and women Christian leaders must learn to follow the Holy Spirit's leading, saying yes to the prompting of the Holy Spirit and obeying. This happens in unique ways for women leaders, however. When a female leader feels unsure about her leadership decisions, following the Holy Spirit's direction gives her confidence and strength. Rachel Bailey described it this way: "In every decision I had to say, 'Lord, you're going to have to guide me in this because I'm not qualified in this area of ministry, but I love your people.'" A woman leader's lack of confidence makes learning to depend on the Holy Spirit necessary early on in her spiritual journey. As a woman leader hears the direction of the Holy Spirit, she must learn to trust that prompting and step out in faith and obedience. When she does and she sees the evidence of God's faithful hand at work in the lives of those entrusted to her care, her faith grows.

16. Willard, *Renovation of the Heart*, 14.
17. Willard, *Renovation of the Heart*, 22.
18. Willard, *Renovation of the Heart*, 64, 77.
19. Scott, *Dare Mighty Things*, 215.

Several women experienced seasons in the middle of their leadership journey when they were so busy doing ministry that they neglected their relationship with Jesus or found their identity first in loving and leading the church rather than in Jesus. In seasons of overwork, they became more focused on the validation of the people they served than on the one who called them. One woman put it this way: "What we do as a ministry leader can become just a job. Our Sundays are work. Every time we have a service that people come to experience Christ, we're working. There have been times that I have put my relationship with God on the back burner." As a woman approaches burnout, rejection, or failure, God refocuses her on serving Jesus as the center of ministry rather than serving the church.

Spiritual Authority Formation

Developing spiritual authority is essential to female ministry leader emergence. Ministry leaders must be spiritually respected before they can pastor.[20] Through spiritual formation, we develop spiritual authority. Watchman Nee explains, "Without sanctification there can be no authority."[21]

God can redeem painful experiences of women leaders in beautiful ways as they submit their lives to him. Wilmer G. Villacorta recognizes a power paradox surrounding female leadership: "Vital spirituality is born in contexts of little inclusion and opportunity—in places of powerlessness."[22] This leads to a female leadership approach that seeks to build up others before oneself and give away power. In this, God's promise in 2 Corinthians 12:9 is realized: "My power is made perfect in weakness." Through this "downward ascent," a woman leader gains spiritual authority—a humble, selfless, and vulnerable power.[23] Mother Teresa was a globally influential woman leader who demonstrated a spirituality rooted in powerlessness that illuminated the world around her.[24] This kind of power demonstrates the kind of servant leadership Jesus calls us to: "Whoever wants to become great among you must be your servant, and whoever wants to be first must be slave of all" (Mark 10:43–44).

Spiritual authority is a delegated authority from God and is paradoxically rooted in submission. As we submit to God and the authorities in our lives, we develop spiritual authority. Pastors Mike Bonem and Roger Patterson

20. Scott, *Dare Mighty Things*, 215.
21. Nee, *Spiritual Authority*, 183.
22. Villacorta, *Tug of War*, 43.
23. Villacorta, *Tug of War*, 49, 116.
24. Villacorta, *Tug of War*, 18.

encourage those serving in second-chair[25] leadership roles: "An attitude of submission is not a loss of authority. It is recognition of the source of authority."[26] When female and male leaders submit themselves to Jesus and to the church leaders God has called them to serve under, they gain the authority of those they serve. When leaders step out from under the authority of the leaders around them, they lose that delegated authority. Unless emerging leaders learn to submit to authorities, they will not develop spiritual authority.[27] Women leaders who have been taught to submit from an early age have an easier time developing spiritual authority than those who have not had to learn this spiritual discipline.

EGALITARIAN THEOLOGY RELEASING AND VALIDATING FEMALE LEADERS

The church I grew up in was part of the Foursquare denomination (founded by a woman). Several pastors on staff were women, and one preached regularly. Every independent Pentecostal church I have since belonged to has had female staff pastors and preachers. No one publicly argued to limit women's roles in church leadership; however, I heard few theological justifications for women in ministry leadership. Passages of Scripture that seem to limit women were generally glossed over with "Culture was different back then."

While I felt called to full-time ministry as a teenager, I wasn't sure what that meant for me. I read the Bible and struggled with passages that seemed to present a barrier between me and ministry. I needed to settle the issue for myself, so I asked my father to help me purchase some Bible study resources. I wrote a paper for my college freshman English class examining the difficult passages and what the Bible says about women and leadership, concluding that God does not put limits on female leadership, but culture does. This work settled my theological questions, and God brought me on a journey of realization over the next two years that he had called me not just to be a musician who served the church with my musical gifts. God asked me to see the bigger picture of what he was doing and take responsibility for building the church as a pastor. I heard my first sermon explaining egalitarian theology at a women's conference when I was thirty-eight. Every woman leader in

25. A second-chair leader is a man or woman who is serving in a church leadership team but is not in the first chair, which is the senior or lead pastor role. They are not the primary leader of their organization, but they do carry a leadership role.

26. Bonem and Patterson, *Leading from the Second Chair*, 41.

27. Clinton, *Leadership Emergence Theory*, 177.

this study who grew up in a theologically egalitarian charismatic church like mine had a similar experience. Our churches did not teach a fully fleshed-out theology of female leadership.[28]

Today more than ever, however, the theological question is front and center in every discussion of female church leadership. On the internet and in social media, thought barriers between movements have been erased, and arguments have been reduced to memes and "gotcha" tweets. Pastors in environments that have historically taken egalitarian theology as a given find themselves answering questions about the role of women in the church. Soon after my husband and I assumed the pastorate of a historic Assemblies of God (AOG) church, a young man who grew up in this egalitarian church asked my husband why I was leading or preaching, given what Scripture says about women in ministry. The AOG has "16 Fundamental Truths" that an individual seeking ordination must affirm to receive ministry credentials.[29] These doctrines provide the essential basis for fellowship. The AOG also has a position paper, "The Role of Women in Ministry," that clearly articulates its egalitarian position as it pertains to the local church (it does not address a theology of the home).[30] Because the AOG considers egalitarian theology to be a "nonessential," one is not required to embrace egalitarian theology to be ordained in the AOG. As a result, even though the movement embraces egalitarian theology, local churches may not. An AOG woman senior pastor described to me an encounter with her former AOG pastor when she was working for him as a children's pastor. When she shared that she felt God calling her to senior pastoring, he told her that an AOG church would never elect a woman as a pastor, so she should let that idea go. I met an AOG senior pastor who does not believe women should lead and so doesn't empower them in his local church, despite the position paper of the movement. Theological barriers exist, even in egalitarian movements.

Egalitarian theology is important for the church, perhaps more than ever, and explaining the theology behind our praxis is essential to the development of a new generation of men and women leading in churches.

The Impact of Egalitarian Theology on Female Leaders

In this study, egalitarian theology was one of the most significant parts of the spiritual journey for women leaders. Every female leader I studied believes that God intends no limits for female leadership and that any perceived

28. Morgan, "Female Leaders in Egalitarian Churches," 103.
29. "Assemblies of God 16 Fundamental Truths."
30. "Role of Women in Ministry."

biblical restrictions come from mistaken translations of the original language or flawed exegesis and hermeneutics of the reader.[31] Most of these women developed as leaders inside a theologically egalitarian environment. Those who grew up in egalitarian churches had not wrestled with the controversial Bible passages that seem to limit female leadership. Learning to understand and articulate egalitarian theology came later in life, either because of seeing controversy on social media or from encountering resistance to their preaching or leadership from complementarians attending their churches.

I spoke with women who were discipled in complementarian environments and learned egalitarian theology later. One woman, Mary Thompson, grew up staunchly complementarian. As she developed, her leadership gifts became impossible to ignore. God was calling her to serve the church with those gifts. "As the gifts and calling and the picture of who God called us to be became clearer, my husband and I started asking different questions." They began to study egalitarian theology, and after deep work, Mary found herself emerging on the other side of the theological fence. "I grew up being against female ministers. I spoke out against it. And so it was very comical when God really revealed my calling in ministry." In two noteworthy cases, the women's husbands recognized their leadership gift and God's call on their life before they did. This realization created cognitive dissonance for the couples, causing them to wrestle with their previous interpretation of the Bible's teachings about God's plan for women. As these couples became convinced that God has not placed limitations on women, the inner conflict was resolved and the women were able to step into their calling.

Egalitarian marriage is also an essential part of female development, commonly described as the "mutual submission" of Ephesians 5:21. Husbands and wives are mutually submitted to each other and co-submitted to Christ. This creates equal responsibility and authority for husbands and wives in the home and family. The support provided by a husband equally engaged in the home empowers a wife's ability to lead outside the home.

Interestingly, not every household represented in this study is purely egalitarian, however. While every participant believes that God does not put limits on female ministry leadership, many of them hold an adapted

---

31. CBE International has developed a wealth of resources exploring debated biblical passages and identifying errors in translation and interpretation that have historically been used to subjugate women, both in the home and in ministry leadership. For example, the Greek word *kephāle*, translated "head," has very different modern implications than the metaphor did two thousand years ago. A tiny sample of these include Majola, "Power of Bible Translation"; Haddad, "Tracking Errors in Bible Translation"; B. Miller, "Misinterpreting 'Head' Can Perpetuate Abuse."

complementarian perspective of marriage. They believe the husband is the head of the household and should lead the home and be the tiebreaker in decisions at home. Many female leaders find this to be a relief rather than a burden. Instead of feeling weighed down by the pressures of leadership both at church and at home, they are able to defer to their husbands at home. Katie Ellis explained this dynamic: "In most of my relationships, I am the leader, the one making the decisions. I'm okay with my husband making decisions for us at home because it takes a weight off my shoulders."

In all these quasi-complementarian marriages, the husband seeks agreement from his wife before making decisions. Furthermore, his headship in the household does not mean that the couple defaults to traditional gender roles in the marriage. With the husband's increased responsibility for the home also comes an increased responsibility to serve within the home, meeting both his wife's and his children's needs and empowering his wife into ministry leadership.

The Pentecostal movement's historic focus on experience over theology produces more pragmatic approaches. Rather than worrying about a well-articulated theological defense, Pentecostals are more likely to recognize extra-biblical validation of a woman's ministry, including anointing, gifting, and ministry fruitfulness. These are proof enough of God's validation in these circles. One Australian woman pastor expressed confusion about why the church continues debating about women in ministry leadership. "This doesn't make sense to me. Shouldn't we just start by identifying the gift on the person and go with that?" Inside her Pentecostal church, spiritual gifts reveal God's design for women, and further biblical exploration is unnecessary.

Once a Pentecostal female leader encounters people outside her egalitarian tradition, however, she must learn to articulate a biblical theology of female leadership. This becomes essential for the development of women who are called to have impact beyond their local churches and movements. However, this typically doesn't occur until a woman begins preaching and encounters theological resistance from those in the audience from complementarian backgrounds. Many Christians from non-Pentecostal traditions require biblical proof of God's validation of female ministers and place less value on experiential proof.

Learning egalitarian theology develops confidence in a female leader. Women who question their own leadership or are questioned by others find egalitarian theology incredibly empowering. Discovering that God purposely designs and creates women leaders and wants to use them for building the church produces confidence in God and his call. As one woman put it, "Egalitarian theology feels like permission, and affirmation, to do what

God designed me to do." Another spoke of egalitarian theology as a solution for ministry "sticky floors," or self-imposed limits: "I had very low confidence for many years, and the road to leadership was a long one for me—a sticky floor, not a glass ceiling. Egalitarian theology showed me that gender doesn't come into play in a call to leadership, just our *yes*." Another described how egalitarian theology validates her leadership: "It gives me the confidence to obey the Lord in the calling he has placed on my life. Egalitarian theology also helps me to not have to look to others for 'permission' to be in ministry leadership. It gives me more open influence in people's lives."

For many of these women, egalitarian theology either gave them the release they needed to pursue the calling God had laid on their hearts or provided validation of their ministries later when they needed to defend their own credibility.

Male church leaders are not required to mount a defense for the validity of their ministry leadership, but women leaders rely on the men around them to be able to articulate egalitarian theology well and defend their female colleagues.[32] If male local church leaders don't understand egalitarian theology well enough to articulate it, then women leaders in these environments will be limited in their influence development.

Egalitarian Theology: Inviting Female Leaders into Partnership with Male Leaders

Now that we understand what egalitarian theology is and how it impacts the development of women leaders, we need to understand how it is practiced. Women leaders have unique experiences that impact their missional approach. The term *egalitarian missiology* provides a framework for understanding the intersection of egalitarian theology and God's mission through the local church. Egalitarian theology invites female leaders into equal partnership with male leaders. This theology initiates a ministry praxis of mutuality that reflects the unity of the Godhead to accomplish God's mission. As missiologists Arthur F. Glasser, Charles E. Van Engen, and Shawn B. Redford note, all Christians, including women, are called to "full-time involvement in the task of making Jesus Christ known, loved, and served throughout the world. All have been given spiritual gifts to make this service possible."[33] Women leaders bring their unique contribution into God's mission as an expression of their spirituality.

Egalitarian theology does not simply place women into ministry leadership roles. It shapes how male and female leaders together carry out God's

---

32. Catford, "Women's Experiences," loc. 514 of 8092, Kindle.
33. Glasser, Van Engen, and Redford, *Announcing the Kingdom*, 264; see also 1 Cor. 12.

mission. God's perfect design for partnership was revealed in the garden of Eden when God made male and female in his image and then commissioned them to caretake the garden together (Gen. 1:27; 2:15–18). As Gretchen Gaebelein Hull observes, "Men will bring a male perspective and women a female perspective. When both minister together—in line with their mutual creation in the image of God and in fulfillment of Jesus' prayer in John 17:20–23—they will begin to mirror the unity, equality, harmony, and cooperation of the Godhead."[34] This egalitarian mutuality does not diminish or devalue the role of men but instead elevates women leaders to stand alongside their male partners to steward the work of God.

WOMEN'S THEOLOGICAL REFLECTION

An egalitarian missiology amplifies the mission theology of women. When women are leading on the front lines of God's mission, they bring their unique experiences into their reflections. Lederleitner describes this as a theology-making process: "As they face hardships and difficulties in their journeys, [women leaders] find ways to make meaning of what they are encountering in light of what they believe about God and his mission."[35] Missiologist Frances S. Adeney explains women's mission theology as a from-below-to-above approach rooted in personal experience that is contextual and often is narrative-based. Female mission theology is widely diverse, but themes include selflessness, embodiment, empowerment, relationality, invitation, celebration of diversity, unity, respect, humility, receptiveness, willingness to express emotion (even in scholarly works), dialogue and listening, working in community, education, and healing.[36] Lederleitner explains a feminine missiology that demonstrates humility:

> Leading in God's mission is quite different from other forms of leadership. . . . It cannot be self-focused, not if it is truly healthy and if it is going to reflect the image of the One in whose name we are working.[37]

Lederleitner continues,

> God's plan for his mission seems to be to form relationships with flawed individuals and invite them to serve alongside him. All the while, these people

34. Hull, *Equal to Serve*, 226.
35. Lederleitner, *Women in God's Mission*, 87.
36. Adeney, *Women and Christian Mission*, 29, 31, 53, 59, 92–93, 98–99.
37. Lederleitner, *Women in God's Mission*, 66.

frequently fall short, making poor decisions, and at times they model behaviors that cause many in the world to question God's goodness. Yet if these flawed human beings serving and leading with God in mission keep humbly coming back to him, confessing their sins and failures, he lovingly mentors them and they begin to grow and develop in remarkable ways.[38]

Theological reflection is beginning to progress beyond the old, tired arguments of egalitarian versus complementarian theology to discover new themes of God at work through women, transforming them from "theology-followers into theology-makers."[39]

Every generation needs new theology that contextualizes old truths in new experiences and expresses them in fresh ways. As Western culture becomes increasingly de-Christianized, establishing outposts of kingdom culture amid the dominant secular culture will be a cross-cultural, missionary work. As women step into kingdom leadership, the resultant egalitarian missiology enriches both men and women on mission with God.

SUMMARY

The journey of a woman's ministry leadership development begins with her calling. She must recognize and respond to God's invitation to ministry leadership. This is often disruptive to the plans and progress she has already made toward her chosen career path. Saying yes to Jesus is a powerful decision that changes the course of her life. Often someone else must confirm her calling for her to take the first step. As she takes her first steps of obedience, she begins to discover her unique gifts and design for ministry. God shapes her spiritually, discipling her. As she grows in her submission to God, he gives her spiritual authority, which grants her the respect of those she leads. She must grapple with the theological implications of her leadership. Egalitarian theology empowers her as a full participant in God's mission and sets her up for developing her own unique theological contributions to the church.

38. Lederleitner, *Women in God's Mission*, 94–95.
39. Adeney, *Women and Christian Mission*, 67.

4

FEMALE LEADERS FORMING LEADERSHIP COGNITION

ASPECT 2

When I was a teenage girl, my youth pastors encouraged me to call myself a leader. I went to leadership meetings and served in small ways, like setting up chairs, playing with the worship team, and making copies. I had no formal title or leadership responsibilities, but they were cultivating a mindset in me to recognize my influence with others so I could steer them toward serving Jesus. I struggled internally with the word *leader*, feeling like an imposter. I was fairly certain no one cared what I did and doubted that anyone beyond my friend group even knew my name. I didn't see myself influencing anyone. Nevertheless, I felt called by God to leadership, and so I kept going.

I had an interesting encounter recently, in one of those oh-my-gosh-the-world-is-small kind of moments. A woman I pastor wanted to introduce me to a good friend of hers who is a missionary in a Muslim-majority country, so we went for coffee. We realized at that meeting that we had met before. This missionary was about five years younger than me, and she had been a young teen in the youth ministry where I served on the worship team. I did not remember her, but she certainly remembered me. As we reflected on those days, she told me that she had viewed me with awe and admiration, like a rock star, and that I had inspired her to serve Jesus. I was deeply shocked to hear that I'd been influential in her life. I had no idea. Even though I had leadership influence in those days, I did not yet recognize myself as a leader.

A woman needs to learn to think differently as she becomes a leader. The second process of the internal development of a female leader involves her cognitive development, her mind and how she thinks. Leadership-thinking formation involves an identity shift in a female leader's view of herself and others. In addition to other ways of self-identifying (perhaps as daughter, as mother, as wife, or with regard to career or hobbies), a woman comes to identify herself as a leader with a greater responsibility for others. As she grows, she gains confidence in her leadership abilities and begins to think about the big picture. She also learns to cultivate her mental health.

This chapter covers the various parts of a female leader's cognitive development:

- developing a leader identity (having role models)
- developing confidence in leadership abilities (taking risks)
- thinking big picture (envisioning)
- cultivating mental health

DEVELOPING A LEADER IDENTITY

Developing a leader identity is essential for women early in their leadership journey. A woman needs more than gifting, skills, a title, or a position to emerge as a leader; she needs to embrace a new identity and conceive of herself as a leader called by God. Simply discovering giftedness and developing new skills is not enough for female leaders to emerge. For women to become leaders, skills learning must be accompanied by new-identity learning. A woman must learn to view herself as a leader and recognize her influence as it develops. This requires her to move past cultural or social programming she may have encountered throughout her life that associates authority with masculinity and the implicit messaging that to be a leader is to be unfeminine.[1]

Female Leader Role Models across Generations

Early in a woman's leadership identity development, she needs a role model with whom she can identify. When a young woman sees another

---

1. Adeney, *Women and Christian Mission*, 111, 113–14.

woman doing something that looks attractive, in a style that she likes or with similar gifts, she begins to think that this kind of leadership might be possible for her.

Study participants recognized that fundamental shifts in female church leadership models have occurred. Today's female church leaders represent a broader range of styles, roles, and gifts than the women leaders from even a single generation past.

Many older women in this study had few women leader role models when they were young and did not feel drawn to the women leaders they did see in their local churches. They could not identify with the ministry roles, styles, or gifting that they saw. Pastor Leanne Matthesius spoke of her struggle to find role models: "In the last century, types of women's ministry were limited; if you weren't a kids church worker or a musician, then there was not a whole lot of scope for you." Pastor Donna Crouch described pioneering a new identity: "I didn't see a woman preach in person until 1996. So as a woman pastoring in 1987, I was an anomaly—the odd man out—trying not to do things like a guy." Often God called women to lead in ways they had never seen modeled by other women.[2] To see themselves as leaders, baby boomers and members of Gen X had to pioneer a new idea of what that might look like—an identity that matched their unique gifting and passions.

The absence of role models is less often the case for younger generations. Brittney Baird is a millennial co-senior pastor who did not come from a ministry background but felt called to ministry and then married a pastor. Even when she began ministering, she didn't have many female role models: "At the beginning of my ministry journey there was no social media. I hadn't been to conferences or any other churches. So at the very beginning, I definitely thought if you were a woman in ministry, you played the piano or you sang, or you were in the nursery, or you were on the hospitality team, cooking. It was definitely conflicting for me because I always felt like a natural. I just felt like a leader even before entering into a church, and I couldn't do any of those things." Female roles in her egalitarian church weren't narrowly defined because of theological barriers. There just weren't enough female leader role models in various areas. However, the ministry roles that women of prior generations had pioneered became a foundation for Brittney to build on.

Rejecting old role models that don't fit is a key to women leaders embracing their full, authentic selves. A willingness to forge a new kind of role is essential for a woman to manifest her leadership calling and bear the ministry fruit God has planned for her.

2. Lederleitner, *Women in God's Mission*, 175.

What people see female leaders doing becomes a guide for what they expect from the next generation of leaders. Brittney described her search for role models as a quest to understand what her church family would expect of her leadership. By understanding what other women pastors were doing in other churches, she hoped to figure out what she should be doing. She wanted to form appropriate expectations for herself through role models.

The Impact of Female Leader Role Models

The baby boomer and Gen X generations had to creatively forge new identities outside the box, beyond what they had seen in their own churches. With the rising influence of churches in which women are pioneering new leader identities and with the rise of social media, a greater diversity of role models for xennials, millennials, and Gen Z is far more prevalent.[3] These role models are vital for creating a starting point of possibility for leadership for younger generations. If a woman can see herself in a female church leader, then she can begin to think that this kind of leadership might be possible for her as well.

As important as female role models are for women, they are perhaps even more important for men. When women leaders pioneer new, nontraditional roles for women inside a church, they give the male leaders in that context a new way to think about women. When male leaders need to fill a leadership opportunity, if they have not seen a woman successfully navigate the responsibilities involved, they will probably not consider asking a woman to lead. While this is true of leadership and preaching roles, it is also true of other male-dominated leadership roles like church production or security team leadership. A woman leader can create new norms for men for how to give women opportunity, how to interact with them, and the kinds of influence they can be trusted with.

More influential women advanced their leader identity a step further. More than just a leader, they saw themselves as a leader of leaders at their core and internalized being purposed to develop other kingdom leaders. They conceived of themselves as becoming role models for others. As a woman sees her potential in a role model or takes what she sees and pioneers something new, she becomes increasingly aware that she can become a role model for other developing leaders. This is a cyclical process over time.

When a woman recognizes herself as a leader, she grows in influence. As she grows in influence, she increasingly internalizes a leader identity. This

---

3. As I mentioned earlier, I divided these generations into ten-year increments. I grouped generations as baby boomer: 1955–64; Gen X: 1965–74; xennial: 1975–84; millennial: 1985–94; and Gen Z: 1995–2002.

internal identity work cannot be minimized as inconsequential. It must be prioritized, especially early in development.

Leader Identity Formation

Mary Lederleitner lists five steps to developing a leader identity. The process begins with a woman thinking leadership is masculine. Then a period of dissonance and confusion follows as she begins to sense her own leadership potential. She then develops a resistance to thinking about leadership as masculine. She begins selectively to think about herself as a leader and sometimes to trust that identity until finally she gains self-confidence in her leader identity in a mixed-gender environment. Organizations should foster groups that encourage women in their leader identity development, help them identify their purpose, and connect their leadership to that higher purpose.[4]

A sense of purpose comes to women ministry leaders when they experience a mandate and calling to leadership given by God. A leader must be honest with herself about her unique design and calling and accept the mantle of leadership.[5] The identity work that a woman leader undertakes is often initiated and always undergirded by her call from God into ministry.

A mentor or a coach can catalyze a woman's identity formation by recognizing and identifying leadership potential in her. A leader's encouragement gives a woman permission to view herself as a leader and as unique, even when she doesn't identify with role models she has seen. Pastor Sharon Kelly describes feeling as if she could not be anything like the female leader role models she had and so could not be a leader, but a mentor freed her from the constraints of the role models she saw: "My mentor explained to me that not all leaders are the same. There's no leader-shaped cookie cutter. That was really important for me to realize." Mentoring speeds along leader identity formation.

As a new pastor in a church that has not previously seen many women pastoring, I feel one of my most important responsibilities is to support the next generation of female leaders in my church. I need to recognize and call out the budding leadership gifts in young women entrusted to my care. Those who have not yet seen a role model they resonate with are sometimes reluctant to accept the pressures of leadership. I can help expand their ideas about what ministry leadership looks like by introducing them to new role models

---

4. Lederleitner, *Women in God's Mission*, 39–41.
5. Lederleitner, *Women in God's Mission*, 38–39; Ely, Ibarra, and Kolb, "Taking Gender into Account," 480.

through social media and encouraging them that God designed them to be unique, free, confident, and purposeful.

DEVELOPING CONFIDENCE IN LEADERSHIP ABILITIES

In addition to the unique journey of identity formation a woman leader must embark on, she must also develop confidence in her leadership abilities. Every study participant recognized that developing confidence is a vital part of a female leader's cognitive development. Her thinking must change for her to have influence. She must move beyond her lack of confidence, get comfortable with her natural leadership style and strengths, avoid comparisons, become comfortable with risk-taking, and learn to make and *own* her leadership decisions.

The Female Confidence Deficit

Confidence does not come easy for many women, and experts point to a variety of reasons for this. Even when women are successful, they are prone to devalue themselves and are susceptible to imposter syndrome, fearing their self-perceived incompetence will be exposed.[6] Women consistently underestimate their own abilities, predicting their own failure. A woman may naively not recognize she is experiencing gender discrimination and assume her own incompetence is the reason for her marginalization.[7] Susan Vinnicombe and Val Singh theorize that women are socialized to be less confident and that young girls are trained by their mothers to be attached. Because of this, they tend to be anxious instead of independent.[8] Image-conscious Western culture has also negatively impacted women's confidence. Women battle their bodies instead of being comfortable in their own skin.[9]

These factors likely contribute to the confidence gap between the sexes. Sheryl Sandberg and Nell Scovell and Anna Fels point to studies indicating that while women typically underrate their own performance, men typically overrate their own performance. Women are more likely to internalize negative feedback, leading to low self-esteem, and believe that failure is due to an

6. Imposter syndrome is when "women fear they will be found out or unmasked as unworthy of the success they have attained or the positions they have won." Vinnicombe and Singh, "Women-Only Management Training," 302.

7. Adeney, *Women and Christian Mission*, 149.

8. Vinnicombe and Singh, "Women-Only Management Training," 298, 302.

9. Lederleitner, *Women in God's Mission*, 191–92; Gross, *Women's Voices*, loc. 1108 of 3081, Kindle.

inherent internal flaw.[10] This gender difference starts early. A friend of mine was awakened in the night by her five-year-old son, who had regrettably peed in his bed. She groggily got up to take him back to his bedroom and stripped him of his wet pajamas. She then started stripping down the urine-soaked bedsheets. As she did, she noticed her young son posing nude in front of a full-length mirror, flexing his arms. He glanced back at her, smiled, and said, "Don't I look awesome?" Had this been a little girl, she would likely have felt humiliated and needed comfort. Boys seem to be hardwired with confidence that girls don't have.

Insecurity is not just uncomfortable; it also negatively impacts a woman's future performance and success. Women often struggle with perfectionism and hold back from attempting things until they are certain of success. Their lack of confidence often causes them to stop competing. Without competition, females do not win—the very thing that grows confidence. Low confidence causes inaction, even though women perform as well as men when they do act.[11] In addition, an insecure woman has a difficult time hearing criticism. If her defenses are up, she will not be able to hear difficult feedback, stunting her own growth.

Virtually every female leader in this study had to overcome a lack of confidence in her leadership, and some are still struggling—even as very successful, influential leaders. This insecurity comes from a variety of sources. A third of the women leaders identified some form of imposter syndrome at the root of this insecurity—feeling that they are underqualified and lack gifts and resources.[12] A woman leader's ability to process through her insecurities is essential to her longevity. Her sense of calling is the surest defense against quitting when facing her own unrealistically high standards for herself and her leadership.

Gaining Confidence

The female leaders in this study were quick to differentiate between confidence and arrogance. Humility seems to be an essential part of female leader identity, which causes women to steer clear of anything that feels like self-promotion. This is part of identifying with Christ. Nancy Beach defines humility as identifying the contributions of God and others around us in our success. This kind of humility is compatible with self-confidence.[13]

10. Sandberg and Scovell, *Lean In*, 29–30; Fels, *Necessary Dreams*, 145. See also Kay and Shipman, "Confidence Gap."
    11. Kay and Shipman, "Confidence Gap."
    12. Vinnicombe and Singh, "Women-Only Management Training," 302.
    13. Beach, *Gifted to Lead*, 36, 39, 41.

External influences are important for women leaders gaining confidence. A lack of role models caused significant self-questioning in participants as well as resistance to their leadership from others. When a female leader did have a female role model who had accepted herself and was comfortable and confident in her own unique style and gifting, then the junior female leader was able to imitate this self-acceptance. This transition was essential for women progressing in leadership influence. Pastor Holly Wagner explained this well: "When a woman sees someone who's confident in who they are and free to be who they are, then that releases her to be who she's supposed to be. I just decided to live out who I really am. And that's when our church grew." When Holly modeled this self-acceptance, her ministry became attractive to others.

A woman's leadership being validated and encouraged by others helps bring self-acceptance. Women grow more confident when they are trusted by other leaders, given leadership opportunities, and hired by a church that affirms female leaders. A woman understands that when someone entrusts her with a leadership opportunity, they are demonstrating confidence in her abilities. A woman can borrow other people's confidence in her until she has successes of her own. If someone I respect believes I can do it, then I must be able to do it!

A woman becoming comfortable with her natural leadership style and gifts is an essential part of her journey toward confidence. Every female participant regarded this as an important process in her development. Self-awareness of gifts and style is necessary before a female leader can be confident in her unique leadership design. Self-awareness is an aspect of emotional intelligence that we will explore at length in chapter 5. One emerging leader said, "Gaining confidence in my own leadership abilities and decision-making came from self-awareness of the areas that I excel in and the areas that I'm not as competent in." This is also connected to developing authenticity, which is another component of emotional intelligence.

Confidence and increased influence are linked. Women with more influence report having more confidence in their own leadership abilities. More leadership experience and gaining more authority grow the confidence of women. Women are typically willing to accept leadership roles only if they feel enough self-confidence, but if women will simply start by saying yes to leadership opportunities, increased confidence will come.

Avoiding Comparison

Comparison kills confidence. Women leaders must learn to avoid comparing themselves to others. Young women leaders struggle with comparing themselves not just to other women but also to the male leaders around them who seem to find leadership easier or appear further along. Women compare themselves on many fronts, from appearance to status. Ministry leaders struggle in particular with comparing their gifts and levels of influence to those of other leaders.

Early on, women leaders emulate their role models. They model themselves after what they respect, and this provides a pattern to follow. However, as a woman becomes self-aware of her own giftedness, comparing her progress to that of available role models (who may have very different gift sets and ministry callings) can potentially lead her to devalue her own unique ministry contribution. To grow in influence, a woman leader must be able to set aside anxiety about being different or insecurity about not being good at what another woman is good at and lean into her own unique God-given design. One pastor said, "I watched my [female] pastor be comfortable with herself, which taught me to be comfortable being my true self. That really set me free. I don't have to fit into a certain mold. It's so easy to compare yourself to other women or think you have to do something the same way that someone else did it." When women stop comparing themselves and trying to copy someone else, their self-acceptance produces confidence in their own leadership abilities.

Avoiding comparison is connected to increased influence. In the same way that budding female leaders need to unplug from unhelpful role models, emerging women leaders need to avoid comparing themselves to other women leaders (more on this in chap. 11). As women grow to become influential leaders and mature in age, they learn to stop comparing themselves to other leaders. Instead of being worried about what other women are doing or not doing, they can value the diversity of callings around them without feeling judged or devalued by the differences among them.[14]

Taking Risks in Faith

Confidence is important in decision-making. A female leader becomes more confident in making and owning decisions as she grows. Most of the study participants recognized that confidence in decision-making and risk-taking are important in female leader development. Without the confidence to make important decisions, a woman cannot lead effectively.

Women leaders need courage to take leadership risks. Taking risks may be easier for men because of the connection between prenatal exposure to androgens and a willingness to take risks.[15] A meta-analysis of 150 studies exploring the risk-taking tendencies of males and females found that many factors impact risk tolerance, including self-esteem and social environments.

14. Lederleitner, *Women in God's Mission*, 43.
15. Schmitt, "Truth About Sex Differences."

The difference in risk tolerance between men and women may also be caused by a gendered difference in competitiveness.[16] When testing men and women for risk aversion in corporate takeovers, C. Bram Cadsby and Elizabeth Maynes found that women tend to align with the decisions and strategies of others in their group instead of forging different paths.[17] This could be a safety measure.

Women leaders' willingness to take risks comes later in their development and is associated with influential leadership. Most of the women in this study who recognized risk-taking as important in leadership were in senior positions of leadership. In positions of lesser authority, the risks are smaller and affect fewer people. When a female leader's authority increases, her decisions have further-reaching impact. Women's more collaborative, others-oriented leadership perceives risk not as personal but as collective. A woman leader is conscious of the wide-ranging, harmful impact of a failed risk, making her naturally more cautious. The later development of risk-taking may also be connected to a woman leader learning to broaden her awareness to consider the entire organizational picture rather than just one department. Instead of thinking about just the personal risk, she learns to consider the organizational risks.

Fear holds women back from engaging in challenging assignments. Despite the risk, these challenges potentially build skills and influence. Sandberg and Scovell encourage women to move past fear and view challenges as learning opportunities.[18] This mental shift begins by changing the cultural narrative that women need to be rescued. We need to replace this with the idea that women are God-designed to be *ezer-kenegdo*—strong warrior-companions to men.[19] To reduce fear, female leaders can look for links between what they already know and have accomplished and what lies ahead.[20] More advanced female leaders in this study explained that hearing God's direction and choosing to obey provide confidence that a risk should be taken and faith that God will support the risky step. Simply put, influential Christian women believe that every significant and important undertaking requires faith, and that faith requires risk.

Women's leadership coaches often recommend taking action as a strategy for confidence building. Katty Kay and Claire Shipman prescribe action because it forces women to work hard, perform, and develop skills, and their successes in turn produce confidence.[21] Tara Sophia Mohr recommends women take a "leap action," something that can be accomplished in a few weeks and

16. Byrnes, Miller, and Schafer, "Gender Differences in Risk Taking," 379.
17. Cadsby and Maynes, "Gender, Risk Aversion," 57.
18. Sandberg and Scovell, *Lean In*, 10, 15, 24, 62.
19. James, *Half the Church*, 114.
20. Tarr-Whelan, *Women Lead the Way*, loc. 1327 of 4551, Kindle.
21. Kay and Shipman, "Confidence Gap."

that stretches a woman beyond her comfort while connecting her to those she wants to influence. Leap actions are learning opportunities.[22] When a leap action pays off, women become less afraid of the next opportunity.

Christians call this a "faith step" or a "leap of faith." When a female leader becomes convinced that God has put an opportunity before her and feels a sense of urgency to answer that call, she is ready to take a leap of faith. Her courage comes not so much from confidence in her own abilities as from confidence that this action must be taken, and that God has asked her to take it. She has confidence that when she steps out in faith, God will equip her by his power with the spiritual gifts she needs to accomplish what he has called her to do.

Once a woman has taken that step of faith, there are two possible outcomes. Either she is successful in her efforts and learns about her own giftedness, or she experiences some degree of failure. A woman can grow in confidence in the wake of failure by changing the way she views the experience. Instead of her internalizing this with the message, "I am a failure because I failed," she can externalize the experience. This kind of thinking says, "Now I know what doesn't work. I have learned something." Figure 4.1 shows this progression.

To grow in confidence, female ministry leaders need to preprogram their default response to be yes when opportunities arise.[23] Saying yes to God keeps them from the female tendency to overthink the opportunity and find all the reasons to hold back. A church ministry leap action might be saying yes to planning an event or launching a new program or outreach. If a woman says yes to leading a short-term initiative and then experiences success, she gains self-awareness of what she is good at. This awareness provides her with the confidence she needs to tackle bigger challenges.

When I was a young woman supporting my youth pastor husband, my primary role was coordinating the youth worship team. He was the face and the voice of our ministry team, but I was more musically skilled and organized. My pastors recognized something in me that I did not. When the church needed a new worship pastor, they asked me to step in temporarily. I did not believe I had the ability to lead the worship ministry of the entire church, but I agreed to fill the role on an interim basis for a maximum of six months. Instead of filling the role with someone else more qualified, they hired an older, experienced worship ministry coach to help me develop the ministry skills I did not yet have. This man traveled to Chicago twice monthly to teach me how to lead a worship ministry. After two years of the coach's support,

22. Mohr, *Playing Big*, 166.
23. Lederleitner, *Women in God's Mission*, 7, 35; Tarr-Whelan, *Women Lead the Way*, locs. 1272–1363 of 4551, Kindle.

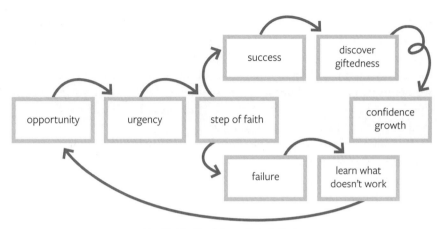

Fig. 4.1. The Confidence Growth Cycle

I no longer needed the help, and the ministry grew and thrived. I continued to lead that ministry for another decade. If I had been presented with the opportunity outright, I would certainly have declined it and would not be writing this book today. But because my pastors presented me with a small commitment, I had the space to develop confidence for the larger commitment.

We need to teach women to be brave, to sacrifice, and to take risks to tackle the problems of our day.[24]

THINKING BIG PICTURE

In addition to developing a leader identity and developing confidence in their leadership abilities, female leaders need to develop the skill of thinking big picture, or envisioning. Unfortunately, they often underperform in this area, especially when compared to men.[25] Envisioning involves four abilities. The first is recognizing parts of society where people are not flourishing and viewing them as opportunities. Instead of avoiding these problems as too difficult, a visionary gravitates toward these issues and recognizes cultural trends. The second ability is visualizing a better future for the group, dreaming about good things that could happen. The third ability is creating a strategy for building that flourishing future. The fourth ability is vision casting, or the ability to share the compelling story of this better future with stakeholders.

For emerging women leaders to become influential, they must learn the skill of envisioning. In this study, only women who were level 5 leaders (see

24. Scott, *Dare Mighty Things*, 154.
25. Ibarra and Obodaru, "Women and the Vision Thing."

Lois McKinney's five levels of leadership in chap. 2) said they recognized the importance of envisioning in their development. Without the skill of envisioning, female leaders stay stuck in middle-management roles, where they focus on strategy and the implementation of someone else's vision. Many women leaders tend to hesitate to present a vision for the future. However, those who have a well-defined vision for the future have more confidence.[26] Without vision, a leader is not leading.[27]

As emerging women leaders develop confidence and become more comfortable with risk-taking, they are ready to think big picture. For an entrepreneur, this means engaging the problems in a community that might be overwhelming at first and dreaming about what a different future could look like. In a redemptive process, a woman leader's struggles become the seeds for her vision for mission as she glimpses a better future. As a plan begins to emerge, she must talk about her dream with others and allow them to weigh in, and she must rally others around her calling. As she paints a picture of what could be, she inspires others to see that same picture and join the work of bringing it to life.

Those leading inside an established organization should delegate administrative details to others and focus on the big picture, developing a vision for the entire organization. This means seeing beyond the boundaries of one's own responsibilities, taking responsibility for the success of the entire organization, and being willing to make difficult, risky decisions. These steps are essential for shifting from middle management to the executive level, according to leadership-development expert Rebecca Shambaugh.[28]

CULTIVATING MENTAL HEALTH

Even if a female leader develops a leader identity and confidence in her leadership abilities and learns to think big picture, poor mental health can negatively affect her cognitive development. The presence of anxiety leads to a need for control that limits her ability to trust God, herself, and others and to make risky decisions. One female leader described this connection between control and anxiety: "I felt like I've got to control this. I've got to systematize this. And then eventually before you know it you wake up one day filled with anxiety because you're trying to maintain this thing you built." Anxiety caused this leader to feel as if success rose and fell with her rather than allowing her to develop dependency on God, and it made her afraid to rely on others and to take risks in faith.

26. Fels, *Necessary Dreams*, 11, 161, 183.
27. Ibarra and Obodaru, "Women and the Vision Thing."
28. Shambaugh, *It's Not a Glass Ceiling*, loc. 394 of 3062, Kindle.

Healthy leadership thinking comes from a healthy mind. Women spoke of seasons when struggles with anxiety caused them to hold too tightly to organizational control or when the church felt out of control, producing anxiety. Risk-taking can produce anxiety, so risk must be balanced with a leader's anxiety tolerance. This is particularly true later in leadership development, when a woman has built both a reputation as a successful leader and a significant organization many people depend on. The more a leader has to lose, the more anxiety they deal with in risk-taking. Leaders fear the loss of what they have worked hard to build. If anxiety builds up, this can lead to burnout quicker than overworking.[29]

In busy seasons, a female leader who neglects her spiritual life can begin to think her work's success is dependent on her. She takes the burden of leadership entirely on herself, which weighs down her mind. Instead of relying on God, she makes the mistake of self-dependence.[30] The root of this is the sin of pride. The painful and ironic consequence is that pride in leadership accomplishments can impede future growth. Pride may make a leader risk averse, reluctant to let go of previous seasons of success and to take obedient steps forward in an effort to protect the past.

A healthy mind moves a leader forward at a pace at which anxiety can be managed. It stays in an attitude of God dependence, not taking credit for God's work. A healthy mind does not onboard the anxiety of others but stays in an attitude of faith and obedience to God's call.

SUMMARY

The second major area of development for women leaders is cognitive development. Women need to develop a leader identity. They often base this identity on the role models they have observed. A lack of quantity and diversity of female leader role models means that often women must pioneer a new identity without a pattern to model. Women leaders must also develop confidence in their leadership abilities. Women often struggle with low confidence, particularly in leadership. They must learn to avoid comparing themselves with other leaders and to take risks in faith. Resultant successes will build their confidence. As women leaders continue to grow, they must begin thinking big picture, which is essential to influential leadership. As they do all these things, they must work to maintain a healthy mind by managing anxiety and relying on God.

29. Cuss, *Managing Leadership Anxiety*, 6.
30. Cuss, *Managing Leadership Anxiety*, 12.

5

FEMALE LEADERS FORMING EMOTIONAL INTELLIGENCE

ASPECT 3

y parents put me and my siblings into piano lessons when I was six. My sister and brother quit after a few years, but I stuck with it. I started playing for church events at about age twelve. Once I got a taste for playing with a band, I was hooked. I enjoyed playing, singing, and writing music. I became self-aware of my musical gifts. When I felt called to ministry, I gave my abilities to God. I was a musician with a heart for ministry. Later, as a worship pastor, I realized that I was good at administrating and motivating a team. The opportunity to lead enabled this discovery. The emergence of my gifts produced more opportunities to lead at an executive level in our church, and these opportunities enabled the discovery of my giftedness for project management. This was an unfolding process.

The process of self-awareness was not all sunshine and roses, however. I also learned what I'm not good at. I still cringe to remember occasions of failure or mediocrity and facing the negative feedback from my team members or leaders. Most worship pastors lead worship while singing. I was a worship pastor, but I was not a great singer. I had to recognize that no matter how much training and practice I put into singing, it was never going to be one of my strongest gifts. Regardless of my own expectations for what God had called me to do, I painfully discovered that my ministry was going to look different. I had to learn to manage my disappointment and embarrassment so that they didn't control my behavior. To grow, I had to receive the difficult truth about where I am not effective. I learned that ministry isn't about me and what I want to do; it's about serving others.

I met others on my team who loved to sing and wanted so badly to be great worship leaders, but God had designed them with different gifts. These folks continually pushed themselves into circumstances where they faced rejection and humiliation instead of the validation they craved. Too many got stuck there. One woman had tremendous project management skills that could have been so valuable in planning church services, but she would not value what she was naturally good at and was frustrated by what she perceived as externally imposed limits on her ministry.

I've had to work on my sensitivity when dealing with others, both in what I perceive and how I communicate. I am not as crippled by other people's opinions as some are, but sometimes I misread people's feelings. Developing what John D. Mayer and Peter Salovey call "emotional intelligence" is an ongoing process in my life.[1]

Leadership consultants agree that female leaders need to develop emotional intelligence (EI),[2] which consists of four primary domains: self-awareness, self-management, social awareness, and relationship management.[3] Daniel Goleman, Richard E. Boyatzis, and Annie McKee write that "great leadership works through the emotions" and that the mood and tone of a leader directly impact the motivation, commitment, and morale of followers.[4] People are more willing to stay on a team when their leader is optimistic and enthusiastic.[5] Skillful guidance of one's emotions is necessary for successful leaders,[6] and this requires emotional self-regulation as well as self-awareness.

This third internal development process shapes the soul of a female leader. Developing EI differs from spiritual development and cognitive development in that it addresses how we process emotion. Because EI is necessary to many other processes of development, its development is essential. Developing EI is a process that happens over the life of a leader and has direct connections to leadership influence emergence. As a female leader gains more EI, she

1. Ovans, "How Emotional Intelligence Became a Key Leadership Skill."
2. Tarr-Whelan, *Women Lead the Way*, loc. 1498 of 4551, Kindle; Cole, *Developing Female Leaders*, 69; Eagly and Carli, *Through the Labyrinth*, 75.
3. Goleman, Boyatzis, and McKee, *Primal Leadership*, 43–44.
4. Goleman, Boyatzis, and McKee, *Primal Leadership*, 17.
5. Goleman, Boyatzis, and McKee, *Primal Leadership*, 18.
6. Bradberry and Greaves, *Emotional Intelligence 2.0*, 43.

also gains more leadership influence. The components of EI especially key to female leadership development are the following:

- developing self-awareness
- processing criticism
- learning self-regulation
- developing inner motivation
- embracing authenticity
- developing empathy

DEVELOPING SELF-AWARENESS

Rebecca Shambaugh writes that self-awareness is the primary characteristic of effective female leaders.[7] The journey of developing self-awareness is therefore an essential one for female leaders. Self-awareness allows women leaders to discover their blind spots and grow. As a female leader grows in self-awareness, she discovers her unique giftedness and God-given design—what she is uniquely designed to do for the kingdom of God. Every female study participant acknowledged that self-awareness was an essential part of her development.

Female leaders experience a lack of self-awareness of their giftedness early in their journey, which leads to a lack of confidence in their leadership. Self-awareness develops through opportunity and practice. Brittney Baird said, "Over time, when I was given opportunity, I was able to pinpoint that leading comes easy for me; leading is natural to me." As in my own experience, leadership opportunities provide a mirror for a woman to see what she is good at and what she is not good at.

As female leaders mature, they discover their strengths and weaknesses. Instead of getting stuck after discovering weaknesses, female leaders need to either correct their weaknesses with training, coaching, and practice or use a collaborative approach to borrow someone else's strength. Self-awareness is important not just for discovering strengths and weaknesses, however. Self-awareness of one's motives for ministry leadership is also vital. A female pastor explained to me that she regularly evaluated her own motives. This self-evaluation enabled her to realize when she needed to adjust her motives in ministry relationships. She could reorient herself around the needs of others rather than looking for them to achieve her ministry goals.

Self-awareness is especially important for women with latent leadership gifts who are married to pastors. Such women in this study had to engage a

7. Shambaugh, *It's Not a Glass Ceiling*, loc. 322 of 3062, Kindle.

process of self-discovery to recognize their own calling, distinct from their husband's calling. Only when these women figured out what they are gifted to do did they feel confident in their divine calling and begin to grow in leadership.

Women leaders need feedback to gain self-awareness of blind spots. Women whose husbands are in ministry leadership can receive helpful feedback from their spouse. Those without this support need other sources, such as mentors. Sadly, most emerging female leaders do not receive honest, real-time feedback, and so their growth is stunted, and their self-awareness limited. Kadi Cole encourages pastors to clearly define expectations and communicate them to the women on their teams.[8] Clear feedback from supervisors, peers, and team members is useful for developing female leader self-awareness.[9] However, comprehensive feedback is typically given annually, while women leaders may benefit from more frequent, consistent supervisor feedback combined with self-assessment. Where this kind of feedback is not available, women leaders should seek external coaching to help them discover blind spots.[10]

What is clear from the data is that the development of self-awareness has a direct impact on the growth of influence. Self-aware women are more influential. The sometimes painful process of developing self-awareness is vital to female leadership development.

PROCESSING CRITICISM

Criticism can either empower or cripple its receiver. Because many women struggle with self-esteem issues, negative feedback may shut down a female leader, but it's necessary for gaining self-awareness. Women leaders must be able to cope emotionally with criticism, process it in a positive way, and recognize opportunities for growth.

Most women in this study agreed on the importance of learning how to process criticism in a positive way. Without EI, women process negative feedback as hurtful and damaging rather than as a tool for growth. Instead of internalizing criticism as "I'm a bad leader" or "You are rejecting me," female leaders need to learn to internalize criticism as "I made a mistake that I can correct."

One of the male pastors I interviewed observed that the women on his team frequently wear "protective armor" to defend against criticism because of their insecurities about their femaleness in leadership. Early in a woman

8. Cole, *Developing Female Leaders*, 83, 134.

9. Ely, Ibarra, and Kolb, "Taking Gender into Account," 481; Cole, *Developing Female Leaders*, 132; Hopkins et al., "Women's Leadership Development," 353.

10. Vinnicombe and Singh, "Women-Only Management Training," 304.

leader's development, hearing criticism can cause her to shrink down and feel inadequate in her leadership, particularly if the criticism is related to her femaleness. This can be a major barrier to growth and development.

Most of the female participants acknowledged that they have not received much feedback, positive or negative. If female leaders are wired to be defensive because of innate insecurity, then it is possible that they are not receiving feedback because their leaders have given up providing what seems to be unwanted feedback about their mentee's leadership development. The ability of female leaders to process criticism is an essential part of moving beyond this stalemate.

As a female leader grows in spiritual maturity, she recognizes the importance of participating in Jesus's ministry in others' lives as well as the urgency to maximize her impact. She can then move beyond the self-doubt that criticism creates. Being ineffective in an area matters only because it points to a growth opportunity. It cannot disqualify her because her strengths are needed. She cannot afford to shrink back because others need her ministry leadership to grow in effectiveness. She is motivated by the needs of others, which cause her to pursue growth, even if it is painful to become self-aware of her leadership weaknesses. Her focus shifts from self to others, a mark of spiritual maturity. Learning to process criticism is a part of this spiritual development.

A helpful strategy for avoiding being blindsided by criticism is to ask for feedback from bosses, peers, and employees.[11] By taking initiative to address blind spots, two things happen. First, a woman gains control over how and when feedback is given, so she can be emotionally prepared for criticism and hear it privately. Second, when those around her become aware of her desire to grow and address their concerns, they are less likely to be angry and aggressive when they deliver criticism and more likely to be diplomatic and reasoned in their approach. A softer delivery can make criticism easier to receive.

Arianna Huffington advises women to give themselves permission to feel rejection as an emotional response to criticism but then to quickly move on.[12] Tara Sophia Mohr encourages female leaders to depersonalize feedback. Instead of internalizing criticism as personal failure, female leaders should view it as valuable information revealing the needs of the person providing it. If the individual is a stakeholder in the leader's vision, then useful feedback should be carefully considered and unhelpful criticism ignored.[13]

11. Shambaugh, *It's Not a Glass Ceiling*, locs. 429–68 of 3062, Kindle.
12. Sandberg and Scovell, *Lean In*, 49.
13. Mohr, *Playing Big*, 101–2.

LEARNING SELF-REGULATION

Learning to manage emotional responses, or self-regulation, is also a vital part of female leadership development, particularly in the context of experiencing leadership pain. Leadership experts Alice H. Eagly and Linda A. Carli encourage female leaders to maintain emotional control in professional environments to avoid being perceived as weak.[14] This is perhaps easier said than done when facing difficult feedback. Women leaders in this study described their difficulty controlling their tears while hearing correction from a boss.

Sandy described to me the challenge of emotionally regulating herself while hearing difficult and direct feedback. Her personality is sensitive, and she has very high standards for herself. She is emotional and quick to tear up, even when she doesn't want to. She has a hard time not crying when she is disappointed in herself. She feels leadership failures deeply and has had a hard time controlling her feelings. She recognized that her pastor was holding back feedback about her leadership, checking in with her feelings before communicating with her. On a good day, she took a deep breath and told her pastor, "I need help. And I know that for you to help me, you will have to tell me things that are hard to hear. I know I need to hear them. So I will do my best not to let the tears flow. But if they do, keep talking. It's just water. I'll be fine. I want to hear you and get better. Please keep talking." When Sandy recognized that she has a hard time emotionally regulating herself, she took initiative to communicate that she is not as fragile as she appears to be to prevent her pastor from feeling awkward and avoiding giving needed and wanted feedback. Sandy gave verbal permission to her superior to continue to offer coaching, regardless of her tears, making sure that the superior understood that while she was still learning how to self-regulate, she wanted the feedback.

Other women spoke of learning to emotionally self-regulate by bringing their feelings to Jesus in prayer and releasing their tears there, privately. This might involve asking for a break during a difficult conversation to step away for a few minutes of prayer and release. Women who have been hurt by careless comments or experienced the pain of betrayal or rejection need healing, and Jesus is available to strengthen and bring hope.

Self-regulation is important not just in difficult conversations with superiors but also in difficult conversations with the people a woman leads. To self-regulate, a female leader needs to have self-awareness of her own feelings about the situation at hand. She needs to control her emotional response (anger, disappointment, etc.) to the problem and to the other person's reaction to being

---

14. Eagly and Carli, *Through the Labyrinth*, 244.

confronted. Leanne explained, "I think the minute something becomes overly emotional or heated and aggressive, you then give opportunity for people to throw out the message because of the messenger." If an important message is delivered without emotional control, the recipient may dismiss the leader's correction as an overreaction or as coming from questionable motives, and the opportunity for learning is lost. The chances of a positive outcome are far more likely if the leader regulates her emotions. Younger leaders struggle with having difficult conversations and having successful outcomes, and a lack of self-regulation is likely why. The data shows a connection between emotional self-regulation and the development of influence, indicating the importance of this skill in the development of a female leader.

DEVELOPING INNER MOTIVATION

Inner motivation is another component of EI. It keeps female leaders moving forward when things are difficult or discouraging. For the women in this study, the motivation to pursue the call of God to be a female leader happened early in their lives.

The women were concerned not just about being motivated to continue in leadership, however. They were also concerned about what motivated their pursuit of influence. About three-quarters of the women recognized how important it is to be aware of their motivation for wanting to develop authority.

While many of them had an inner drive for achievement and success, it was important to them that their motivation be others-oriented and not self-serving. This work in motivation formation is closely tied to the development of spiritual maturity and the foundational Christian call to humbly love others before ourselves. Karolina Gunsser-Grant, a solo female lead pastor in Australia, explained, "I realized quickly how to diagnose my own motivation. I measure my own leadership by asking myself: *Am I helping those around me become all that God has intended them to be?* That question has helped me stay grounded. It's helped me keep my relationships pure in my motive."

When a woman is given an opportunity to preach to a room full of men and women, it is powerfully validating of her leadership. This is particularly true when the men give the female preacher their full attention. It lends credibility, but it can also lead to ego development and pride. Katelyn Beaty describes the seductive nature of celebrity, which she defines as "power without proximity," and its promise to provide fame.[15] Leaders who lack confidence and look to others to provide their sense of worth may struggle with a desire for celebrity, which is so

15. Beaty, *Celebrities for Jesus*, 14.

valued by our culture. Pastor Holly Wagner challenged women to examine their motivation for wanting to preach. The motivation for capturing the attention of men should not be validation or the need to feel accepted. What matters is that men can receive the ministry of Jesus through what a woman is communicating.

One woman attributed her season of waiting on leadership to God's sovereign work. During that time, God was purifying her motivation before entrusting her with significant influence. "God put my dreams on pause so that I could really work on growing in my emotional intelligence and spiritual maturity and to make sure that the motivation for leadership was not about my name or my leadership but about fulfilling the calling that God had on my life." This kind of shift in motivation is vital for female leaders who struggle with confidence and needing affirmation. Female leaders need to learn how to minister out of love and compassion for those they are leading rather than a need for affirmation from others. Without the correct inner motivation, ministry longevity is threatened. Seasons will come when a leader's popularity wanes, and if her motivation depends on affirmation, then she will not make it through times of leadership backlash.

Almost universally, the women in this study communicated discomfort with marketing themselves to others. When someone tries to gain respect or opportunity by talking up their accomplishments and abilities, this communicates a self-oriented motivation. The more influential participants tended to believe that self-marketing was not as important as the less influential participants thought. So while influential women may be better at recognizing and talking about their own skillfulness, they recognize that self-promotion does not necessarily create more opportunities. On a practical level, society expects women to be humble and avoid self-aggrandizing, which limits the effectiveness of self-promotion. On a spiritual level, self-promotion is the opposite of many of Jesus's instructions to avoid bragging (see, e.g., Matt. 5:5; 6:1–7).

As a female leader develops EI, her primary motivation for pursuing ministry leadership grows into a desire to be obedient to God's calling. This is a mark of ministry maturity. As leadership influence grows, regular self-diagnosis of motivation is essential to spiritual health.

EMBRACING AUTHENTICITY

Learning to lead authentically typically comes later in female leadership development. The more influential female leaders in this study emphasized the importance of embracing authenticity. The more influence a woman has, the more likely she is to describe herself as leading authentically, with no disconnect between her leadership persona and her sense of self.

Authenticity is developed over time. In the early years of ministry, a woman leader experiences significant social pressure, from both her leaders and those entrusted to her care, to behave according to the environment's norms for women. These expectations come from men who believe women should occupy certain roles and have certain qualities, as well as from women who look for specific types of traditional role models. (We will explore typical environmental pressures, such as the need to embrace a more masculine style to be accepted as a leader, in greater detail in later chapters.) A woman leader must consider her thoughts and feelings about the expectations she experiences and determine whether the person others want her to be is congruent with her unique identity. She may spend a season split between what she believes about herself and whom she feels she must be for those in her ministry. This creates cognitive dissonance, which produces leadership pain over aspects of her uniqueness that feel rejected.

Once a woman leader gains self-awareness and then confidence, however, she feels freer to be her true self. Authenticity for a female leader shows up in her leadership presence, what she wears, and her Voice (more on this in chap. 10).[16] Authenticity development is important for leaders both in interpersonal conversations and in public communication. With increased authenticity comes increased ministry influence and authority.

Leadership presence has to do with how a woman carries herself around other people. When a leader with presence enters a room, people notice. Relaxed and confident leaders move freely and assertively rather than using small movements. Their facial expressions are relaxed and open. Their chins are up. When they speak, their voices are loud enough to carry through the room. They make eye contact and connect with others in the room, making them feel seen. These leaders convey a true, authentic version of themselves rather than a calculated performance.

Society has expectations for a pastor's physical appearance. While male pastors have had the traditional suit to guide them, women pastors have not had a clear pattern to follow except for the expectation to dress modestly.[17] Women preachers have felt pressure to follow the fashion of dress of their role models. Embracing one's personal style in fashion is part of learning to lead authentically. This comes as an inner release, when a woman unhooks herself from societal expectations for feminine appearance or inner pressures to look like another successful female leader.

One female participant said, "I decided I don't have to wear heels when I preach. It's such a little thing, but I had to give myself permission and be

---

16. *Voice* is capitalized in reference to free self-expression, and it is lowercased in reference to physical speech.

17. Payne, *Gender and Pentecostal Revivalism*, 65.

okay with that. I can wear shoes that still look good, but I feel comfortable in flats, and they are more my style." This woman grew up as an athlete and tomboy and felt uncomfortable trying to dress like a "girly girl." This doesn't mean that women leaders should look masculine. They should be true to what they like and feel comfortable wearing. Some of the women rejected the ultraconservative maxi skirts and buns of their parents' generation in favor of edgy high fashion. Others embraced a boho, laid-back style instead of the pantsuits worn by female television preachers. Even in the face of criticism from church members who prefer that women leaders look more traditional, they stayed true to themselves.

Having an authentic Voice means that when a woman leader speaks into an issue, she does not parrot someone else's delivery style or thoughts. She has done the work of thinking through the issue, and when she speaks, she communicates her thoughts clearly and logically, owning them as her own. The confidence to speak authentically comes with time and experience. Seminary education is a powerful catalyst for developing a woman leader's authentic Voice.

As more advanced leaders show their authenticity with confidence, their example helps younger female leaders develop confidence in themselves. One woman described being inspired by her female pastor in the early years of her ministry journey: "I saw her not care what other people thought about her, which is really hard to do. This sounds crazy, but if she wanted to wear leather pants, she wore leather pants. This set me free and kept me from trying to fit into a mold." As she watched her pastor embrace authenticity without trying to be anyone else, she was freed to accept her own uniqueness as suitable for leadership and to lead authentically herself.

DEVELOPING EMPATHY

Empathy is another component of EI. Empathy is the ability to connect with what someone else is feeling and thinking. It is different from compassion, which sits at a distance. Empathy comes in close. Developing empathy is key in a woman's leadership development, particularly in how she interacts with those entrusted to her care.

Pastor Meghan Robinson said, "To be a leader you need to be a good reader of people. Leadership has a lot to do with people being willing to follow. And so you have to be able to read people in order to know what they need in any given circumstance." Empathy allows a female leader to recognize someone else's feelings and cues her to adapt her leadership approach. She can adjust both what and how she is communicating to best connect with and inspire the person to whom she is talking.

Empathy is particularly necessary when negotiating with someone with equal power or a peer. It helps a leader understand how to create a win-win situation. When negotiating with someone with less power, a person with empathy knows when and how hard to push as well as when to be gracious and patient. A female leader can adjust her communication approach based on what she senses the other person feels. A woman in this study described using empathy to discern the motivation level of volunteers: "I'm personally very highly motivated for ministry, so I've needed to realize that I'm dealing with people who have different circumstances and things going on in their lives. It's my job to just love them there and be patient, as patient as people were with me." Another woman told me how important it is to learn to read what people are experiencing and be sensitive, giving grace to people. She connects learning empathy to the spiritual gift of discernment as a by-product of spiritual maturity. Learning empathy is particularly important for female leaders with task-oriented or black-and-white-oriented personalities. Those who are focused on the task at hand can miss the social cues that indicate someone is not on board, or they can miss signs of early burnout.

Empathy begins with deep listening, not only to the words people are saying but also observing body language and patterns of behavior. Facial expressions and body language provide important cues. Is this person shut down and hunched over or energized and engaged? When someone who used to be reliable is no longer consistent, they are communicating that something is not right. Empathy requires a female leader to lower her defenses and take on the perspective of someone else, even if temporarily. Empathy also involves thinking about the whole life and all the obligations of a person and adjusting expectations for those who have significant obligations, such as young children or sick parents.

As a leader, if I am guiding a course correction, I need to ask myself, How is this person experiencing my words? If I am inspiring someone to greater levels of commitment or service, I ask, How is this person experiencing this moment? Are my words a weight or a springboard? What I sense from that person guides my approach, whether gentle care is needed or a challenge to stretch them.

While female leaders must be able to understand the challenges and barriers faced by those entrusted to their care, they cannot allow themselves to get stuck, frozen by others' struggles. Kendra, a young female leader, became entangled in empathy several years ago. An unhoused woman with an infant and likely a substance abuse problem showed up in our church lobby one day. Kendra began to help this woman, providing diapers and formula and driving her to appointments. Without involving other leaders, Kendra, who has a big heart, ended up making huge sacrifices. She became so concerned for this family's well-being that she moved out of her apartment to stay with a friend and allowed the family to live in her apartment (rent free). Kendra just wanted to do the right thing. While Kendra was well-meaning, the end of this story is painful. Kendra went through an incredibly difficult, emotionally exhausting, lengthy process to get her apartment back, and her empathy did not result in this woman gaining independence and stability.

Steve Cuss describes three types of leaders. The first type, enmeshed leaders like Kendra, have too little emotional distance between themselves and others, having confused codependency for empathy. These leaders deal with the contagion of the anxieties of others. The second type, detached leaders, have too much emotional distance and have not learned empathy. The third type is a differentiated leader. This leader can differentiate between where she ends and the other person begins. She is connected to another person but still maintains emotional distance that allows her to recognize and acknowledge the sources of anxiety in that person without absorbing their anxiety. Differentiated leaders connect deeply but move people forward.[18]

Female leaders must help people move past their perceived limits into the fullness of what God calls them to. Empathy helps a leader stand in someone else's shoes, survey the land as they see it, discern God's leading, and strategize a way forward. Empathy says, "I know this is hard, but let's take that next faithful step together."

SUMMARY

Female leaders develop EI in unique ways. Social expectations for women don't typically include leadership roles, so they must develop self-awareness of their own gifts to be able to recognize their leadership calling. Effective leaders must also be aware of their weaknesses. Women's lack of confidence means that criticism about their weaknesses is often painful and difficult to hear. Female leaders must learn how to process criticism in a way that does not shut them down but moves them forward in growth. To be able to both receive difficult feedback and deliver it, female leaders must learn emotional self-regulation. As they develop, women leaders find an inner motivation to keep going when things are difficult, one that is not based on validation from others. They also discover their unique design and increasingly lead with authenticity. Influential women leaders develop empathy, allowing them to connect deeply with people while moving them forward into what God has called them to.

18. Cuss, *Managing Leadership Anxiety*, 119, 121.

6

FEMALE LEADERS
FORMED BY HOME LIFE

ASPECT 4

I magine, if you will, two women. Both are young mothers on their church's leadership team. One woman, Emma, is the discipleship pastor, and the other woman, Victoria, leads the children's ministry. They both feel called to ministry leadership and are gifted and well respected by their church. Even though Emma is well trained and gifted to lead, after eight months in her role, she resigns. Victoria continues in her role for ten years before being promoted to the executive pastor role. What is the difference?

The biggest challenge to female ministry leadership longevity is a woman's home life. Victoria's husband was incredibly proud of her giftedness. He ran a successful HVAC company and volunteered in the toddler room on Sundays. He used his flexibility as a business owner to juggle after-school pickups for their kids and doctors' appointments. He cooked dinner and put their children to bed on nights when Victoria had late meetings at church. In his mind, this was not extraordinary; it was his responsibility as a dad. Emma's husband was also in ministry. He was a campus pastor for the church and carried an extraordinarily busy ministry schedule. Emma's husband expected her to prioritize his ministry obligations over hers and care for their children whenever he was busy. He had the higher-profile ministry role and felt Emma needed to prioritize her responsibilities at home. Their church salaries could not support paid childcare, and without family nearby, Emma could not see any solution except to wait until her children were older to answer God's call. While this is a fictional story, a lack of support at home happens all too often for women leaders.

Family and home are forces that shape a woman's leadership development differently than a man's. Married men often see the transition from their mother's care to their wife's care as seamless, which can put extra pressure on wives. Women find it harder than men to answer God's call to kingdom leadership because they face expectations from family and society that create additional pressure and work.[1] Developing women leaders, particularly young mothers, often have a divided focus between home and ministry. The issues surrounding a female leader's home and ministry responsibilities were the most widely discussed topic of this study.

J. Robert Clinton describes this category of development as "social base processing," which is the personal, social support a leader gives and receives, including economic, emotional, and strategic support. This includes family life.[2] A social base is the foundation a woman has at home. God uses social base processing to shape a leader for his purposes. A divided focus between family and leadership does not handicap a woman leader but shapes her uniquely. Married women, single women, and mothers of young children are all shaped by their home lives but in different ways.

SINGLE WOMEN IN MINISTRY LEADERSHIP

Many women start their leadership journey as single women, and some never marry. In some ways, as the apostle Paul says, this is better (1 Cor. 7:8, 32–34). Single women can give themselves to God in prayer, worship, and service wholeheartedly. They have an advantage in ministry because they don't have to worry about how obeying God's call to enter his mission will impact their children or their spouse. This is freeing for those called to celibate lifestyles.

But single women also face barriers in their leadership development that married women do not. Single women in this study had achieved only level 1 or 2 of leadership (see Lois McKinney's five levels of leadership in chap. 2). Many reported feeling treated like a second-class leader in church cultures that place a high value on marriage. Christian expectations about marriage, particularly for women, mean that women experience an increase in social

1. Lederleitner, *Women in God's Mission*, 8.
2. Clinton, "Social Base Processing," 10–11.

status when they get married. This affects their leadership influence. This is not to say that women must get married to become church leaders. But married women often find it easier to be promoted than single women.

Single women in ministry often work long hours and are relied on to carry out the work of ministry that happens in the evenings and on weekends. Churches assume that single women have more time and energy than women with husbands and children. These dynamics can easily lead to overwork and burnout if a single female leader is not careful about creating margins for her own self-care. A single woman leader is better equipped to thrive in her home life if she identifies a primary partner in ministry, whether male or female, to help carry the load of ministry. This partnership creates a support so that ministry does not overwhelm her home life. When she sets aside time for her home life or rest, she has someone looking after ministry responsibilities.

Even a woman who has no desire to marry and has chosen singleness suffers from seasons of loneliness, particularly if she is not close to her family. Heavy ministry schedules can lead to neglecting her social life, and even friendships suffer when given the leftovers of her time and energy. Single women don't get the benefits of the complementary strengths a spouse can bring to things like making financial decisions, home maintenance, and buying a car. When a close family member of a single woman gets sick or injured, her family often expects her to be the primary caregiver because they view her as having fewer responsibilities and so more capacity to help. In truth, without a spouse to help at home, a single woman leader is often exhausted and stretched beyond her capacity to manage both family and ministry needs.

A single woman leader needs to develop an inner circle of close friends to thrive. This group provides similar kinds of support as family and might include close family members. These friends are a team with whom she gets vulnerable and shares her intimate life, from the tedium of daily routines to major decisions. They go on vacation and have fun together. These friends have permission to hold her accountable for character development and goal setting. A single woman leader also needs a team to help her manage household responsibilities. She needs a financial planner, a handyman, a mechanic, and even a housecleaner she can rely on. This team can help with the responsibilities of a female leader's home life similar to the way a husband can.

Single women easily fall into the trap of giving their entire being to ministry and doing too much, neglecting other aspects of their lives. Single women in ministry leadership who do not feel called to a celibate life will often face difficulties finding a husband because they are too busy for a social life. A woman leader who devotes her entire life to Jesus in ministry will find that the list of potential partners gets considerably shorter each year. If she wants to marry, she must choose her spouse carefully to ensure he shares her values and will champion her leadership call.

In seasons of singleness, women leaders come to rely on Jesus intimately in a way many others never discover. Donna Crouch was a single woman for the first eight years of her ministry journey. She believed that she would likely never marry. She was working so hard as a youth pastor that she didn't have time to develop a relationship with a man, much less get married. In that season, she embraced the message of Isaiah 54:5, "Your Maker is your husband—the LORD Almighty is his name," and that her legacy of children would be the young people she mentored in ministry.

Single women leaders sometimes engage in ministry alone but can work in pairs. This ministry partnership might be with another woman, but it also might be with a man she is not married to. She must navigate boundaries in this relationship carefully, especially if the man is married.

MARRiED WOMEN IN MINISTRY LEADERSHIP

Married women leaders process their experiences at home differently. Every married participant in this study described the vital work of developing a husband-wife ministry partnership. Another common theme was the challenge of navigating family needs and a busy ministry work schedule.

Husbands can empower, strengthen, and encourage their wives' kingdom calling. A husband's view of his wife's leadership development has a significant impact on her ability to develop leadership gifts and fulfill her kingdom calling. Participants agreed that without the support of her husband, a female leader simply cannot develop influence in the church. Without her husband's support, either her ministry leadership ends or her marriage ends. In two instances in this study, this was the case. One female pastor reported that a contributing factor to the end of her first marriage was her husband's increasing lack of commitment to ministry, which became a point of significant tension. Influential women leaders figure out how to lead alongside their husbands.

Egalitarian Marriage and Husband-Wife Ministry Partnership

Egalitarian theology in praxis is more than simply women leading in the church. Egalitarian theology shapes marriage partnerships in the home, putting husbands and wives into equal partnership. Empowering a wife requires more than a perspective change, however. Pentecostal environments where egalitarian marriage is not clearly understood or practiced create additional hurdles for women leaders who feel called to serve the Lord in their ministry leadership but also want to love and serve their families well. Cheryl Catford observes, "The female leader is expected to place home and family priorities before church involvement but in reality, her life will be one of constantly juggling ministry, family and domestic demands."[3] Without adequate support, the demands of both home and church can be overwhelming for female ministry leaders. Elizabeth Loutrel Glanville found that these dual demands on married female leaders can limit their opportunities in a way that male leaders do not experience.[4]

Egalitarian theology provides an opportunity for married couples to lead together as ministry partners, but figuring out how to lead alongside a spouse doesn't happen quickly. It requires an extended process of figuring out each other's personalities, gifts, and passions and time for each partner to get comfortable in those areas and let the other lead in their strengths. One woman described leadership in her marriage as a relay race: "He doesn't have to be in the lead all the time, nor do I have to be in the lead all the time. This shared leadership has made us a stronger team." This couple passes the baton of decision-making in their ministry. Frequently, this baton passing was a struggle early on as they decided on lanes of authority and giftedness. But as they clearly defined ministry responsibility and authority and figured out how to communicate well, the work became increasingly smoother. In coequal and traditional ministry partnerships (more on these below), the female leader has to have influence and spiritual authority in her own right; she cannot be successful simply borrowing her husband's influence to exert power. Participants described having to work through challenges involving control, mental health battles, and unequal ministry motivation. Couples had to learn to differentiate between their marriage and their ministry partnership and set boundaries to protect their marriage.

Almost every study participant agreed that a husband who celebrates and supports his wife's leadership is important—even crucial—for a married woman leader. When a husband views his role as stewarding his wife's calling, he carries a sense of responsibility for her leadership success. Leanne said her husband recognizes that stewarding her calling is a significant part of his. "I didn't have big aspirational ministry dreams, but I had a husband who saw something in me and believed it was his job as my husband to steward and draw it out."

This was certainly true for my husband, John, and me. I was already a full-time worship pastor leading a large team at a large church when we

3. Catford, "Women's Experiences," loc. 643 of 8092, Kindle.
4. Glanville, "Leadership Development for Women," 33, 190.

got married. He respected my leadership from the very beginning and was committed to my ministry leadership longevity. He made significant sacrifices in seasons to prioritize my ministry opportunities over his because he believes that a significant part of God's plan for our partnership is for him to provide the support he can to enable me to become all that God has planned. In seasons, I have given the same kind of support and sacrifice to him as well.

This kind of support requires a husband to be not insecure but completely comfortable in his own calling and confident of his gifts. This kind of man verbally affirms his wife's leadership and does what he can to create leadership opportunities for her and validate her leadership. This includes sharing home responsibilities equally. Mary Lederleitner found that empowering husbands are not focused primarily on their own comfort. They are not competing with or threatened by their wives; they wholly support and encourage their wives to develop their full potential. Furthermore, they are joyful in their wives' achievements.[5] Without this kind of support, female ministry longevity is very difficult to maintain. For women whose husbands occupy center stage and expect their wives to take a supportive, secondary role to their calling, leadership development will likely be delayed.

Husbands and wives may work closely together in ministry, or they may not. Either way, they must figure out their roles in their ministry partnership outside the roles they have in their home. This begins with discerning together each partner's giftedness and finding ways to support each other in obedience to God's calling. How husbands and wives relate to each other in their church environment and the nature of their roles at church may well create a different way of interacting than the dynamics in their home environment. If a couple does not discuss this difference and clarify how they will relate in each of the two spheres, problems will arise.

Models of Husband-Wife Ministry Partnership

Not only does marriage correlate with increasing levels of leadership, but the way a husband and wife relate as leaders also impacts the wife's influence. I found a trend correlating influence with successful husband-wife ministry partnership. Married women who are more influential have figured out how to have both a successful marriage and a successful ministry partnership. This means that each partner has figured out their ministry calling and how to relate to their spouse within a ministry leadership context. It also points

5. Lederleitner, *Women in God's Mission*, 149.

to the importance of married women establishing a leadership relationship with their husbands to affect influence growth.

Not every couple will lead the same way. This study identified five models of husband-wife ministry partnership when the wife is a ministry leader.[6] Each type of ministry partnership works a bit differently. Different partnership dynamics within a marriage depend on the leadership gifting, calling, and experience of each spouse and their personalities.

The first model is a *separate ministry partnership*. In this partnership, both spouses are in ministry, but they lead in separate ministry lanes. My husband and I had this kind of partnership for most of our marriage. I was an executive pastor at our church, and he was an evangelist, doing itinerant preaching and leadership coaching with other churches. We were both in ministry leadership, but our roles did not overlap.

The second model is an *independent ministry partnership*. In this model, a woman is in ministry leadership alone, and her husband is not directly involved in ministry or is in a behind-the-scenes role. Judy West is an executive pastor of leadership development at a megachurch. Her husband serves behind the scenes at their church. He is a surgeon who sees his primary ministry role as supporting hers, financially, emotionally, and practically.

The third model is a *co-ministry partnership*. Kent and Alli Munsey lead this way. Both husband and wife carry the title "lead pastor," and they split responsibilities according to their passions and gifts. He looks after finances, operations, vision, and strategy and is the primary teacher. She looks after the management and systems of ministry, creative ministries, church experiences and events, and preaches regularly. Married couples leading together can create some organizational messiness and it gets complicated when the spouses have similar gifts and passions. A successful partnership requires great communication and clarity about who makes final calls in various aspects of ministry. Young married couples in this study who had role models of ministry couples leading together started with co-ministry partnerships and had to figure out lanes of gifting and authority early on.

A married couple may co-pastor a church without each spouse having equal organizational authority. The spouse who is more experienced, trained, or gifted in leadership is often the more senior leader. The fourth model, a *nontraditional ministry partnership*, is one in which the wife holds more organizational power in the church than the husband, but they lead alongside

6. These models of partnership update Clinton's six ministry partnership models: internal/external ministry, co-ministry, independent ministry, alternate ministry, delayed ministry, and dysfunctional ministry. Clinton, "Social Base Processing," 16–17.

each other with a shared title. One woman in this study described her ministry partnership this way: she is the campus pastor with greater authority that gives her the final say on all ministry decisions. She has more experience, leadership gifting, and training than her husband. Her husband leads alongside her with the same title and provides input in decision-making but yields to her authority. They are both fully present and involved in the day-to-day work of ministry. Often he has more of an operational role, while she sets vision. Women in independent ministry or nontraditional ministry partnerships often began ministry before they were married.

An *adapted traditional ministry partnership*, the fifth model, looks more traditional. While the husband and wife share the same title and the wife does have ministry leadership responsibility and authority, her husband has greater authority due to greater gifting, experience, ambition, or availability. She may work part-time rather than full-time in ministry in order to care for children. She does not have merely a title, like "pastor's wife," with no true leadership function. She often leads women's ministry and perhaps other departments of the church as well.

The various partnerships are outlined in table 2.

TABLE 2. Models of Husband-Wife Ministry Partnership

Partnership Model	Description
Separate Ministry Partnership	A female leader leads alone, and her husband has a separate ministry role in a different lane of ministry.
Independent Ministry Partnership	A female leader leads alone, and her husband is either not involved in ministry or serves in a behind-the-scenes role.
Co-ministry Partnership	A female leader leads alongside her husband with coequal authority and responsibility. They have the same role (and possibly title) and divide lanes of influence by gifts and passions.
Nontraditional Ministry Partnership	A female leader leads alongside her husband in the same role, but she has more authority and responsibility than he does because of greater gifting and/or experience.
Adapted Traditional Ministry Partnership	A female leader leads alongside her husband in the same role but has less authority and responsibility than he does because of less gifting, experience, ambition, or availability (frequently due to young children) than her husband.

Older couples frequently started with a more traditional partnership, but the husband had an increasing awareness of his wife's leadership gifts and his church's need for her leadership strengths. As he recognized this, he brought more of himself into the home and looked for her input in ministry decisions. He invited her into ministry roles and gave her authority in their church.

He empowered her leadership, and their partnership style shifted to either an adapted traditional ministry partnership or a co-ministry partnership. Partnership goes both ways, as husbands in ministry need the encouragement and support of their wives as well. A couple can share the weight of ministry leadership in partnership.

JUGGLING LEADERSHIP, CHILDREN, AND THE HOME

Motherhood creates dynamics and responsibilities for female ministry leaders that are different from how fatherhood impacts male leaders. Motherhood may be perceived as a distraction from ministry leadership, but it shapes women in beautiful ways. Glanville found that the motherhood season develops women ministry leaders to become more flexible, people-oriented, compassionate, and empathetic.[7] Motherhood requires selflessness that deeply forms character. This season creates challenges for women leaders, however. Mothers today face more cultural pressure than mothers of previous generations (like the pressure to spend more leisure time with their children or host picture-perfect birthday parties), even though studies show they invest an equal amount of time in their children.[8] Female ministry leaders face difficult decisions when they become mothers and want to be home with their children but feel called to ministry.[9] Nancy Beach claims that achieving a balanced life is impossible, so women leaders who are also mothers should release the feelings of guilt they experience.[10]

Motherhood Support

Many study participants described the difficulties of being a mother and a wife and on a church staff. These women are not interested in taking a break from ministry leadership for their motherhood season; they wish to be engaged in leading while also being great mothers and wives. Six women explained that doing both ministry and family well simultaneously is essential and nonnegotiable. Their sense of calling is so great that they feel they cannot stop leading. Some mother-leaders had seasons of part-time ministry when their children were very young, and others continued in full-time ministry after a maternity leave.

7. Glanville, "Leadership Development for Women," 201.
8. Eagly and Carli, *Through the Labyrinth*, 53–56.
9. Scott, *Dare Mighty Things*, 95.
10. Beach, *Gifted to Lead*, 94.

The primary home support need of a mother-leader is childcare. Most experts point to fathers as the best solution for this need. Alice H. Eagly and Linda A. Carli's secular perspective is blunt: "For women to achieve full access to leadership in society, men will have to step up and share more equally in family responsibilities."[11] When a father is fully engaged in child-rearing, he shares the load of responsibilities at home. Every generation of Western fathers since the baby boom has been more involved with their children.[12] These involved fathers have faced cultural backlash, however. Psychiatrist Anna Fels recognizes that men have often been "socially penalized for prioritizing family over work" and their manhood doubted in jokes about "househusbands."[13] A 2009 survey found that just 9 percent of people in dual-earning marriages said they shared housework and childcare evenly.[14] Shared parenting is a work in progress, but equally sharing responsibilities in parenting empowers mothers to fulfill their kingdom callings. Ruth Haley Barton notes that a mother needs her husband to fully participate in parenting and understand it as part of his own God-given ministry assignment.[15]

It is obvious, therefore, that egalitarian marriage is essential to female leader support. If a husband does not see himself as an equal partner in the home, then he will resent time spent caring for children while his wife prepares a sermon or runs a meeting. Both male and female leaders in this study stressed the importance of both partners carrying an equal responsibility for household chores and childcare. The need for an egalitarian marriage was especially true of women at leadership level 4 or 5. They recognized that having a well-managed home was essential to fruitful ministry. How home management responsibilities were assigned to each spouse was not based on gender but on skill, passion, and busyness. The husband and wife had regular conversations to adapt to new seasons, redefining marriage roles and responsibilities to make sure that both partners could win at life and ministry. One participant said, "We both work hard to come shoulder to shoulder and work as a team, but we have had a lot of conversations to define what our roles within the home need to look like in order for us to accomplish the mission that's in front of us."

Raising children is a distinctly female leadership development issue. While fathers are also parents, participants believe that even in egalitarian marriages, mothers are hormonally and instinctively more aware of their children's needs.

11. Eagly and Carli, *Through the Labyrinth*, 81.
12. Eagly and Carli, *Through the Labyrinth*, 84.
13. Fels, *Necessary Dreams*, 252.
14. Sandberg and Scovell, *Lean In*, 106.
15. Barton, *Equal to the Task*, loc. 2266 of 2871, Kindle.

Specifically, when children are sick, mothers are typically the default choice to stay home with them. The mothers in this study were not resentful of this; in fact, they wanted to care for their sick children. This was a role they preferred to occupy.

Trying to do both ministry and family well makes life very busy for women in ministry leadership, frequently creating family tension and stress. One female leader (in a nontraditional ministry partnership) described the chaos of busy ministry combined with the responsibilities of parenting: "My husband had to be out of the house at 6:30 a.m. to go do bump-in.[16] I was trying to prepare to preach my sermon while feeding breakfast to two kids and getting them and myself dressed. My phone was ringing nonstop from volunteers calling with questions because we were in a new venue. I was just trying to get out the door to get to church. And I thought, wow, this is just so intense!"

The women in this study frequently had very high standards for themselves early on. They wanted to perfectly manage their home while building significant leadership influence. A female leader describes the feelings of self-inflicted pressure:

> As women, sometimes we feel like we have to do everything. We have to be there for our husband. We have to be amazingly wise. We have to have our pantries organized. Especially with social media and Pinterest, you feel like your whole life has to look great and be labeled and organized and color-coded. But no one shows you that those influencers online have help to actually do those things. So then women leaders are killing themselves, burning the candle at both ends, trying to lead churches with their husbands and be what Pinterest says you have to be.

If mother-leaders lean toward a ministry leadership focus, then they deal with mom guilt, feeling as if their kids are getting cheated. One woman leader dealt with depression after her young child began to prefer the nanny over her. These women have to wrestle with these issues and find ways to be present for the things that really matter to their children and also be present for the things that really matter in ministry leadership. They want their children to feel as if they are the priority all the time. Others feel guilty about not being in the office or at church when they choose to spend time with their children. The women in this study had to come to terms with the fact that they could not do everything by themselves and needed help. They needed help inside

16. A "bump-in" is the lengthy process of setting up equipment and supplies to do portable church services in nonpermanent venues. This process can take three hours or more weekly for set up and another three hours or more for tear down.

their homes, and they needed help in the office from their ministry team. It's not possible to do everything all alone as a superwoman.

Busy fathers aren't always available to provide enough support, however. Women leaders with children at home note the importance of child-rearing support from paid workers, friends, or family members. Some of the women struggle because they lack childcare support, either because their church does not provide daycare or because the quality of available childcare is poor. Other participants have childcare provided by their church, either through a church daycare or through the church hiring nannies, babysitters, or life assistants for their female staff. A life assistant helps not only with ministry tasks but also with managing personal life and home life.

The women leaders explained that they had to take initiative and request that childcare support be made a church budget item so they can do what they need to do. Those who did not ask the church to pay for this kind of support were often financially burdened by the high cost of childcare relative to low ministry salaries. One empty nester expressed regret over not asking for a salary increase. Over all her years of earning, she had made just enough to cover the cost of childcare. Some of the women receive volunteer childcare from close church members, and others have family nearby who provide childcare support. These women are willing to be vulnerable and resourceful, recognizing that they will find ministry leadership very difficult without childcare help. In some cases, women leaders have full-time childcare help, and in others they have part-time help. Whatever the form, childcare allows female leaders to continue leading while mothering.

Mothers in this study talked about needing great self-awareness to discern their heart's desire about how to split their time and focus between ministry and family. One said, "Every day I hold myself accountable to my mindset, my heart attitude, and my agenda. And I will never look back in regret." Those who embraced the stretch to do both, however, found that motherhood expanded their capacity to do more ministry leadership. Learning to rely on the support of others to manage home life is a leadership skill, as is becoming more efficient. Motherhood teaches women to juggle many responsibilities, a skill also needed in ministry leadership. If a mother keeps an open heart, then applying these new skills to ministry expands her leadership capacity.

As women leaders age, the needs of their families change. Older study participants described the significant financial, time, and energy demands of their extended families, from aging parents needing care to siblings in need of help. However, women's immediate family responsibilities lighten as children grow up. Baby boomer leaders described how their children becoming older and more independent gave them more time and freedom to devote to ministry leadership.

Domestic Support

Women leaders also need support managing their households. Studies reveal that women carry the bulk of domestic responsibilities. One study found that having a husband creates an extra seven hours of housework per week for a woman.[17] Another study found that women carry 75 percent of the household responsibilities, while yet another found that for every hour of housework performed by a husband, a wife works seventeen hours.[18] These numbers all point to the same conclusion: in the home, women are responsible for more than men are. Many working women manage a "double work shift," taking on childcare and chores in the evening.[19]

Despite the heavy load of domestic work women carry in addition to career pressures and financial responsibilities, women feel guilty about having dirty houses.[20] Beach encourages female ministry leaders to face these feelings with a trade-off strategy: either accept a dirty house or hire a cleaner (if they are able to afford one).[21] Glanville notes that the female ministry leaders in her study were better equipped to flourish in their ministry and leadership development when they had household help.[22]

This isn't always as simple as hiring a cleaner, however. Women in this study deal with shame about having to hire home support for cleaning or other tasks and embarrassment about needing this help. They feel they should be able to manage this very basic responsibility. Others dine in restaurants frequently or use volunteers from their churches to help with home management. To deal with guilt and shame, one woman leader intentionally decided that her time at home would be focused on family relationships rather than tasks. She prioritizes her family over the home.

CHURCH STAFF CULTURE AND POLICIES THAT EMPOWER HEALTHY HOMES

Mother-leaders in this study identified flexibility in office hours and work location to be essential to flourishing in leadership. "Being given flexibility in the office has been fantastic and created the opportunity for me to be able to

17. University of Michigan Institute for Social Research, "Exactly How Much Housework Does a Husband Create?"
18. Cole, *Developing Female Leaders*, 87; Eagly and Carli, *Through the Labyrinth*, 74.
19. Vinnicombe and Singh, "Women-Only Management Training," 298.
20. Scott, *Dare Mighty Things*, 95–96.
21. Beach, *Gifted to Lead*, 98.
22. Glanville, "Leadership Development for Women," 215–16.

continue leading," one said. An older participant noted that technology and the internet have made this flexibility possible. Early in her leadership, she needed to be present in the office. Now she is able to work remotely.

Some mothers are able to work from home when they need to or go to the office just one or two days a week. They described having meetings in the office but frequently working at home. Other mothers work in the office only during school hours. One is able to bring her children into the office with her. Some women make themselves available for ministry at night after their children go to bed. Smaller churches that might not be able to provide supports like childcare can compensate for this by granting this kind of flexibility to their leaders who are mothers.

Unfortunately, flexibility comes with the hidden cost of always being available. Some church cultures encourage women to work anywhere at any time. While this makes it easier to mother, women can often overwork themselves based on their own expectations and have trouble creating boundaries.

The more senior a female leader, the more flexibility and control over her schedule she has. Flexibility in office hours and location was perceived to be a sign of earned trust from leadership and team members. Flexibility was a reward of fruitful ministry and so a type of leadership validation. Women reported feeling very grateful for this flexibility and did not have entitled attitudes about it. This sense of gratitude kept their attitudes positive during seasons when they did not have as much flexibility. Some women reported experiencing reduced flexibility during busy ministry seasons. Certain responsibilities, like preaching during Sunday services, come with less flexibility.

Some mothers described needing and receiving the freedom to take seasons off from ministry. Many women stepped back to working part-time or took time off completely when children had significant needs. One takes summers off from ministry to be with her children. They believe their families should take priority over ministry leadership. One woman told me, "I believe that my first ministry is to my family." For Karolina Gunsser Grant, stepping back to part-time hours when her children were small was not a matter of personal preference or being overwhelmed but a matter of self-awareness of her own heart and spiritual maturity. She believed that stepping back was in obedience to the Holy Spirit's leading. She did not relinquish her role or her leadership responsibilities, but she did cut back the number of hours she worked in the office.

> I was full-time up until I had my first child, and I remember so vividly the week before I was supposed to go back to work after the maternity leave period. I had told myself that I would have to go back to work full-time. And some women

do and that's great. But I felt the pressure of that, and I heard the voice of the Holy Spirit say to me, "Who's telling you that you have to go back full-time?" And I realized it was me. And it was the upbringing I had that informed that pattern of thinking.

Churches that are committed to female leaders as people, beyond the ministry function they perform, hold leadership opportunities for them so they can jump back into leading when the time is right.

Flexibility is a cultural value that is sometimes grudgingly given or resented by men. A boomer male senior pastor commented on his personal struggle leading women who are mothers, stating his preference for empowering mothers with older children so the church does not have to deal with leadership instability.

Women in leadership also deal with managing reproductive issues. Several were required by leadership crises to return to work just a few weeks after childbirth. Others had to juggle breastfeeding and ministry travel or had to preach soon after childbirth. Finding places to pump around the office, coping with a menstrual cycle while preaching, and struggling with hormonally influenced mood swings were also challenges for some women.

Ministry travel is stressful for mothers, but avoiding travel limits peer relationship development. Several mothers said that travel is stressful but necessary. Mothers see that their children struggle when they are away. One woman leader who had to travel internationally several times a year with her husband to fulfill her church and denominational responsibilities said, "I definitely feel the stress of travel. I would love consistency for my kids. They don't love it when we go away." Increased influence means increased travel requirements for women, and if this happens while children are at home, this creates stress. Women with good family support are better equipped to deal with extensive travel associated with leadership responsibilities. Women without good support may opt to wait until their children are grown for travel that brings expanded influence. Those who choose to travel with young children must make peace with the complications and stresses this brings.

SUMMARY

Women leaders are formed by their home environment. Single women are shaped through the absence of support they experience in their home life and must create support through close friends who become family, both practically and emotionally. Married women leaders cannot become influential without the emotional and practical support of their husbands. Egalitarian marriage, in which each partner takes equal responsibility for decision-making, childcare, and domestic chores, is a powerful support of female leadership. Married couples must figure out their partnership as ministry leaders, defining how they will interact and what their roles will be in their ministry context. Partnerships look different depending on the ministry giftedness, calling, and experience of each spouse. Mothers in ministry leadership need childcare support and support with running their homes. Churches can empower mothers in leadership by providing resources for childcare or home help. Church staff policies that provide flexibility in when and where women work enable women to both take care of their families well and maintain their ministry leadership responsibilities.

7

FEMALE LEADERS FORMED BY MINISTRY ENVIRONMENT

ASPECT 5

D ebbie Rhoads started going to church as a teenager after her mother became a Christian. She loved her youth ministry and how her youth leaders poured into her. She realized that she wanted to spend her life loving and discipling young people in the way she had been loved and discipled.

Debbie was excited to be hired as the children's director. But she didn't realize the significance of the complementarian theology embraced by her church: the only other ways a woman could serve were as a secretary or in women's ministry. She soon encountered resistance to her leadership, particularly because her husband was not in ministry with her. She could stand in front of children and teach a lesson, but she was not permitted to lead the children in a salvation prayer because some of the children were boys. Leading a boy in a salvation prayer was considered taking authority over a (future) man and thus inappropriate for her as a woman. She could make a salvation appeal but was required to hand off the prayer to a man to "seal the deal." This became incredibly difficult for her. To comply, she tried to train male volunteers to close her lesson, but the men would not or could not pay attention to the important nuances of leading children through this moment of decision. (Never mind the absurdity that Debbie could train a man to administer the salvation call but could not present it to a male herself.) So Debbie trained her preteen son to lead children in a prayer of salvation.

Debbie was deeply frustrated by these limitations and could not understand why she was placed under such restrictions. She knew she was created to lead children to Jesus and felt stifled in her calling. But she decided that at the end of a Sunday, children heard and responded to the gospel, so she submitted to the limits, telling herself it was worth it.

After moving to a new, egalitarian church, things began to change. She discovered that the limits on female leadership that she had been taught her whole life weren't the only way to understand the Scriptures. She began to wrestle biblically and theologically with her calling in search of the right way forward. She found freedom as she explored a more holistic reading of God's design and purpose for women leaders. She stepped into children's ministry leadership again, this time with no limits on her leadership. She grew in leadership confidence and became comfortable simply being herself. Her senior pastor recognized the leadership gift and ministry fruitfulness in her life and began to promote her into more significant leadership opportunities, eventually inviting her into the church's executive leadership team. Debbie recently wrote *My Brand New Life*, a book for children exploring their salvation journey, published through Kidology. A supportive environment triggered inner work, grew Debbie's leadership, and transformed her as a leader.

A woman leader continually considers and responds to her ministry context. This environment shapes her as a leader even as it shapes the nature of her leadership. She has experiences with people, policies, culture, circumstances, and events as she responds to God's call. God uses these experiences to form her leadership character, values, and capacity. As she develops, her potential is realized through opportunities, and her responsibilities grow.[1]

Researchers and reflections from women leaders point to a variety of environmental issues that women leaders encounter that impact their leadership development. As each woman in this study developed, the culture of the organization she was immersed in deeply impacted her as a leader. Church culture determines acceptable roles for women, value for feminine voices, and opportunities for female leaders. This chapter considers hindrances to female leadership development, leadership opportunities for female leaders, female leader sponsorship, and supportive work environments for female leadership.

HINDRANCES TO FEMALE LEADERSHIP DEVELOPMENT

Women leaders frequently begin their leadership race at a disadvantage, starting further behind their male colleagues because of hindrances they must

1. Clinton, *Leadership Emergence Theory*, 81.

overcome. These are often unseen forces that push against their forward progress, causing leadership development to be more difficult and slower for them.
Women leaders face hindrances such as theological and cultural resistance,
gender bias, a pay gap, and sexual harassment and abuse.

The women in this study had positive and successful leadership development experiences overall, but they did encounter significant challenges along
the way. These leaders had to come to terms with the resistance they faced
and decide to move forward despite the obstacles.

Theological and Cultural Resistance

Over half of the women pastors in this study faced theological resistance from
outsiders or newcomers to their churches—their egalitarian churches. Women
described men getting up and walking out of a sermon in protest or turning their
chairs around and facing the back of the auditorium while a woman preached.
Some of this resistance was not theological but cultural. Well over half of the
women in this study faced traditional cultural expectations for women that op-
posed female leadership. In regions where male church leaders abound, women
leaders can be startling to church attenders. One woman said, "We've had people
come in church who are surprised that we would allow a woman to preach or
surprised that we lead a church together." Women leaders must recognize and
reconcile with these cultural expectations that create awkwardness.

When the women leaders encountered theological resistance, they had to work
through their thoughts and emotions surrounding it. Their sense of calling propelled them forward, and they accepted that not everyone was going to support
their leadership. They did not debate theology with dissenters, but they were
willing to have theological conversations with those who were genuinely open.
They used warmth and love to disarm a conversation, convincing rather than
arguing. They expressed compassion for those who were bound by religious rules.

Gender Bias

Western cultural attitudes toward women have changed dramatically in
the past century, but the residue of old perspectives still permeates our social
atmosphere. Social psychologists Alice H. Eagly and Linda A. Carli recognize
that cultural constructs of gender roles drive conscious and unconscious bias
against female leadership and associate leadership with masculinity.[2] This
shows up in the business world, where both male and female leaders disregard
women for promotion, assuming that they cannot execute leadership roles

2. Eagly and Carli, *Through the Labyrinth*, 125.

while effectively managing their family responsibilities.[3] Women have also been stereotyped as poor problem-solvers, undermining their leadership.[4] Without opportunities to lead, women cannot demonstrate their competency.

These unflattering stereotypes (among others not mentioned here) impact what women believe about their own leadership potential. The longer women encounter barriers to leadership, the less willing they are to push through them.[5] Those who do often abandon their feminine uniqueness and values to blend in with male leadership.[6]

Gender bias is often not overt (like illegal discrimination) but subtle. Women's leadership experts and business consultants Herminia Ibarra, Robin J. Ely, and Deborah M. Kolb point to what they call "second-generation bias," which is not an overtly discriminatory approach but "something in the water" that indirectly prevents female leaders from flourishing in an organization. This can manifest in an organizational lack of flexibility, poor networks for women, excessive expectations, and too few role models.[7]

Bias impacts women in ministry leadership as well. Robyn Wilkerson refers to this as the "stained glass ceiling" that prevents women from achieving God's leadership call for their lives regardless of training or gifting.[8] Sometimes women leaders even face resistance from other women who prefer masculine ministry.[9] In egalitarian contexts with predominantly male leadership teams, Frances S. Adeney identified passive resistance to female leaders through a prevailing attitude that men are the "real people." People with this attitude seek to preserve male leadership and ignore or exclude female leadership.[10]

When I was an executive pastor, part of my responsibilities included training the male pastors I supervised in preaching and teaching. The primary preachers in our egalitarian church were our co-senior pastors, a married couple. But when they did not preach on a Sunday, the person tagged to preach was almost always one of the two male pastors I supervised, not me. This was true even though I had more theological education and more ministry experience and was a little bit older than these men. The assumption was that our church family would rather listen to a man than a woman—even though we were theologically egalitarian. I had to consistently guard my thoughts and attitudes to celebrate the opportunity given these male pastors entrusted to

3. Barsh and Lee, "Unlocking the Full Potential of Women."
4. Prime, Women "Take Care," Men "Take Charge," 4.
5. Barsh and Lee, "Unlocking the Full Potential of Women."
6. Vinnicombe and Singh, "Women-Only Management Training," 300.
7. Ibarra, Ely, and Kolb, "Women Rising," 486.
8. Wilkerson, Shattering the Stained Glass Ceiling, loc. 163 of 3455, Kindle.
9. Lederleitner, Women in God's Mission, 175.
10. Adeney, Women and Christian Mission, 144, 147.

my care rather than feel resentful or entitled. I had to coach myself not to be discouraged or to question my own giftedness or calling to teach.

Over half of the female participants in this study disclosed having faced some type of gender discrimination on their journey. Typically this meant they had to work harder to prove their leadership abilities before they were trusted. To be validated and accepted, they had to live up to higher standards than the male leaders. One woman described it this way: "I had to prove myself as a leader to gain the respect of men in leadership alongside me, to get to the point that they celebrated the gift that's in me. Now they celebrate the gift in other women who are in leadership at our church. But I do think that I had to gain my 'street cred.'"[11] These standards mean that as they were developing, few other women occupied executive leadership roles on their teams and these women felt alone. Without opportunity and a great deal of encouragement, women do not progress in their leadership development—even in environments where they are wanted and valued. They are already so hard on themselves that unspoken high standards can be crippling.

Nearly half of the women in this study had difficulties because of their strong, dominant personalities. They are frequently unfairly judged and given feedback that they are intimidating or seem unavailable or unapproachable. Their strong opinions are interpreted as pushy or emotional, or they are considered "bitches." Men feel disrespected by the strength of women's opinions or just dislike them outright for their strength. Men sometimes bully these women, shutting them down in conversations, or sabotage their opportunities. These actions produce insecurity that slows down female leadership development.

Survey participants described a variety of hindrances (see table 3). The most significant hindrances reported were difficulties developing networking relationships with male pastors and gender discrimination in ministry settings. Forty-five percent of the surveyed women had experienced these two issues. These findings point to the significance of the challenges in male-female ministry relationships. Most significantly, the more influential a woman leader was, the less likely she was to have experienced gender discrimination and difficulties networking with male pastors. Most of the women who reported experiencing these hindrances were level 2 leaders. This indicates that these issues are significant barriers to developing influence. Women who have experienced gender discrimination get stuck at level 2 leadership and do not become widely influential leaders. This means that these barriers are not merely perceived barriers or emotional problems of women but genuinely impede the development of significant influence.

11. "Street cred" in this context means leadership credibility.

Pay Gap

The second-generation bias shows up in the ministry pay gap. In 2017 male senior pastors made an average of $15,000 more a year than their female counterparts, even though the women pastors were better educated. This pay gap has been improving, however: in 2015 male pastors made $25,000 more than female pastors in equivalent roles.[12] A few years ago, a male senior pastor told me that the benefit of hiring women for executive leadership roles was that they were cheaper than men because they accepted lower pay. The inequality in pay creates financial hardship for women in ministry, thereby negatively impacting their leadership.

Women in this study also deal with wage inequality. Sometimes their salaries go entirely toward childcare.[13] Curiously enough, while they face very real inequalities, they do not seem bothered by them. In their view, if a woman is raising children, she should accept that her divided focus means lower pay. Others are happy to work full-time for part-time pay to enable other staff hires or as a kingdom sacrifice. One noted that being underpaid made her more hesitant to lead, however. Equal pay demonstrates a church's support of a woman's leadership. Financial stability in the life of a female leader and her ability to spend money on presenting herself well, childcare, or a comfortable home show those in her world that the church values her leadership. Empty-nest women leaders expressed regret about the significant financial sacrifices they had made, putting their entire salary toward childcare costs. The regret was not continuing in ministry leadership but that they had not insisted on increased financial support from the church.

Sexual Harassment and Abuse

The #ChurchToo movement that emerged out of #MeToo sadly brought to light instances of sexual harassment and abuse existing within the church, which should be a safe place for women. The women of this study had mixed responses when asked about their experiences with sexual harassment and abuse in the church. None of the women who spoke with me reported experiencing this kind of trauma. However, 11 percent of the surveyed women

12. Emmert, "State of Female Pastors."
13. To determine whether it makes economic sense for both partners to work outside the home, a married couple may weigh the income of the spouse who earns less against the cost of childcare. Because of both the gender pay gap and the traditional social roles of mothers as caregivers, this is typically a question of whether a wife will work outside the home. While the responsibility for the cost of childcare belongs to both a father and a mother, when decisions are made about childcare costs, they are often weighed against the wife's income potential as the lower-wage partner.

leaders reported experiencing sexual harassment or abuse from other ministry leaders, which is noteworthy. These findings reveal sexual dysfunction and sin in the churches of the surveyed women that were not reported by the interview and focus group participants. This may be in part because the interview and focus group churches were chosen based on the apparent health of their environment, whereas the survey likely captured women leading in ministry environments that were not as healthy. It also may be a result of the anonymity of the survey versus the confidentiality of the interviews and focus groups. The women I interviewed are part of my context and have varying degrees of relationship with me. They may have been less comfortable sharing their experiences of sexual harassment or abuse than the women who were certain of their anonymity.

TABLE 3. Anonymous Survey Reported Hindrances to Female Leader Emergence

Hindrance	Percentage of total surveyed women affected
Difficulties developing networking relationships with male pastors	45%
Gender discrimination in ministry settings	45%
Theological opposition	30%
Wage inequality	28%
Difficulties obtaining mixed-gendered mentorship or sponsorship	23%
Sexual harassment or abuse from other ministry leaders	11%

LEADERSHIP OPPORTUNITIES FORMING FEMALE LEADERS

Studies agree that emerging women leaders need learning-by-doing leadership opportunities. These opportunities function as testing grounds, part of early development.[14] Granting these high-quality leadership opportunities, or "developmental job experiences," is an essential component of cultivating female leaders. When women are given less-challenging, low-risk assignments, their successes are smaller, and their learning is limited. Without recognized big wins, women are overlooked for leadership advancement.[15]

Kadi Cole encourages male leaders to regularly put women leaders onstage during church services to communicate women's authority, to demonstrate confidence in their leadership, and to encourage women to speak their opinions

14. Clinton, *Leadership Emergence Theory*, 137.
15. Hopkins et al., "Women's Leadership Development," 358–59; Eagly and Carli, *Through the Labyrinth*, 216.

in meetings. However, these leadership opportunities need to have real leadership responsibilities with real authority and not be merely for show. Defining clear roles for women leaders is essential to their success.[16] Halee Gray Scott agrees, encouraging ministries to create opportunities to increase the visibility of female leaders, allowing them to display their abilities and achievements.[17]

In unsupportive environments, opportunities for female leaders are scarce. Elizabeth Loutrel Glanville found that a woman's delayed timeline of leadership development is sometimes the result of a lack of leadership opportunities. Granting a ministry opportunity communicates confidence in the person given the opportunity, and the experience gained through the opportunity creates competence. A woman's ability to see herself as a leader is severely undermined by a lack of opportunity and failed opportunities.[18]

In churches where a culture of female leadership is still developing, volunteer opportunities can have a significant impact and should not be undervalued. Success in small opportunities leads to relationships with leaders, which can lead to larger opportunities. Many women leaders in this study came to their role not through their education or professional ministry experience but through volunteer opportunities in their churches that opened doors to support staff roles. Accepting a supporting role (e.g., an administrative assistant) to a key ministry leader creates an opportunity to build a relationship with that leader. That relationship can then lead to an opportunity for a staff leadership role.

Female ministry leaders often do not feel recognized for their accomplishments, however. Mary Lederleitner's and Frances S. Adeney's research found that many female ministry leaders watch the male leaders around them advance, and they feel invisible, unnoticed on the sidelines.[19] To address this recognition gap, Ibarra, Ely, and Kolb encourage organizations to intentionally recognize female leader accomplishments, even if they are less significant than their male counterparts' achievements.[20]

When women in hindering environments do get challenging opportunities, sometimes these opportunities are impossibly difficult, leading to failure, burnout, and stress. Organizational psychologists Michelle Ryan and Alexander Haslam call these negative opportunities a "glass cliff."[21] Cole recommends that ministry teams that recognize this pitfall in their environment rally around women in difficult assignments and discuss the

16. Cole, *Developing Female Leaders*, 25, 45, 141.

17. Scott, *Dare Mighty Things*, 118.

18. Glanville, "Leadership Development for Women," 145, 157–59, 160–61.

19. Lederleitner, *Women in God's Mission*, 115–16; Adeney, *Women and Christian Mission*, 25.

20. Ibarra, Ely, and Kolb, "Women Rising."

21. Eagly and Carli, *Through the Labyrinth*, 220.

challenges.[22] How a woman leader responds to and performs in a difficult assignment is crucial to her future opportunities, because while men are often promoted based on their potential, women's chances for advancement are based on past performance.[23] Lederleitner found that many women ministry leaders feel continual pressure to prove themselves to be competent leaders.[24]

Many women self-sabotage their own leadership by rejecting promotions and opportunities because they worry that a new role or task will impact other areas and relationships in their lives. Lederleitner encourages churches to give women time to consider new leadership opportunities so they can figure out how to fit all the pieces together. Once a woman finds a strategy, she may come back with a "yes."[25]

Almost every female participant identified leadership opportunity as a crucial element of their development. One participant said bluntly, "I don't think we can really form as a leader without opportunity to lead." Opportunities help a woman recognize her calling and gain self-awareness of her giftedness. This is important in forming a leader identity. Opportunities provide a means of transforming giftedness into skillfulness, then increasing influence.

One participant reflected on how important leadership opportunity was for practicing the skills she was being taught: "You need a lot of learning and training, but it's not until you actually apply it in ministry that you realize, hey, I can do this! I'm good at *this*, but I'm not good at *that*." Training and opportunities provide women leaders with ministry experience and increase their confidence over time. These opportunities typically start out small. One woman noted that she received lots of encouragement from leaders who saw her potential, despite evident failure. As she was faithful with opportunities, she acquired more skills, and this led to bigger opportunities. Healthy church environments reward success with bigger opportunities, so saying yes to lower-stakes opportunities is a critical step for women. In these smaller opportunities, female leaders demonstrate their leadership capability before being invited into bigger opportunities.

THE SIGNIFICANCE OF FEMALE LEADER SPONSORSHIP

An opportunity is most beneficial to a woman when it is offered by another leader and she does not have to ask for it. Some leaders in this study seemed

22. Cole, *Developing Female Leaders*, 52–53.
23. Barsh and Lee, "Unlocking the Full Potential of Women."
24. Lederleitner, *Women in God's Mission*, 117.
25. Lederleitner, *Women in God's Mission*, 200.

to find the idea of a woman asking for an opportunity for herself to be distasteful, associated with self-promotion. These women described trusting God to open doors of leadership opportunity. Cole encourages church leaders to recruit women to lead and not wait for them to volunteer.[26] Sponsorship happens when someone else opens a door of opportunity. Sponsorship is vitally important for female leadership development because often women cannot create their own opportunities. Women leaders need sponsors who open doors of opportunity for them.

Women in executive roles rarely sponsor other women, even in churches. This may be because women view leadership opportunities as scarce and are self-protecting or because they are too busy to notice the women waiting in the wings. John G. Stackhouse Jr. appeals to men to recognize their power and to use it to empower women into ministry leadership.[27] Without male sponsorship, many women will not be able to step into their God-given calling, and the kingdom will suffer for it.[28] Scott encourages churches to foster male-female partnerships through the creation of sponsorship programs that encourage male-female interactions and work to integrate women into predominantly male relational networks.[29]

Having powerful male leaders recognize the leadership potential of women and ask them to start leading is so important. These men give women clear leadership roles. One woman in this study observed that because women in the middle of an organizational hierarchy don't hold significant power, they are not able to open doors for other women. Men at the top who hold power need to open doors of opportunity. If they don't, women stay stuck. Male sponsorship opens doors for women to step into leadership roles. A male senior pastor described choosing a female leader to sponsor. He had enough of a relationship with a young female leader to recognize the significance of the leadership potential in her, and slowly over time that young woman became self-aware of her own calling and gifting. When these two elements were both in place, he gave her an opportunity. His awareness of her potential came only through relationship, and if his church's leadership culture had prevented male-female relationships, this sponsorship would never have happened.

Several female leaders in this study felt their leadership opportunities had been limited in some way. They recognized that women frequently received opportunities for support roles rather than for executive roles. They said that women had to work harder than men to prove their capability before receiving

26. Cole, *Developing Female Leaders*, 13.
27. Stackhouse, *Partners in Christ*, 124.
28. Lederleitner, *Women in God's Mission*, 165, 171.
29. Scott, *Dare Mighty Things*, 190.

leadership opportunities. Participants did observe, however, increasing opportunities for female leaders in recent years, particularly in large churches and as women assume denominational leadership roles. Cultural shifts have also created pressure to make leadership opportunities available to women.

Many of the most influential women in this study had to work hard to be exceptional leaders before they were noticed and selected for leadership roles. Their leadership skills were what opened doors for them, not a sponsor who advocated for them when all they had was potential. They advanced when others recognized their ability, fruitfulness, and already proven leadership talent.

SUPPORTIVE WORK ENVIRONMENTS FOR FEMALE LEADERSHIP

Women leaders have unique support needs because of their life experiences, motherhood, and social expectations. In a work environment, women leaders need a female-affirming culture, flexibility, and the ability to take a nonlinear leadership journey. This type of environment helps women leaders grow in leadership.

Female-Affirming Culture

Participants described an organizational culture that cultivates female leadership. They each experienced aspects of this culture in various ways, painting a complete picture. In this kind of environment, women are empowered and present at every level of leadership. Women are on the church board and in executive-level positions, and they have strong voices and the final say on major decisions. Women preach regularly in the pulpit. These powerful women are recognized publicly as role models for younger women and attract strong young women. More advanced leaders mentor younger leaders in leadership and public speaking. Women are senior pastors or co-senior pastors with their husbands, leading and preaching as full partners. Unmarried men and women pastor together in partnerships. Both men and women have equal opportunities for leadership roles, and up-and-coming leaders are viewed not as threats or consumables but as resources to be cultivated. Women's voices are invited, wanted, and valued in leadership conversations, and so are men's voices. A male senior pastor said, "The environment that we have is one of empowerment. It's one of trying to push women forward and trying to give them opportunities to lead and speak up."

A female-affirming culture does not view a woman as merely a help to her husband's leadership. In these ministry environments, a wife can hold more organizational authority than her husband. Some churches in this study were looking for husband-wife teams and will not promote a single man or a husband whose wife is not an equal leadership partner. Other churches treat spouses separately and are willing to promote a female leader without her husband's involvement. Or they are willing to give her leadership authority in the church above her husband, who may not be called to vocational ministry or might have less leadership gifting and experience.

In this culture, calling and gifting matter more than gender. There is time for growth and development. Women are encouraged to take initiative and take the lead. They do not need to ask for permission before taking action or making a decision for their sphere of leadership. The men and women look for female leadership talent in unlikely places. For example, they promote personal assistants to executive-level pastoral roles or promote children's pastors to campus pastors, blazing nontraditional, nonlinear career paths.

The culture is honoring, regardless of gender or achievement. Women are valued and honored publicly before they are successful, and they become successful leaders because they have been valued and honored. One woman explained how being in an environment where her opinion was wanted, asked for, and valued brought gifts to the surface that she did not realize she had. It brought her confidence and self-awareness. Conversely, another woman leader who did not initially develop in a female-affirming environment experienced a lack of external support, which caused her to question her budding leader identity and pushed her development backward. An advanced female leader asserted that without the right environment, a female leader's development is stunted.

In a female-affirming culture, people think about how spaces can empower women leaders. Office space accommodates nursing mothers and daycare facilities. Open spaces bring safety and transparency to male-female one-on-one conversations.

In this kind of environment, emerging men and women leaders can form authentic relationships with other leaders and build strong leader identities and confidence. Young male leaders are trained to recognize and understand the developmental needs of female leaders, preparing them to develop female leaders when they are in a position to do so.

Flexibility

Women want more from life than career or ministry alone. They want work and home to be entwined.[30] This isn't necessarily about achieving balance,

---

30. Tarr-Whelan, *Women Lead the Way*, loc. 854 of 4551, Kindle.

which implies that home and ministry are separate and therefore battling for time. This is about weaving together home and ministry responsibilities and ensuring that those entrusted to their care in both spaces thrive. Women struggle in work environments that expect long hours in the office.[31] While local church leaders may not need to travel extensively, they are frequently called on for evening and weekend commitments, which can cause a conflict of interest for women leaders with young families.[32]

It is possible for women leaders to have successful careers and strong families, however. The key ingredient, vital for women to thrive both at home and in ministry leadership, is flexibility. In the era following the COVID-19 pandemic, corporate culture is shifting in response to the need for flexibility, and the church needs to recognize the opportunity this shift presents for women leaders.[33] Churches looking to build pipelines of female leaders should grant greater flexibility to women in the ministry workplace without diminishing their authority or opportunities.[34] Flexibility is so important that women will negotiate with employers for it.[35] Women's leadership consultants agree on the need for flexibility, even if they disagree on the conditions of it.

Working long hours in an office doesn't necessarily create the best employees, and it is not necessary in an era when people have learned how to collaborate in online meetings.[36] Flexibility might look like female leaders choosing their hours and their locations for work (typically, Sunday services are an exception to this flexibility). Flexibility might look like church teams designing expectations for ministry leaders based on results rather than hours logged (and giving this kind of flexibility to both male and female leaders).[37] Churches that depend on volunteers cannot avoid weekend and evening hours (times when volunteers are available), but church staffs can build flexibility into their daytime hours to compensate.

The fruit of flexibility is leadership health. Families are healthier because women are fulfilled in their ministry calling and have the flexibility to do both work and home life well. Staff members are loyal to their organizations and pastors, bringing longevity and stability to a church leadership team.

31. Barsh and Lee, "Unlocking the Full Potential of Women."
32. Cole, *Developing Female Leaders*, 48.
33. Krivkovich et al., "Women in the Workplace 2022."
34. Lederleitner, *Women in God's Mission*, 187; Beach, *Gifted to Lead*, 91.
35. Ely, Ibarra, and Kolb, "Taking Gender into Account," 483.
36. Eagly and Carli, *Through the Labyrinth*, 207.
37. Cole, *Developing Female Leaders*, 129.

A Nonlinear Leadership Journey

Women leaders' career paths often do not follow the direct route of those of their male counterparts. Men move upward from rung to rung, but when women navigate seasons of motherhood or other family responsibilities, they may step downward or pause entirely. Glanville notes that the motherhood season often makes a female ministry leader's journey nonlinear as she cycles in and out of ministry as children are born. Some women wait to enter ministry until their children are older.[38] A female ministry leader's journey is unique.[39] Margaret M. Hopkins and her colleagues encourage organizations to support women with intentional career planning that takes these seasons into account, and they encourage organizations to hold managers accountable for providing this kind of development.[40]

Some women in this study wanted to reduce their ministry workload while their children were young, slowing down their influence progression, and they were happy to make this sacrifice. Other women chose to move from more powerful positions in their church's leadership hierarchy to positions of lower status because they felt these roles were better suited to their passions and gifts. Women leaders are typically less concerned about climbing a ladder of power, and so a movement "downward" should not be seen as a demotion due to incompetence. Leaders in a ministry context should recognize that this nonlinear nature means not that a woman will be less focused on the ministry work before her but that her value system is different from those of her male counterparts. Women want to be very strategic about how they structure their lives and leadership, and a supportive work environment will allow for a nonlinear leadership journey.

SUMMARY

Women leaders are shaped by their ministry environment. They face theological and cultural resistance, gender bias, a pay gap, and even at times harassment and abuse. Women need opportunities and sponsors to open doors of leadership opportunity for them. The most supportive ministry leadership environments have a female-affirming culture, offer flexibility, and allow a nonlinear leadership journey.

38. Glanville, "Leadership Development for Women," 154–55.
39. Lederleitner, *Women in God's Mission*, 24.
40. Hopkins et al., "Women's Leadership Development," 359–60.

8

FEMALE LEADERS FORMING INFLUENCE THROUGH LEADERSHIP RELATIONSHIPS

ASPECT 6, PART 1

Leadership creates relationships that wouldn't likely exist otherwise. In 2024 I'll celebrate twenty-five years of pastoral ministry. In that time, I've ministered in three churches and navigated transitions away from two churches. As I have most recently transitioned from an executive pastor role in Chicago to a lead pastor role in metropolitan Washington, DC, I've been struck by how my relationships in Chicago have changed now that I no longer pastor there. Some relationships have become friendships, while some women leaders in the church still reach out to me for ministry advice and help. Other relationships, with people I once interacted with almost daily, seem to have quietly subsided. Without localized mission bringing us together, we no longer have places where our lives intersect. While I miss these wonderful people, this is the nature of leadership relationships. The best leadership relationships become deep friendships that continue through different ministry seasons, but many relationships are just for a season, for a unique God-designed purpose.

In previous chapters, we explored the three internal aspects of female leadership development and the two external aspects. As women leaders receive the necessary environmental supports and progress in their inner development, they begin to form leadership influence. This influence is cultivated through leadership relationships. Leadership relationships reach up, down, and across and create personal influence, or power. The reach of a woman's influence can be measured as it grows.

THE DEVELOPMENT OF PERSONAL POWER

Power creates leadership capacity. Andy Crouch notes that the word *power* makes us uncomfortable. But even if we rename it *influence, leadership*, or *authority* so that we feel better about it, it is still at its core *power*. Instead of avoiding power, we should view it as a gift from God to steward well, tied to our role as image bearers of God.[1] Influence is part of authority. Douglas McConnell differentiates between being "in authority," which is power derived from a position in an institution, thus granting the leader the power of that institution, and being "an authority," which is power derived from personal expertise, skill, or another type of influence.[2] A leader can also have influence derived from relationships, virtuous character, personal charisma, transactional rewards (a paycheck), or threats (getting fired). A poor leader may use negative means, such as coercion or manipulation, to influence those around them.[3]

God forms Christian leaders, entrusting people to their care to cultivate human flourishing. Over a lifetime, a leader gains power that enables them to complete their God-given assignment in building the kingdom. Without power, a leader cannot lead. When women leaders increase their power, they have increasing capacity to fulfill God's mission.

Often women in the church develop influence through their relationships, their skills, or their expertise without being granted the authority of a position. Women are most often promoted into positions of authority after they have already developed influence on their own as an authority in a particular field. A potential female church leader might have Bible knowledge, skillful social media usage, or musical gifts. The organizational power that comes from a formal church leadership position strengthens a female leader's ability to rally people around a vision, make decisions, and manage a team. This doesn't always come easily for women, however.

Anna Fels found that women sometimes struggle to take authority because of its connection to dominance, which is decidedly culturally unfeminine. Dominance is power misused, however. Fels defines dominance as "the failure of a

1. Crouch, *Playing God*, 10, 12.
2. McConnell, *Cultural Insights for Christian Leaders*, loc. 2650 of 5152, Kindle.
3. Raven, "Bases of Power," 1–4.

person in power to acknowledge and respond to the wishes and needs of those with less power."[4] Despite a hesitancy to use power—even in the right ways—women leaders impact their contexts through their influence and authority.

Five Levels of Leadership in Local Church Ministry

As explained in chapter 2, we can measure a person's authority within a church based on position, organizational power, and reach, such as social media followership. A female church leader's increasing influence can be determined based on her level of leadership (see fig. 8.1). I used these five levels to categorize the leadership influence of study participants.

These five levels are progressive. Over a woman's leadership lifetime, she may progress into new levels of leadership authority. Not every woman is called to greater influence, but many are. Influence growth is not always linear for women leaders. A woman may have seasons when she has reduced leadership influence—for example, while she is on maternity leave.

A female ministry leader typically begins at level 1 with unpaid leadership roles. These are often leadership roles in small groups or teams within her local church. A woman leader grows to level 2 as she gains authority. She may accept a support staff role at her church or become a senior leader in a smaller church. These women are often responsible for fifty to a hundred people entrusted to their care. When a woman progresses to level 3 leadership, she might have an executive staff position or be a campus pastor in a large church. She might be a senior pastor in a midsized church. She is now responsible for leading other leaders who care for and shepherd people in the church. As her authority continues to grow, she might become a senior pastor of a large church or perhaps have a leadership role in a denomination. At this level, level 4, a woman leader must lead leaders of leaders who care for people. Her ability to replicate and reproduce is essential. She may be church planting or working on another strategy for church multiplication. At level 5, a woman leader has international influence in her organization and beyond, extending her influence through the internet, writing, and hosting or speaking at major conferences that gather church leaders from other churches. Other church pastors look to her for guidance in pastoring. Level 4 and level 5 female ministry leaders are exceedingly rare.

Other types of influence, including spiritual authority and personal influence, cannot be quantifiably measured.[5] But as women leaders engage in the

---

4. Fels, *Necessary Dreams*, 155.
5. Spiritual authority is an extension of God's authority through one's relational position as a daughter or son of God, while leadership authority is an extension of institutional power through one's position in the organization.

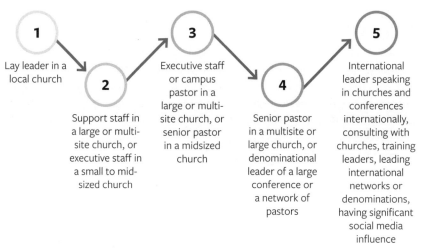

Fig. 8.1. Development of Leadership Influence

seven processes of development, their influence grows. Over time, greater influence gives them positional authority to lead larger groups of people and direct more resources toward their vision for God's mission. The hierarchical structures in large churches and denominations are a trellis for a female leader's influence to grow on. These large institutions have structured pathways for leadership relationships, opportunities, and platforms for large-scale communication.

Accumulating power for personal gain is not the aim of Christian leadership. The heart and goal of Christian leadership is selfless sharing, which is the basis of spiritual authority (Phil. 2:3–5). Wilmer G. Villacorta calls this a "power out of weakness" that leads to a deeper connection with God through sharing power.[6] This kind of generosity of influence builds deep connections with other people as well. Growth in influence requires careful reflection and self-awareness to guard motives through healthy pacing and accountability.

Ironically, the personal difficulties, hindrances, and resistance women leaders experience in ministry may sift out those with selfish motives, safeguarding church authority from narcissistic female leaders. This is perhaps why we hear about public fallout due to abuses of power by male leaders far more often than we hear of abuses of power by women in ministry leadership roles. Women looking to accumulate power selfishly simply do not persist through the hindrances. Women leaders in church ministry survive only if they are others-centered because church leadership simply has too few personal

6. Villacorta, *Tug of War*, 3.

benefits for women. This means that women leaders' motives are typically trustworthy.

God has different purposes for different women leaders, and not every woman is called or destined to be an international leader. Women are needed and valuable at every level of leadership. But surely God has called more women to international leadership than we see around us today. For the women who do feel called to it, we need to provide pathways for them to grow in influence as they carry God's mission forward. It is not merely a nice idea but a spiritual responsibility of church leaders to steward the developing gifts and callings of God in these women, recognizing that these women's leadership is part of God's plan for the church body. All Christians are called to support female leadership emergence.

Women church leaders occupy each of the levels of leadership and need leadership training to expand their influence. J. Robert Clinton observes that most leaders are trained to be levels 1 to 3. Since needed skills differ with each level of influence, Clinton recommends training be grouped by leadership level.[7] Women volunteering in their first year of ministry have very different training needs than women pastoring churches and training for denominational leadership roles. It follows that women leaders benefit from being grouped by their level of leadership for additional training. This study examined women in each of these five categories to discover what types of training are needed to achieve each increasing level of leadership influence.

Mapping Influence Development in Female Leaders

This study tracked female leaders' rise in influence through several variables. One variable was leadership role promotions. Women moved from volunteer leadership, to being hired as support leaders, to leading departments on church staff, to overseeing staff as executive-level leaders, to senior pastoring, to having significant influence beyond their local churches through denominational/formal network leadership roles, writing books, and speaking at conferences and other events. The most significant variation to this trajectory was women who planted churches, often co-pastoring with their husbands, and were at the top of their organization from early in their ministry journey. Another variable was social media, particularly Instagram, which is the preferred platform in my context of local church ministry. Instagram is particularly popular with users from age eighteen to forty-four, the age group most churches are attempting to engage.[8] The most influential female

7. Clinton, *Leadership Training Models*, 34, 64, 78.
8. McLachlan, "Instagram Demographics in 2022."

participants in this study have more than forty-two thousand followers on Instagram, and there is a direct relationship between progression in their local church leadership and their social media influence. (See appendixes D and E for the leadership influence of study participants.)

Interestingly, a third of the study's female participants indicated that they are not interested in increasing in power within their organization simply for the sake of personal progress. In fact, two campus pastors indicated that they would prefer to move backward into positions of less power inside their local churches because they feel their gifts and passions are better suited to different roles where they feel more fruitful. This attitude requires a great deal of self-awareness as well as spiritual maturity and humility. One woman pioneered a new role for herself inside her church, building partnerships with organizations within her city. Rather than focusing on building her own influence within her local church, she focuses on building the influence of her local church within society.

Accumulating power is not the top priority for these women, and this is a distinctive of female ministry leadership. These women want to maintain their freedom and flexibility above all else, and if accumulating more power means they have to lose freedom, they are far less interested in a promotion. Conversely, women in senior pastor roles of well-established churches noted that they have more freedom than those in midlevel and executive leadership roles. These same women noted the stresses of church planting while having a young family. Women don't always recognize the benefits that come with rising into leadership roles with greater responsibility, which often come with more flexibility and higher pay.

FORMING INFLUENCE THROUGH CULTIVATING LEADERSHIP RELATIONSHIPS

Relationships are essential for female leaders—and not just for creating opportunity for advancement. Leadership relationships are central to gaining leadership influence. For female ministry leaders, impact is measured through relationships.[9] A female leader forms relationships based on her leader identity within her ministry context with those who have a shared purpose. She forms relationships up, across, and down: with more advanced leaders, her peers who lead in other contexts, and those she develops. As she builds leadership relationships and expands her interactions, she gains influence. A female leader needs more advanced leaders to mentor her as well as to validate her

9. Lederleitner, *Women in God's Mission*, 103.

leadership to others. She develops other leaders and connects with or builds peer networks of leaders.

Leadership is created through forming relationships where both parties have a shared purpose, and a leader exerts power to influence the path of progress toward that goal. Leadership exists in the interactions between people. Joseph A. Raelin describes the practice of leadership as a "process co-formed with others and through an interactive relationship."[10] Without these interactive relationships, leadership doesn't exist.

Even though women are naturally wired for relationship and can connect and empathize deeply with others, female ministry leaders must learn to relate to others in a new way, through leadership relationships.[11] Leadership relationships require specific skills and behaviors. Women can struggle with developing relationships that involve a power dynamic.[12] Women's leadership style is often highly democratic and participatory, flattening hierarchy.[13] Women sometimes feel as if professional relationships are contrived and inauthentic and so devalue them. Many women neglect "politics," operating on the assumption that their leaders will evaluate their good work and promote them based merely on merit. They often find political maneuvering distasteful.[14] Despite the awkwardness of these seemingly contrived relationships, they serve important roles in female leader emergence. If women leaders reframe these as leadership relationships, recognizing the people as important allies in achieving a God-given vision and mission, then they will begin to experience the value of these relationships. While personal relationships provide emotional and practical support, leadership relationships provide a shared vision for God's kingdom advancement.

As women leaders are shaped by their environments, they in turn learn to shape their environments through their developing influence. Leadership influence is formed in relationships, and women leaders need multiple types of relationships to grow their leadership skills and influence.

As a woman develops as a leader she gains followers, adding to her influence. People begin to trust her and are inspired to engage with her vision. Mentors, leadership coaches, and sponsors accelerate her influence growth as they validate her leadership by sharing their power with her. Their affirmation of her leadership by giving her leadership positions or speaking

---

10. Raelin, *Leadership-as-Practice*, 72.
11. TenElshof, "Psychological Evidence of Gender Differentiation," 239; Schmitt, "Truth about Sex Differences."
12. Schmitt, "Truth about Sex Differences."
13. Eagly and Johnson, "Gender and Leadership Style," 249.
14. Vinnicombe and Singh, "Women-Only Management Training," 302.

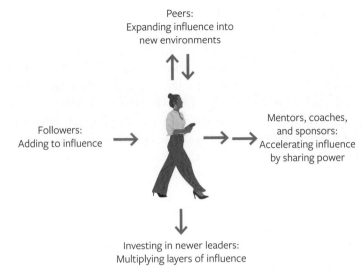

Fig. 8.2. Influence Development Model

opportunities causes people who already trust these mature leaders to also trust and follow her leadership (assuming her character is worthy of respect). As a female leader invests in new leaders, she multiplies layers of leadership influence. As those leaders influence others, she gains new groups to influence indirectly. Those people entrusted to my care are also entrusted to the care of my spiritual leaders. As a female leader develops peer relationships with other leaders, her relationships create bridges for her to influence new environments. This might happen indirectly through the advice she gives a peer that is then implemented in a new ministry context. This influence might also be direct influence, through guest speaking at a peer's church event, providing team training for another church, or doing online ministry. See figure 8.2 for a model of how influence grows.

Let's look at each type of leadership relationship.

Mentorship and Training

When I was twenty-three, my pastors, Steve and Melodye, decided to develop me for worship ministry leadership. I had musical skills for playing the piano and singing, and I was showing signs of being able to organize myself and others well. What I didn't know about ministry was a much longer list, including how to plan the flow of a worship service. Pastor Steve invited me into a weekly one-on-one meeting with him to plan services. In the early days of these meetings, he asked me what songs I was considering for Sunday and gave me feedback about my choices. He helped me, a young white woman, think more deeply about song choice, considering things like the needs and preferences for worship of the older people in the room or the Black and Latinx members of our congregation. Then he would tell me what he wanted the rest of the service to look like. I'd take notes and then communicate to people who needed the information. After I learned this way for a year or two, Pastor Steve asked me to start bringing him a draft of the entire service plan. He would review it with me and offer small improvements or full changes. As the years went on and I gained experience, he rarely changed the plans I put in place. Eventually these planning meetings subsided and I planned worship services without direct supervision.

This kind of practical mentorship not only taught me the skills for planning and executing high-quality and impactful worship experiences but also gave me authority in our church. I became Pastor Steve's mouthpiece. He communicated to people on our team about church services through me. This arrangement worked so well that after five years or so, he began to use me to communicate on his behalf regarding other aspects of church life, and I became the executive pastor for this megachurch before I was thirty. I knew the team relied on me to keep everyone on track and knowing what they needed to do.

As explained in earlier chapters, female ministry leaders need role models to provide examples and sponsors to create leadership opportunities. They also need mentors to provide coaching.[15] Margaret M. Hopkins encourages women to cultivate male and female mentors and to define objectives for these relationships.[16] Leadership mentors identify callings, gifts, and potential in female ministry leaders. They provide leadership and organizational advice, encouragement, identity affirmation, and friendship.[17]

While the benefits of mentorship are self-evident, women typically have few opportunities to be mentored by another woman because of a lack of women in senior-level positions providing mentorship to women.[18] Obtaining male mentorship in ministry is often challenging once a young woman graduates from her youth ministry because mixed-gender mentoring in ministry can be tricky.[19] Men are often hesitant to provide mentoring to female leaders,

15. Barsh and Lee, "Unlocking the Full Potential of Women"; Cole, *Developing Female Leaders*, 81; Hollywood, "Comparative Study of Feminine Dimensions," 244.
16. Hopkins et al., "Women's Leadership Development," 357.
17. Eagly and Carli, *Through the Labyrinth*, 253; Tarr-Whelan, *Women Lead the Way*, locs. 2140–58 of 4551, Kindle.
18. Scott, *Dare Mighty Things*, 117.
19. Lederleitner, *Women in God's Mission*, 179.

especially young women. Female leaders who have been mentored, however, are often more satisfied, more highly paid, and more competent.[20] Without mentors, the emergence of female ministry leaders' influence can be delayed, and they can be left feeling devalued and inadequate.[21]

Mentorship in Female Leadership Development

Women in this study explained that early in their leadership development they needed role models they could admire from afar, but once they started leading, they needed mentors to come alongside them in their journey and coach them. Every woman in this study acknowledged that she needed and wanted mentors, but well over half of these women experienced a lack of mentorship. Gen Xers and boomers were particularly disadvantaged by the lack of female leaders who came before them, leaving them with few mentors to shape them. One female baby boomer shared that her pastor's wife could not mentor her in leadership because she did not have the skills or experience and was often dealing with her own children and life challenges. As a double difficulty, women lacking self-confidence were awkward in conversations with a mentor and had difficulties keeping a mentor engaged and interested. A lack of mentorship is strongly correlated with level 1 and 2 leaders, indicating that a mentor is often needed to move a woman into higher levels of leadership and influence.

Male mentors were key in the development of influential women in this study. By far, most of the women who had mentors had *male* mentors. Many had male youth pastors who recognized their potential and invested in their development, but they did not have mentors later as an adult. Many women took it upon themselves to pursue a mentor and took the initiative in building this relationship. Others were promoted into positions that directly reported to a senior pastor. Nearly a third of the women in this study were formerly personal assistants to male senior pastors. They identified time spent in meetings listening to their pastors talk about leadership direction, vision, and culture as mentorship, and eventually their pastors recognized this as a developmental process and promoted them. Five women in this study were directly promoted from personal assistant to campus pastor.

Nearly three-quarters of the participants described being indirectly mentored in nonpersonal relationships. They considered listening to sermons and podcasts, watching leaders on social media, and reading books and articles by respected leaders to be valid forms of mentorship when personal

---

20. Hopkins et al., "Women's Leadership Development," 355–56.
21. Glanville, "Leadership Development for Women," 145, 160–61.

relationships were not an option. With the shortage of female mentors, this adaptation was important. The shortcoming in this system is that without personal relationships with mentors, these women experienced a lack of feedback, which is essential to building self-awareness. Almost half of the women in this study experienced difficulties due to a lack of feedback about their leadership. Church planters particularly struggled to get feedback due to a lack of mentors. To help create self-awareness, these leaders needed to bring in outside consultants to provide feedback about their leadership. Those who did receive feedback needed good emotional intelligence to be able to handle criticisms of their leadership.

Ministry Training

Training was important for every female participant. Only a third of female participants had received formal training through a Bible college or seminary. This is likely an indicator that women do not typically start out with ministry leadership as their planned career path. However, formal ministry training can both equip women with important skills and knowledge for ministry leadership and increase their confidence. Formal ministry training also creates opportunities for developing relationships with ministry peers and mentoring relationships with professors. Over half of the women in this study received nonformal training from internships, conferences, books, and sermons and talks. Nonformal training was the most common type of training these women received. Few women had received training in public speaking or preaching. Some women viewed themselves as undertrained but did not let that stop them from leading.

Mentors Creating Leadership Power through Validation

Building relationships with more advanced leaders is essential for accessing leadership opportunities. If a pastor does not know a female leader in his church, then he will not have any context for considering emerging female leaders for potential roles. These relationships also provide leadership validation. Two-thirds of those I interviewed discussed the importance of a woman's leadership being validated by someone above her. When an established leader validates a developing leader, the mature leader lends the developing leader their leadership influence and credibility until the emerging leader has earned their own. This validation can turn into sponsorship, which occurs when an established leader creates an opportunity for a developing leader to cultivate influence with others. Validation of leadership comes from public recognition (particularly from senior male leaders), hiring women and promoting them to ministry leadership roles, having female leaders preach on Sundays and outside their local churches, and recognizing God's anointing. These validating leader relationships bring credibility to and trust in a female's leadership, building her personal influence. Male and female study participants agreed that male leaders have power and therefore a particular responsibility for validating the female leaders around them. Single women in this study said that marriage would also be an important validation of their ministry. Marriage increased the authority levels of the women in this study.

Without external validation, a female's leadership can be perceived as overly domineering or controlling and her motives questioned. Nearly half of the women in this study felt uneasy with self-promotion of female leadership. These participants believe they are able to validate their own leadership only through humble faithfulness and fruitfulness over a long period of time. A possible exception to this inability to self-validate is social media followership, which is a quantifiable form of earned leadership influence. Social media influence opens doors of in-person opportunities for women leaders.

The more advanced female leaders in this study were actively working to validate emerging female leaders by having them preach at their events, inviting them to coauthor books, and bringing them into their relationships. If, because of low self-confidence, a woman cannot recognize the validation she is being given, then she is not able to leverage that borrowed influence. Only when her leadership is producing recognizable fruit in others' lives does it become self-validating.

Developing the Next Generation of Leaders

The women in this study were in near perfect agreement that developing younger leaders is a crucial part of their own development. They need to have the leadership skills to inspire developing leaders for kingdom work and to be able to equip these new leaders for leadership. The most advanced leaders had internalized this into their identity, seeing their purpose not in just creating followers or building vision and organizations but in creating change agents who would fulfill their own callings. This is transformational leadership.[22] These women became self-aware of their own giftedness for developing leaders and recognized that they were role models for novice female leaders.

Developing a young female leader begins with cultivating a leadership mentality in her. Advanced women leaders use strategies to cultivate this mentality. They convert task lists into a formal leadership role with regular

22. Brubaker, "Spirit-Led Followers," 141.

responsibilities and people to care for and then assign that role to a woman with a budding leader identity. Or they hand a capable woman a leadership problem to solve. They continue to invest in young leaders by providing coaching and mentoring, particularly through interpersonal communication. Three women who recognized such a need for coaching young female leaders pioneered three organizational networks for developing female leaders. A third of the women leaders described being very relational and building close, personal connections with the young women they were developing. They gave mentees more time and attention than others in their churches. One female co-senior pastor described it this way: "We draw those people in really close because we know we're going to be requiring a lot of them. That's the model." They recognized that if they were going to make heavy asks of these women, they needed to make significant relational deposits into them first. These women often wrestled with the process of developing leaders. Their leadership investments were sometimes undervalued by mentees, and they dealt with the pain of being rejected by women who left their churches after being mentored.

Peer Networks

Women leaders also need well-developed peer networks. Peer relationships provide learning, growth, and spiritual support.[23] They are essential for sharing knowledge, building influence and confidence, and connecting with opportunities.[24] Women leaders need to be able to process the unique challenges they face with other female ministry leaders who understand their experiences. In these safe spaces outside their organizations, women leaders receive emotional support, advice, friendship, and encouragement.[25] Women leaders need relationships not just with mentors and advisers but also with professionals, leaders in community organizations, and social media personalities.[26] These relationships build "social capital," which expands influence, and they provide opportunities for leaders to offer help and advice as well as receive them.[27] Female leadership experts encourage women to spend time daily networking and to look at every interaction as a chance to build a peer relationship.[28]

---

23. Cole, *Developing Female Leaders*, 206; Scott, *Dare Mighty Things*, 135.

24. Hopkins et al., "Women's Leadership Development," 357–58; Cole, *Developing Female Leaders*, 81.

25. Lederleitner, *Women in God's Mission*, 182; Suby-Long, "Role of Transformational Learning," 104; Vinnicombe and Singh, "Women-Only Management Training," 300; Eagly and Carli, *Through the Labyrinth*, 210, 212.

26. Tarr-Whelan, *Women Lead the Way*, loc. 2592 of 4551, Kindle.

27. Eagly and Carli, *Through the Labyrinth*, 210.

28. Ely, Ibarra, and Kolb, "Taking Gender into Account," 482.

Barriers to Women Leaders Developing Peer Networks

Peer relationships are frequently inaccessible for women leaders. Informal networks create relationship-building opportunities, but women are frequently excluded from male-dominated networks.[29] In a 2003 Catalyst study, 46 percent of women reported exclusion from these networks as a limiting factor in their career advancement.[30] These networks provide influence and social capital, confidence, useful industry advice, deal making, and understanding of politics.[31] These "boys' clubs" may exclude women unconsciously, and women may also opt out of belonging to them because they do not value them.

When I was a worship pastor in my twenties, I realized I was leading by trial and error. I had never been part of a worship ministry as large as the one I was leading, and I was guessing what would work to solve problems and then implementing untested solutions. Some of them worked, but others did not. I needed someone with experience in a large church setting to help me think about how to structure the ministry, set appropriate expectations, and cultivate creativity. So I reached out by email to an experienced and popular male worship pastor, asking if I could have a phone conversation with him to ask some leadership questions. His assistant responded to my email by telling me he did not take meetings with women and referred me to a book about worship. I felt embarrassed and confused.

Even though they developed their leadership in churches, the women of this study faced significant barriers in developing leadership within denominational and ministry networks. Building strategic relationships in networks of peers was one of the most difficult learning experiences for the women of this study. Two-thirds of the women leaders in this study struggled to build peer networks. In the early years of their ministry, most of these leaders focused on their families and building relationships with the people they led and followed. Later in their development, they began to recognize their need for peer relationships. They needed peer relationships to provide support, share ideas, prayer, solidarity, learning, and encouragement. Above all, women talked about needing peer relationships to feel as if they were not alone and that they were "normal" as female ministry leaders.

Almost half of the women shared obstacles to building peer networks. Some viewed men as being better at networking and cited a shortage of female minister networks. Most have very little in common with traditional

29. Barsh and Lee, "Unlocking the Full Potential of Women."
30. Catalyst, "Double-Bind Dilemma for Women in Leadership," 19, 26.
31. Hopkins et al., "Women's Leadership Development," 357–58.

pastors' wives—a circle that has more possibilities for networking. (As an executive pastor, I received an invitation to a pastors' wives gathering from a significant Christian leadership network.) Several women also found the idea of networking to be distasteful. The word *networking* connoted awkward, shallow, self-serving relationships. Some worried about whether others were trustworthy, or they felt insecure to engage other female leaders.

Despite their initial awkwardness, female leader networks play a vital role in female leadership emergence. Ely, Ibarra, and Kolb encourage female leaders who struggle with feeling as if they are "using" people to recognize the higher value of networks. Women leaders need to be able to process the unique challenges they experience, and the resultant pain, in relationships with other female ministry leaders who understand their experiences. In these safe spaces outside their organizations, women leaders mutually receive emotional support, advice, friendship, and encouragement.[32]

One woman pastor said, "I definitely reach out and try to build relationships with other female pastors. That can be challenging." These relational networks are essential for sharing knowledge, providing emotional support, building influence and confidence, and connecting with opportunities.[33] Egalitarian male-led ministry networks often exclude women because of mixed-gendered relational dynamics (the Billy Graham rule), and male and female leaders' experiences are not always congruent. Building connections between women leaders is important, but women need structured environments that create opportunities for open, safe dialogue to do this. Conferences and large events typically do not provide enough opportunity for interaction that allows women to build foundations for long-term relationships. Women need longer-term, programmed connections, with regular opportunities for structured personal interaction over months.

Networking with men is a particularly challenging venture. A third of the women in this study encountered overt gender discrimination in denominational or network settings. Women were iced out of conversations at events and encountered passive-aggressive resistance as their opinions were ignored by male pastors. Often denominational networks are male-dominated and do not have women at every level, so women from local churches where female leaders flourish encounter culture shock in these environments. For many, their instinctive defensive reaction is to pull back, to perhaps allow

32. Lederleitner, *Women in God's Mission*, 182; Suby-Long, "The Role of Transformational Learning," 104; Vinnicombe and Singh, "Women-Only Management Training," 300; Eagly and Carli, *Through the Labyrinth*, 252–53.

33. Hopkins et al., "Women's Leadership Development," 357–58; Cole, *Developing Female Leaders*, 81.

their husbands to engage instead, avoiding any issues. No one wants to be disloyal to movements they are helping to build, much less to the kingdom of God. However, as networking relationships are key to advanced leadership development, movements that repress female networking because of the Billy Graham rule or sexism severely limit the potential influence of the female leaders within.

Five women identified the Association of Related Churches (ARC) as a "boys' club" that does not value women's leadership or voices and is particularly difficult to penetrate relationally. A female pastor said, "ARC is one place where there are so many women in this room that have so much to offer, but they're just not allowed to." Two others mentioned the Australian Christian Churches (Assemblies of God Australia) and the Assemblies of God USA as particularly male-dominated in denominational leadership. These organizations espouse an egalitarian theological position, but their practices have not demonstrated this stated value.

Those with husbands in ministry have relied on them to be a bridge to other male leaders and have used them to access information and ideas, but this is not always possible. Many women attempted conversations with male leaders who became visibly uncomfortable when approached by a female leader. Many women rely on their husbands to make the relational connections because walking up to a man at a networking event can be so awkward. One woman described being completely ignored in a pastors' network gathering: "I'll get stonewalled in rooms unless my husband is with me. There are some men who are just uncomfortable talking to me." Another participant described these clumsy exchanges in trying to build peer relationships with men in networks: "What I definitely have done is push my way into men's conversations and made them aware of my role via my body language or forcing conversation." If a woman does not have a husband in ministry, this networking effort can be more daunting. Another participant described the challenge of stepping into denominational leadership without the strength of peer relationships: "This denomination is so social, so relational. If you're not with people golfing on Monday after they've preached in your church—if you're not with people socially, learning more about them, learning what they think—if you're only in formal settings, then you try being the only woman at a big board table with nine men. And the only other woman is the woman taking notes that you get sat with at dinner."

A male pastor acknowledged that his fear of interacting with female leaders has less to do with him not trusting himself and more to do with his fear that others will think the relationship is inappropriate or sinful. This kind of resistance is frustrating and discouraging for women leaders and causes them to feel rejected. A level 5 female leader said, "The fact that women have been portrayed as a threat to a man's ministry is what gets me really mad. And the fact that men are walking around going, 'What problem? There's no problem with women. There's all this opportunity out there.'" This is a cultural issue that needs to be addressed head-on in denominational environments, and better thinking and behavior need to be modeled by executive denominational leaders and megachurch influencers.

Men and women partnering in ministry leadership is not inherently danger-ous or sinful. It strikes me as a particularly insidious strategy of the enemy designed to rein in church leadership because when men and women partner in strength, powerful things happen. We need better frameworks for male-female relationships than those provided by our oversexed culture.

Strategies for Growing Peer Networks

Unless a woman leader can overcome these barriers and build peer relation-ships outside her local church context, her leadership context will be limited to her local church, and she will peak at level 3 or possibly level 4 leadership. Despite the difficulty, women called to broader influence in the church must persevere. The women in this study found ways around the barriers, utilizing strategies such as bridge building, honoring other leaders, cultivating new connections, helping others, and bonding over fun activities. A husband can be a relational bridge, as can a male pastor friend who introduces a female leader to other male pastors. Leaders cultivate new connections by initiating follow-up interactions after becoming acquainted, perhaps via social media, text messages, or setting up coffee chats. Social media also provides a large pool of potential connections for female leaders.

Some women choose to believe that male leaders are well-intentioned but unaware (and a little bit dumb). These women cope with the diffi-culty by believing that the resistance they experience is not personal but cultural. Others recognize the problem but shrug off the pain of rejection and patiently persevere through it, seeing it as a means of spiritual shap-ing, and pioneer for the sake of future generations of female leaders. These women self-regulate to guard their reactions and allow the fruit of their leadership to speak for itself. Others take a more political approach and engage the power dynamics at work. They recognize the male thinking that causes limitations for female leaders and strategize ways around it. They work rooms at leadership events, build relationships with powerful people, and leverage those relationships to create new ones. They refuse to accept limitations.

This study found that male leaders play a vital role in advocating for women as they develop peer networks. A male pastor can initiate a collegial peer relationship with a female leader (with spousal transparency), and then he can introduce her to his network. A husband pastor can play this role for his wife. His support of her is a type of validation, which signals to other men that she is safe, has ideas and opportunities to share, and can offer a valuable relationship. From there, she can build additional relationships with male leaders. A female pastor might never play a round of golf with the boys, but she can be professionally respected and collaborate with male pastors on ministry initiatives. Network building starts with one man intentionally sponsoring a woman leader in a ministry network, vouching for her. One male pastor explained the importance of his sponsorship of female leaders on his team in male networks: "For women to access those higher-level denominational leadership opportunities—whether leading training or leading a district—it required *me* to open those doors, and sometimes I had to push on those doors a little bit to make it happen."

A possible opportunity for peer relationships is female-leader training cohorts. Female-only cohorts provide a unique opportunity to build relationships with women leaders who lead in different contexts. Groups such as WXP for women executive pastors,[34] the Women's Collective Cohort certificate program at Ascent College,[35] and She Leads Circle of 12,[36] provide these kinds of learning communities for women leaders.

Women most often grow peer networks one relationship at a time by intentionally and regularly reaching out to other leaders. Organizations can aid in this process by creating support groups and learning communities for developing female leaders.[37] Villacorta describes this kind of community as providing a sense of belonging and identity. Women gain power through identifying with a group. He encourages building relationships without selfish motives because the pursuit of power and one-upmanship robs us of true intimacy. Villacorta names the humble, selfless desire to share one's power with others the "downward ascent," which is a Christlike approach to building networks.[38] Women who need to build their networks can cultivate them by mentoring other women and centering other women and their needs in relationship development.

Peer relationships must be cultivated over time, and it takes work to make connections. True relationships cannot simply be picked up when someone has a need and then put aside when no longer needed. Female leaders need

34. https://wxpastors.com/.
35. https://ascent.edu/womens-collective-cohort/.
36. https://www.sherises.com/she-leads.
37. Ely, Ibarra, and Kolb, "Taking Gender into Account," 482, 485.
38. Villacorta, *Tug of War*, 31, 33, 101.

to have integrity and honor their commitments by being present for others when they have needs.[39] They should avoid comparing their journey and opportunities with those of other female leaders because comparison leads to envy, which erodes relationships and stunts relational networks.[40]

SUMMARY

Women have more or less power based on the level of leadership they have attained. Women leaders form power, or influence, through leadership relationships. These types of relationships include mentoring relationships in which women develop relationships with more skilled and powerful leaders who coach them, relationships in which women mentor younger leaders, and peer relationships with other leaders who become a resource of emotional support and a community in which to practice and share ideas. These are particularly challenging for women to create, but they are essential to growing in influence.

39. Cole, *Developing Female Leaders*, 203, 206.
40. Scott, *Dare Mighty Things*, 98.

MALE-FEMALE MINISTRY PARTNERSHIPS

ASPECT 6, PART 2

You don't have to think hard to recall a story about a pastor and sexual impropriety. During the period of this study, issues came to light within one of the churches connected to the study. Critics of mixed-gender teams point to such issues as evidence of the inherent dangers of men and women leading together. But in this specific instance, the problems came to light in part because a faithful woman leading on the ministry team cared enough about her pastor to pursue healing for him and their church. Women leaders are often part of the solution, not the problem.

My pastor used to say, "We are all a little bit pitiful." Pastors are humans first, then they are Christians. They are ministers third. We bring all our humanity into our Christianity, and we bring the process of discipleship and inward renewal into our ministry. We don't enter ministry fully formed. We are being formed even as we facilitate formation for those entrusted to our care. This means that humility is vital to our longevity. Without it, sin can destroy our leadership credibility. In this study, the most-discussed topic about leadership relationships was boundary setting in male-female ministry partnerships. This is an especially tricky and important part of leadership development.

Forming influence through leadership relationships is complex and the most significant of the seven aspects. As such, it requires an additional chapter.

FEMALE MINISTRY LEADERS WORKING WITH MALE COLLEAGUES

The dynamics present in mixed-gender relationships create unique tensions that must be recognized and managed. Despite these tensions, healthy male-female leader relationships are essential to female leader development. Healthy mixed-gender relationships are good not only for women but also for men.

Men and women are at their best when working together in partnership.[1] Dallas Willard notes that men and women are very different, and those differences bring unique ministry perspectives and experiences. Each sex needs to learn from the other. Without this mutuality, the church is weakened.[2] Men and women can be protectors of each other, provide emotional support, educate about the opposite sex, learn peacemaking, accomplish tasks more quickly, and offer personal insights.[3] Ruth Haley Barton points to spiritual growth based on the love given and received in these partnerships.[4] Halee Gray Scott encourages men and women to approach each other as co-laborers and allies.[5] Sue Edwards, Kelley Matthews, and Henry J. Rogers advocate for healthy male-female partnerships and envision the family of God in full health, with both genders thriving. Healthy faith families need both men's and women's "ideas, gifts, and perspectives in order to thrive."[6] When men and women work together in ministry, the church reflects the unity of the Trinity.[7] Genesis 2 describes God's design for man and woman working together in partnership to care for the garden. Rob Dixon urges, "We must not rest until we have embodied God's Genesis vision for mixed-gender partnerships."[8] We need these partnerships, and we need them to be healthy.

Male and female callings are interdependent. For men to flourish, women need to flourish, and vice versa.[9] Lausanne 2004 recognized the need for the global church to work toward the "full partnership of men and women . . .

1. James, *Half the Church*, 140.
2. Willard, foreword to *How I Changed My Mind about Women in Leadership*, 10.
3. Edwards, Matthews, and Rogers, *Mixed Ministry*, locs. 603–50 of 2590; Barton, *Equal to the Task*, loc. 2531 of 2871, Kindle.
4. Barton, *Equal to the Task*, loc. 2471 of 2871, Kindle.
5. Scott, *Dare Mighty Things*, 188.
6. Edwards, Matthews, and Rogers, *Mixed Ministry*, loc. 178 of 2590, Kindle.
7. Hull, *Equal to Serve*, 226.
8. Dixon, *Together in Ministry*, 11.
9. James, *Malestrom*, 26.

maximizing the gifts of all" for the purpose of kingdom advancement.[10] To stand in opposition to this mutuality of leadership is to stand against the work of the Holy Spirit.[11] As Willard observes, people are not equal in their gifts or experience, so we need to approach this not merely as a justice issue—women deserve equal status and power—but as an obligation to be faithful to God's unique calling and spiritual and natural gifting of women.[12] What this looks like will be unique to every individual and every male-female team. Those same differences that bring strength also cause misunderstandings.[13] Barton emphasizes the importance of listening and sharing in order to find unity,[14] and she identifies a lack of awareness about how to communicate respect as the core of much male-female relational hurt.[15]

Biblical Male-Female Partnership

The Bible provides us with both a non-spousal model of male-female leadership in Deborah and Barak (Judg. 4–5) and a married ministry partnership in Priscilla and Aquila (Acts 18). Throughout the Bible, imagery of family is used to describe male-female relationships.[16] We are all sons and daughters of God and so are "sacred siblings."[17] Jesus lived out this kind of sibling partnership in countercultural (unmarried) ministry relationships with Mary Magdalene, Mary and Martha of Bethany, and other women.[18] Michelle Lee-Barnewall notes that these relationships set precedent for believers as a surrogate family of brothers and sisters connected by faith.[19] Paul continued this model of partnership. He did not avoid women as sexual temptresses but reached out to them as sisters.[20] Paul practiced interdependent leadership with the women around him.[21] He taught new believers to treat one another the same way they would treat blood brothers and sisters—with great honor—and he referred to his audience as brothers and sisters sixty-five times in his letters to the

---

10. Mickelsen, "Empowering Women and Men to Use Their Gifts," v.
11. Grenz and Kjesbo, *Women in the Church*, loc. 123 of 3642, Kindle.
12. Willard, foreword to *How I Changed My Mind about Women in Leadership*, 10.
13. Statham, "Gender Model Revisited," 425.
14. Barton, *Equal to the Task*, loc. 465 of 2871, Kindle.
15. Barton, *Equal to the Task*, loc. 741 of 2871, Kindle.
16. Edwards, Matthews, and Rogers, *Mixed Ministry*, loc. 750 of 2590, Kindle.
17. Lederleitner, *Women in God's Mission*, 162; Edwards, Matthews, and Rogers, *Mixed Ministry*, loc. 105 of 2590, Kindle.
18. Barton, *Equal to the Task*, loc. 2498 of 2871, Kindle; Edwards, Matthews, and Rogers, *Mixed Ministry*, loc. 257 of 2590, Kindle.
19. Lee-Barnewall, *Neither Complementarian nor Egalitarian*, 86.
20. Edwards, Matthews, and Rogers, *Mixed Ministry*, loc. 480 of 2590, Kindle.
21. Barton, *Equal to the Task*, loc. 382 of 2871, Kindle.

Thessalonians, Romans, Galatians, Philippians, and Philemon.[22] As sacred siblings—or perhaps even as fathers—men have a safe relational framework for mentoring or investing in women to whom they are not married. This paradigm guides both a man's and a woman's perspective of each other as well as their interactions.

Male-Female Partnerships and Sexual Attraction

As women are empowered to fulfill their unique calling in leadership roles in the church, non-spousal male-female interactions will increase. As these interactions increase, the risk of leaders encountering sexual attraction in others or themselves increases. The Western cultural assumption is that male-female relationships will inevitably end up sexual, and this creates unease in these relationships.[23] Our oversexed societal view of everyone as sexual objects makes brother-sister ministry partnerships difficult.[24] This leaves men and women wondering if male-female ministry partnership outside of marriage is truly safe, particularly in light of high-profile pastors who empowered women and then participated in inappropriate sexual behavior. Barton reminds us that these relationships will never be entirely safe, but following Jesus is not about achieving safety.[25]

Men and women in ministry partnerships have interacted in sinful ways. The media ensures we hear about high-profile ministry leaders' sexual failures. Extramarital sex, however, is not where sin begins. Sexual sin begins in the emotional and thought realms first. For women, vulnerability often begins emotionally. Barton warns women against exploiting their sexuality or finding personal validation when someone is attracted to them.[26] Beauty should not be used as a tool to manipulate men for personal gain or for emotional support. Scott agrees, encouraging women not to create greater vulnerabilities in their male colleagues by making themselves sexually available or enticing.[27] This is certainly not to say that women alone are responsible for sexual sin, especially since men are often the sexual aggressors in inappropriate relationships. Women are more likely to be put into awkward positions, trying to manage male sexual advances that threaten their access to opportunity, because they typically have less power than men.[28] For men, socialized hypermasculinity

22. Bartchy, "Undermining Ancient Patriarchy," 69–70.
23. Barton, *Equal to the Task*, locs. 531, 688 of 2871, Kindle.
24. Edwards, Matthews, and Rogers, *Mixed Ministry*, loc. 1463 of 2590, Kindle.
25. Barton, *Equal to the Task*, loc. 2553 of 2871, Kindle.
26. Barton, *Equal to the Task*, loc. 572 of 2871, Kindle.
27. Scott, *Dare Mighty Things*, 189.
28. Murnen, Wright, and Kaluzny, "If 'Boys Will Be Boys,'" 372.

and a higher tolerance for risk make them more likely to cross boundaries. Barton acknowledges the weight of shame that men carry about their sexuality and the difficulty they have viewing women as equal partners and not sexual objects.[29]

The book of James describes the downward spiral of sin (1:14–15). Sexual mistakes begin with attraction, lead to deliberation, and end with consummation.[30] Attraction is not sinful, but it is a warning sign about danger ahead, and men and women would be wise to create barriers and slowdowns. That well-respected ministers have sinned sexually does not make us all powerless to do better. The notion that our sexual urges are so powerful that they cannot be controlled is a cultural myth that has determined how we build male-female partnerships in church.[31] Lustful thoughts can be redirected using self-control, a fruit of the Spirit. Attraction does not mean that consummation is inevitable.

Furthermore, sexual attraction between people is more rare than it is common. Women in this study rolled their eyes at the idea of being attracted to the men on their ministry teams. Not a single woman reported ever feeling sexual attraction for a male ministry colleague. Sheryl Sandberg and Nell Scovell agree: "We cannot assume that interactions between men and women have a sexual component."[32] Scott found that while men and women report feeling attracted to people of the opposite sex, the intensity of the attraction decreases when a person is in a committed romantic relationship with another person.[33] This seems to indicate that married people are not as vulnerable to sexual attraction outside their marriage as our culture trains us to believe. We need to assume the best about a non-spousal male-female ministry partnership, despite failures we may have observed in the past.

MIXED-GENDER (UNMARRIED) MINISTRY PARTNERSHIP BOUNDARIES

Local church ministry is deeply relational, vulnerable, and supportive. Pastors and ministry leaders are charged with forging deep connections between church family members and between themselves and others. Part of the job description is building close, familial relationships with others in the church. Fundamentally, church ministry is not about organizing labor for production,

29. Barton, *Equal to the Task*, loc. 560 of 2871, Kindle.
30. Edwards, Matthews, and Rogers, *Mixed Ministry*, loc. 1807 of 2590, Kindle.
31. Barton, *Equal to the Task*, locs. 228, 2553 of 2871, Kindle.
32. Sandberg and Scovell, *Lean In*, 72.
33. Scott, *Dare Mighty Things*, 180–83.

which can be depersonalized. Church ministry is about people, not projects or products. It is deeply personal and can become intimate quickly. Coworkers are spiritual family members and often have close, personal friendships, where the lines between social time and professional time are blurred. For example, a staff member's participation in a church small group is simultaneously spiritual, social, and professional. Spiritual alignment lowers defenses. Perhaps uniquely, this creates an environment of complex relational dynamics.

Male and female ministry leaders face relational challenges that can cause problems on coed ministry teams. Sexual dynamics between the genders can create awkward tensions or become sinful or outright abusive. Mary Lederleitner's study of women in ministry found that many women experience physical, emotional, and sexual abuse.[34] In the past five years, #MeToo and its daughter movement, #ChurchToo, have created powerful deterrents against such abuses. But while the movements have created safer workplaces for women, they have made things harder for women in other ways.

Since the #MeToo movement sparked, a Lean In survey found that 82 percent of men are worried about being falsely accused of sexual harassment, and nearly half are uncomfortable mentoring, working with, or socializing alone with women.[35] A Pew Research Center survey found that 55 percent of American men think that #MeToo has made it more difficult for them to navigate interactions with women at work.[36] In this climate, nervous men minimize the risk of sexual harassment by avoiding women, causing women to lose the mentorship and sponsorship opportunities that men might provide.[37]

To address these sexual dynamics, teams need to determine an approach for setting boundaries. Strategies for male-female boundaries range from the "Bubble Wrap approach," which is characterized by high boundaries and little interaction, to the "daredevil approach," which has low or no boundaries and high interaction. When boundaries and interactions are low, women are largely invisible, creating great potential for hidden abuse. Scott advocates for the use of a middle approach, with clear boundaries and high levels of interaction (see fig. 9.1).[38]

In this study, the aspect of female-leader-affirming church culture that had the greatest amount of uncertainty attached to it was appropriate boundaries between the sexes. As with so many aspects of culture, this issue can be

34. Lederleitner, *Women in God's Mission*, 114.
35. "How Women & Men Are Feeling After #MeToo | #MentorHer."
36. Wingard, "#MeToo, Fear, and the Future of Women's Leadership."
37. Ledbetter and Kinsman, "Ensuring #MeToo Movement Advances Diversity"; Bennhold, "Another Side of #MeToo."
38. Scott, *Dare Mighty Things*, 184–87.

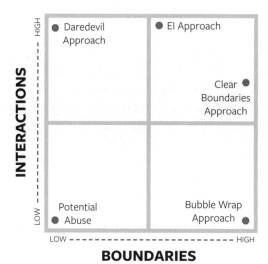

Fig. 9.1. Interactions and Boundaries

polarizing. This study explored the policies and practices of churches with mixed-gender teams, resulting in two mixed-gender boundary approaches that support female leader emergence and best practices for male-female partnerships: clearly defined mixed-gender boundaries and an emotionally intelligent approach. But first we will explore the problems with undefined mixed-gender boundaries and zero-risk mixed-gender boundaries.

Undefined Mixed-Gender Boundaries, Leading to #MeToo

At one end of the spectrum of mixed-gender boundary approaches lies a daredevil approach of undefined boundaries. Here predatory male leaders can abuse women. This catalyzed the #MeToo movement and its ministry equivalent, #ChurchToo, which called these abusive male leaders to account. Only one church of the twenty-four included in this study had direct experience with a high-level leader falling into sexual sin, and none of the women interviewed reported experiencing sexual abuse in leadership.

While most of the male pastors in this study viewed #MeToo as sparking healthy conversations and having positive outcomes, it also made them fearful. They shared a greater hesitancy to build relationships with female leaders, and the women leaders observed this about men in their contexts. One man described how #MeToo made him colder toward his female leaders. He hesitates to compliment and affirm them for fear of how his words will be perceived by them. This is a concerning development, since young female leaders have a great need for affirmation from their senior leaders to develop confidence, an essential component of leadership. Without confidence, women will not accept new leadership opportunities.

Women leaders worry about damage to their churches because of leadership fallout from #MeToo. This is not to say that they are not concerned about victims of sexual misconduct. They worry about the rest of their church families as well and the difficulty of leading through crisis and widespread hurt. While accountability for abuse and sin is essential, the fallout can feed growing distrust for the institution of the church, resulting in the spiritual disengagement of congregants. This is heartbreaking for every pastor.

Because of concern among male leaders about accusation, environments with undefined mixed-gender boundaries are not going to be fertile ground for growing female leaders. A fearful climate can inadvertently lead men to implement a zero-risk approach out of self-protection.

Zero-Risk Mixed-Gender Boundaries

Two participants in this study noted that mixed-gender boundaries in their church leadership tended toward the zero-risk end of the spectrum, eliminating the need for #MeToo to cleanse their churches. A zero-risk approach is often associated with the Billy Graham rule. Graham never permitted himself to meet alone with a woman other than his wife (and presumably his daughter), and many pastors and leaders have adopted this rule. This rule is the remnant of a larger commitment made by Graham and three other men on his team called the Modesto Manifesto, which also included commitments to financial transparency, to support local churches, and to be honest about attendance figures.[39] The part of the manifesto that appears to have been most widely adopted is the commitment never to meet alone with a woman.

The Billy Graham rule creates distance between men and women in ministry. While the rule disrupts opportunity for abuse and prevents unhealthy sexual behaviors by cutting men off from personal relationships with women, it leads to a culture in which men need to stay away from the women on their team, creating a barrier to relationship building.[40] J. Robert Clinton warns that non-spousal male-female ministry partnerships are "dangerous,"[41] and men who agree start to see women as dangerous or impure.[42] This attitude is demeaning to men because it assumes that all men are sex-crazed and in-

39. Beaty, *Celebrities for Jesus*, 37.
40. Scott, *Dare Mighty Things*, 185.
41. Clinton, "Social Base Processing," 13.
42. Barrett, "Healthy Workplace Boundaries."

capable of controlling their urges. It is not a godly perspective and does not align with how the Bible instructs us to treat one another.

This relational distance also robs women of potential leadership opportunities that powerful men distribute, mentorship opportunities with men, and peer networks. When male leaders keep women at a distance, viewing them as threats to their ministry, they never see the potential, gifts, and abilities of female leaders in their churches. Without this knowledge, men do not consider women for leadership roles.

Women in executive roles need to be able to give direct and sometimes difficult feedback to the men who report to them. Providing a performance review in front of a third observer is demeaning to the recipient. One female executive pastor shared that one of her male direct reports used the Billy Graham rule as a reason to avoid these challenging conversations. If a woman leader does not get clear feedback from her male supervisor because a third person must be present or personally oriented meetings must be avoided due to the Billy Graham rule, her growth will be stunted.

Pastors' wives who are not involved in ministry can make navigating these dynamics especially challenging. If a pastor's wife is insecure and relationally disengaged from the women leaders on her husband's ministry team, she can (intentionally or not) create barriers for the women leaders by limiting access to her husband, citing the Billy Graham rule. She might also limit women's leadership opportunities so that women do not work in partnership with her husband, a role reserved for her alone. I've observed that often the role of a senior pastor's wife creates the upper limit for women's leadership in a church. If the pastor's wife does not preach, then she is not comfortable with other women preaching. If she does not lead staff meetings, then she is not comfortable with other women leading these meetings. Senior pastors wanting to develop women for ministry leadership must have frank and open conversations about these dynamics with their spouse to overcome any insecurities that might create roadblocks for other women. Pastors' wives should be empowered into their unique ministry gifts and calling, whether this be accounting, preaching, leading, or hospitality. When a pastor's wife is flourishing in her unique calling, she can be free to celebrate other women flourishing in their leadership calling and encourage her husband to provide the opportunities and mentorship that cultivate women in leadership.

A zero-risk approach to boundaries is sometimes driven by genuine concern for avoiding sin, but it may also be driven by concern for avoiding the judgment of others. A female participant described being passed over for a high-level denominational leadership role that she was qualified for because of the culture created by the Billy Graham rule. The male denomination president was afraid of being closely associated with a woman to whom he was not married.

The Billy Graham rule does not address same-sex temptation. Both men and women will almost assuredly interact with a same-sex-attracted Christian or a gay Christian at some point in their pastoral ministry. A male pastor in his thirties described two occasions early in his ministry journey when, thinking he was going to a group social event, he found himself on an unwanted date with a gay man. On one of these occasions, he was sexually assaulted. The Billy Graham rule does not protect against these situations. The Billy Graham rule also offers young people no protection against abusers. Unfortunately, the rule is simply not nuanced enough to deal with the complexities of our highly sexualized culture. We like things to be simple because simple is easy to follow. But what is best is not always the simplest solution.

The Billy Graham rule is too simple, and having no boundaries is dangerous. Neither extreme creates a culture in which female leaders can thrive in mixed-gender ministry partnerships. What is needed is a middle way.

Clearly Defined Mixed-Gender Boundaries

One middle-ground approach is clearly defined boundaries. Setting clear boundaries should be done openly and by a community of men and women together. Scott encourages men and women to create boundaries at the beginning of their relationship and to include spouses in the process.[43] Beth Backes provides policy advice to churches for protecting women, including sexual harassment training for leadership teams, clear consequences for violations, social media policies, and third-person policies.[44] These are all examples of boundary setting.

Clear male-female boundaries draw lines of "don'ts" for unmarried men and women in leadership. This approach is defined by what not to do, and those who embrace the boundaries put up guards around several parts of interaction. Close to two-thirds of participants described setting boundaries guarding the level of proximity between men and women. An example is not riding in a car with only one other person (family excluded). Half of the participants have boundaries guarding the nature of relationships. Casual friendships with the opposite sex are avoided, and mixed-gender relationships are built only through a spouse. This boundary keeps relationships professional. Two-thirds of the participants follow some version of a rule of three, in which all in-person meetings or conversations over text, email, or social

43. Scott, *Dare Mighty Things*, 188.
44. Backes, "#ChurchToo."

media must include at least three people. This proves difficult when men and women need to hold private meetings to address an issue with a direct report of the opposite sex. One woman pastor explained, "We do have direct reports that are a man reporting to a woman, or a woman reporting to a man. And so sometimes in a one-on-one coaching environment, it doesn't make sense to have a group of three because you really need to focus on that one person."

Some participants also have clear boundaries that guard their reputation or the perception that others may have of their relationships with people of the opposite gender. They want to avoid anyone wondering if something inappropriate might be happening. These reputation-protecting boundaries sometimes conflict with proximity-based boundaries, however. For example, someone adhering to a proximity boundary would meet one-on-one in a public place such as a café to avoid being alone in an office. Someone following a reputation boundary would avoid meeting one-on-one in a café because someone might see them and think it was an inappropriate or even romantic meeting. This also creates a problem for a small church staff when a man and a woman need to meet but no one else is available or in the office. If neither option (meeting alone or meeting in a café) is acceptable, this can create difficulties for developing female leaders.

Many leaders uncomfortably recognized their boundaries are fear-based or rule-based and focused on what not to do. Even though they didn't like this approach, they didn't possess a framework for a better way to go about this.

An Emotionally Intelligent Approach

The second middle way both protects women and creates a framework for healthy male-female relationships. This is an emotionally intelligent approach because it leans on well-developed emotional intelligence (EI) as its guardrail. Self-awareness and spiritual reflection are used to monitor heart condition, sexual attraction, and trust within a team. When an individual recognizes their own vulnerability (attraction) around someone else, they practice self-regulation to guard their thinking, their behavior, and their interactions with this person. Not every individual is treated the same.

Nearly half of the participants use social awareness to gauge what others are feeling and use this to frame healthy conversations. If they recognize someone else is attracted to them, they are careful to guard their own heart for vulnerability. They stay away from topics that lead to intimacy, flirting, marriage advice, or sex. Participants explained that they shape and correct their own thinking about the opposite sex and view them as sisters or brothers, mothers or fathers, or daughters or sons. This approach requires someone to have well-developed

EI. Sometimes the boundaries a person begins their ministry journey with shift with growth in maturity. They may need to begin with clear male-female boundaries, but as they mature in leadership, they may transition to an EI approach.

Barton encourages reflection to identify inner vulnerabilities, such as an unmet need for affirmation. If vulnerabilities exist, they may indicate a neglect of devotional life, needs that can and should be met through a relationship with God, or a need for human connection and affection rather than sex.[45] Edwards, Matthews, and Rogers advise using self-awareness to identify attraction levels, indicating a higher or lower threat. A leader should create relational distance where attraction exists.[46]

Another EI approach is to categorize relationships by type and create different levels of intimacy in different types of relationships. Kadi Cole recommends approaching sponsorship as a public relationship with the greatest relational distance, mentoring as a social relationship with some relational distance, and coaching as a deeply personal relationship. She recommends coaching be same-gender, but sponsorship and mentorship can be mixed-gender. Cole also encourages people to be smart about alcohol use because alcohol can impede a person's ability to use EI.[47]

The EI approach is less about managing risk through rules that guard people's interactions and more about honestly facing oneself, being vulnerably known, and being open to being discipled and accountable in true community. A male senior pastor described the needed inward focus: "Sometimes we try to police something externally that we haven't really empowered internally." Rules that are externally based and aren't rooted in the heart are destined to be broken.

A third of the participants described their church staff having open conversations about healthy male-female relationships. Their teams celebrate and prioritize marriage relationships and provide accountability for pursuing and investing in marriage relationships. Edwards, Matthews, and Rogers encourage including spouses and families in new mixed-gender relationships.[48] They provide a framework for determining relational appropriateness: the three boundary tests. The sibling test asks, "Can this person be trusted as a sibling?" The screen test asks, "Would replaying this conversation on a public screen be embarrassing?" Finally, the secret test asks, "Am I withholding any information from my spouse?" These questions help a person avoid secrecy and provide guardrails for intimacy between unmarried men and women.[49]

45. Barton, *Equal to the Task*, locs. 625–47 of 2871, Kindle.
46. Edwards, Matthews, and Rogers, *Mixed Ministry*, locs. 1499, 1715–42 of 2590, Kindle.
47. Cole, *Developing Female Leaders*, 97, 102, 106–9.
48. Edwards, Matthews, and Rogers, *Mixed Ministry*, locs. 1914, 2267 of 2590, Kindle.
49. Edwards, Matthews, and Rogers, *Mixed Ministry*, loc. 1905 of 2590, Kindle.

Here's a hypothetical way the EI approach works. Matt is a thirty-eight-year-old associate pastor. He has been married for twelve years, and his wife, Beth, is the same age. She faithfully attends Sunday services and helps count the offering. She has a part-time job, but her primary focus is caring for their two children, ages seven and nine. Matt works on a church staff of fifteen people. Five of these team members are women, four in their fifties and sixties and one nineteen-year-old intern. The rest of the team is made up of men of varying ages, eight of them in their thirties or early forties with whom Matt has a close bond. This team of men and women tease each other like a family and work well together under their pastor's leadership.

The senior pastor hires Sally, a thirty-year-old single woman, as the new worship leader. Sally is attractive and outgoing and plays the guitar. Matt has never met anyone like Sally and is immediately attracted to her. His inner alarm bells go off at his reaction to her because he is devoted to his wife, Beth. He has never had this reaction to any of the other women on the team, who are all like younger or older sisters to him.

After some reflection and prayer, he asks his pastor to initiate a conversation with the group of eight younger men on staff about appropriate relationship boundaries on their team. The pastor asks Matt if he is doing okay, and Matt shares that he is feeling vulnerable and nervous about interacting with their new ministry partner, Sally. The pastor encourages him to be careful and keep his prayer life a priority. The senior pastor leads a conversation with the team about serving as a family and viewing and treating each other as brothers and sisters. They have a frank conversation about some smart practices for the team and land on limiting text messages and DMs to office hours (except for emergencies) and that personal problems should be discussed only in a group of three. After the conversation, Matt asks a close friend on staff to hold him accountable to the boundaries they have established.

Matt prays and asks the Holy Spirit to help him navigate the issue with wisdom and integrity. Matt is careful to guard his conversations with Sally to keep them respectful and focused on ministry projects. He keeps his compliments and encouragement focused on her work and keeps emotion out of them. Matt guards his gaze and how he looks at Sally. He guards his thought life, refusing to allow himself to daydream about Sally, and reminds himself that she will be someone else's wife, possibly married to one of his friends. She is worthy of respect. Matt does not touch Sally in any way.

Matt asks his wife, Beth, to reach out to Sally and befriend her since she is new to the church, which she does. He tells Beth he wants to be smart about how he interacts with Sally, so they decide together that Matt will include Beth in group text messages to Sally. Despite the busyness of ministry, Matt and Beth intentionally and regularly invest time in their marriage, having fun, talking, and connecting, with and without their kids present. Matt's pastor checks in with him every now and then to ask how he's doing and how his marriage is going. After a few months of getting to know Sally, the attraction subsides and Matt is able to build a sibling relationship with her, but he keeps his boundaries in place.

While this imaginary story is about imaginary Matt, it could just as easily have been about a woman and her attraction to a man or about same-sex attractions. The EI approach can be helpful to anyone in Christian ministry who finds the need to manage unwanted attractions.

People should value themselves with good self-care and present their appearance at its best. However, especially attractive people are at a higher risk of being either victimized by someone else's ulterior sexualized motives or marginalized by team members as dangerous. Frankly, it's not fair to beautiful people like Sally, but it is a tension to be managed. Team members need to prioritize marital health and have regular conversations as a ministry team about viewing others as kingdom siblings and parents.

Partnerships in Which Women Leaders Can Thrive

Women leaders are most likely to thrive when ministry teams follow either clearly defined boundaries or an emotionally intelligent approach (see fig. 9.2). Leadership teams that follow no boundaries or the Billy Graham rule would benefit by starting with a conversation about the risks and rewards of each approach. Too often, boundaries are determined and enforced by men. Women are disempowered when they have less agency in boundary creation on a leadership team. Several women leaders reported that they felt they did not have agency in boundary setting. The men on their teams decided the boundaries without input. Conversations about boundaries must include women's voices because boundaries have the potential to harm women. The rules we follow should exist because they are best practices, not because they are habits (or relics). Some participants initiated conversations whenever news broke of a high-profile pastor's fall from grace. However, these conversations need to happen well before a moral crisis. Moments of betrayal and stress can trigger reactive, emotional, extreme responses and aren't ideal times for policy creation. Open dialogue between the men and women on a leadership team, with story sharing about experiences and concerns, can begin to create a pathway toward a new culture and a new normal. When boundaries are fashioned together, everyone on the team has buy-in and can hold one another accountable. This is a process that leads to true safety.

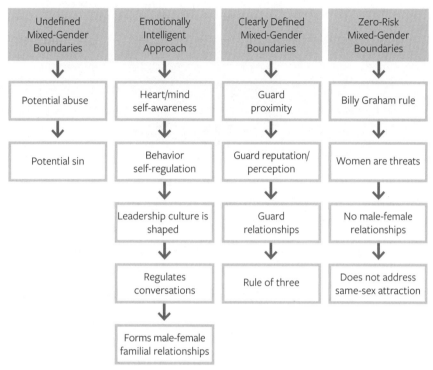

Fig. 9.2. Mixed-Gender Boundary Approaches

SUMMARY

Men and women need a healthy relational framework to work together in ministry partnerships. God has provided examples of how to do this well in the Bible. We are a family of God and sacred siblings, and we need to adopt this mindset rather than our overly sexualized cultural views of the opposite sex. Current approaches to male-female ministry partnerships tend to use either too few boundaries or the opposite, with absolute firewalls between the genders, as typified by the Billy Graham rule. The problem with the Billy Graham rule is that it excludes women from leadership relationships and opportunities. Two alternative approaches offer a middle way. One approach is to establish clear boundaries that create opportunities for high interaction while maintaining boundaries between individuals on a ministry team. The second approach is to use EI to create self-awareness of vulnerabilities and to self-regulate, creating relational distance when attraction is present. Both approaches can be part of a female-leader-affirming leadership culture.

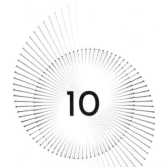

10

FEMALE LEADERS FORMING INFLUENCE THROUGH COMMUNICATION

ASPECT 7

Some leaders love confrontation, and others avoid it at all costs. When my first husband was alive, he took care of the difficult conversations in our ministry, and I was happy for him to carry that load. After he died, I had to deal with a situation in my worship ministry. I was about twenty-five, young, quiet, and reserved. One of the men in the church choir was particularly abrasive. He was critical of everyone and everything and would talk to anyone nearby about his dissatisfaction, snapping and bulldozing his way through people. He clearly had no respect for me. I let his behavior go for longer than I should have—for months. People pointed out to me that he was sapping the team's morale, and I knew I had to deal with him.

I called the man and his wife in for a conversation about how things were going. I had prepared a short list of issues to address and a few Bible verses to offer as spiritual guidance. I felt shaky but pushed through, gently but firmly asking him to change his behavior. I expected him to react negatively. He had an aggressive personality, and he had no problem verbalizing his discontent. To my shock, he listened, and he said, "Pastor Anna, you're right. I need to do better. I'm sorry about how I've been acting." I could see the respect in his eyes for how I had addressed the situation head-on. We prayed together for the Holy Spirit's help. In the weeks that followed, I was amazed at the change in him. He was like a whole new man, laughing, smiling, helpful. He became one of my best leaders. It was a powerful lesson for me about the value of good communication. Still to this day, however, I feel a little bit anxious in confrontation, even when I'm absolutely convinced that I'm right and that the conversation is essential. Predicting how people will react is difficult. I recognize the future of my relationship with this person I care about will be put at risk. Confrontation tests commitment. But without my having this difficult conversation, this man entrusted to my care would have stagnated in his growth. It was my responsibility to give him difficult feedback.

Leadership is formed through relational interactions, and relationships are formed through the building blocks of conversation and language. Leadership communication is a specific type of communication that happens in interpersonal conversations and in large group settings through public speaking.

Every participant in this study recognized that effective interpersonal communication is an essential part of female leadership development. Only the women who had leadership support roles or operational, business-oriented executive roles did not recognize public speaking as a part of their development. Critical in leadership communication are body language and digital communication. Half of the participants discussed leadership presence and learning to use social media as a ministry communication tool. Half of the women also recognized the importance of learning to use their authentic Voice.[1] Voice development is typically a process that emerges later; most participants who spoke about Voice were either Gen Xers or baby boomers and had well-developed platforms of influence.

This chapter begins by examining masculine and feminine language styles and then turns to communication skills for women leaders, effective interpersonal communication, effective public speaking, and social media use.

MASCULINE AND FEMININE LANGUAGE STYLES

Women are socialized to have a style of speaking that is slightly different from that of men. Through conversations, women work to bond with others, while men tend to focus on presenting information to others. Linguist Deborah Tannen calls female language style "rapport-talk" and male language style

1. *Voice* is capitalized in reference to free self-expression, and it is lowercased in reference to physical speech.

"report-talk."[2] Rapport-talk finds similarities and builds connection, while report-talk claims attention by displaying expertise and using entertainment to preserve independence and maintain social status. Private conversations are often rapport-talk, while report-talk is well suited for speaking to larger groups.[3] Sociolinguist Janet Holmes uses similar categories to describe these differences: "male-valued talk" focuses on status enhancing, and "female-valuable talk" focuses on socially connecting and cognitively stretching.[4] The male preference for report-talk makes men more naturally comfortable with preaching and teaching than women. Even though women may be gifted and called to preaching and teaching, they are socialized away from learning the style of speaking required for public speaking.

Judith A. Rolls describes feminine language style as "deferential," an accommodating style perceived as less competent and convincing. This implies that women are socialized to agree with rather than challenge decisions. Leaders speak forcefully and decisively.[5] Therefore, Linda Tarr-Whelan encourages developing leaders to practice avoiding speaking deferentially.[6] The implications are that for women to grow their influence, they need to be given permission to disagree and trained to display their expertise in conversations or public speaking.

When I was a young woman, the men I led alongside gave me subtle and not-so-subtle cues that I needed to hide my intelligence to be accepted. These cues came in gentle teasing or blank, semihostile stares when I used big words they didn't understand. They became visibly irritated if they had to ask what I meant and more often would ignore my statement and move on without responding to it. I was regularly interrupted and cut off by male disagreement before I could fully make a case, but if I interrupted a man, I was perceived as disrespectful. I learned to use short words and short sentences and to make my point as quickly as possible in a room full of men, who resented when I used lengthy explanations with big words and complex ideas to explain something technical. I had to build coalitions with and create allies with men outside the boardroom to be respected in the boardroom. This way I did not have to be aggressive or combative to be heard.

Judith Baxter provides another way to understand patterns of gender and language. Instead of recognizing gender-based speech patterns, she assigns gender to language itself, observing that male and female leaders use both

2. Tannen, *You Just Don't Understand*, 77.
3. Tannen, *You Just Don't Understand*, 88–89.
4. Holmes, "Women's Talk in Public Contexts," 133.
5. Rolls, "Influence of Language Style and Gender," 3–4, 13.
6. Tarr-Whelan, *Women Lead the Way*, loc. 1344 of 4551, Kindle.

transactional and relational leadership language, "conventionally coded 'masculine' or 'feminine'" as the circumstances require. Recognizing differences between male and female lingual styles may cause the female style to be viewed as deficient, disqualifying women for leadership opportunities, and so Baxter likely has a bias for protecting women that may have influenced her findings.[7] To avoid the potential for this negative social consequence, sociolinguist Victoria Bergvall sees gendered language as a continuum rather than two absolutes; this creates a helpful way to nuance the binary nature of these gender labels.[8]

When language is seen as carrying gender, then an entire organization's language can be assessed to assign a gender to the organization's culture. Baxter theorizes that corporations have gendered culture, whether masculine or feminine, based on the style of language used by leaders. Her model identifies three kinds of culture: male-dominated, gender-divided, and gender-multiple. She claims that the gender of an organization's culture has a direct impact on the types of leadership opportunities available to women. Culture is created by the degree to which "supportive talk" and "display talk" are used by both men and women in leadership.[9] "Display talk" exhibits knowledge in extended speeches, where "supportive talk" involves listening, agreement, and affirming short responses so that the other person continues speaking.[10] The implications here are significant. When leadership teams adjust their language choices (intentionally using supportive talk), an organization can change its culture, and that cultural shift can create leadership opportunities for women.

Whether gendered style is assigned to an individual, language, or organization, specific language styles are associated with femininity. Emerging women leaders need to learn to use both display talk and supportive talk, despite social pressure to chiefly use supportive styles in leadership communication.

COMMUNICATION SKILLS FOR WOMEN LEADERS

Finding Her Voice

The process of a woman learning how to engage in display talk is often called "finding her Voice." *Voice* has become a buzzword but is a useful concept in leadership development. Mary Donovan Turner and Mary Lin Hudson define Voice, with a capital V, as the symbol of a person's "distinctive, unique

---

7. Baxter, *Language of Female Leadership*, 14, 74, 168.
8. Bergvall, "Toward a Comprehensive Theory of Language and Gender," 279.
9. Baxter, *Language of Female Leadership*, 18–22, 75, 77–78.
10. Baxter, *Language of Female Leadership*, 71–78.

self."[11] They define a Voiced woman as "one who recognizes her own value and thus accords herself the right to speak."[12] In the face of cultural pressures, organizational pressures, and family pressures, Voice is what enables a woman to value her own authentic, authoritative self-expression, leading to human wholeness. Jackie Roese, who coaches female preachers, observes that women hold back from speaking out from fear that they will be labeled extremists, power hungry, or "bitchy."[13] However, the development of a woman's Voice is essential to her leadership development.[14]

Leadership is built through communication as women persuade others and create influence, but this process is frequently difficult for women. Baxter observes that in business meetings, women often struggle to have their perspectives heard, valued, or put into practice.[15] When gifted female leaders sit quietly, apparently intimidated, uncomfortable, and uncertain how to engage in leadership conversations with men, we lose the valuable contributions of female leaders.[16] This is true not just in business settings but also in ministry. Mary Lederleitner found that women make their best contributions to God's mission through dialogue.[17]

While an organizational culture that values women's Voices is essential to women's leadership development, individual female leaders also bear responsibility for their own Voice development. Nancy Beach challenges women ministry leaders to develop their Voice by becoming experts in their own organizational culture and DNA, owning and communicating their opinions and perspectives, and asking great questions that challenge the status quo. She encourages women to listen to their own lives and tell their stories to find their unique Voice rather than trying to emulate someone else's Voice.[18] Similarly, psychologists Carol Gilligan and Jean Baker Miller found that women develop to their fullest when they learn to value themselves enough to bring their true selves into open dialogue with others, affirming themselves as worthy conversationalists.[19]

A woman who finds her Voice can bring her differing opinions to her leaders. Tara Sophia Mohr found Voice development to be so vital that she discourages overvaluing mentoring, which might cause a woman to depend

11. Turner and Hudson, *Saved from Silence*, 10.
12. Turner and Hudson, *Saved from Silence*, 14.
13. Roese, *She Can Teach*, 9.
14. Suby-Long, "Role of Transformational Learning," 104.
15. Baxter, *Language of Female Leadership*, 12, 15.
16. Edwards, Matthews, and Rogers, *Mixed Ministry*, loc. 1127 of 2590, Kindle.
17. Lederleitner, *Women in God's Mission*, 178–79.
18. Beach, *Gifted to Lead*, 109, 112, 116, 123.
19. Turner and Hudson, *Saved from Silence*, 16.

on someone else's opinions and under-develop her critical thinking skills. She encourages women to learn to challenge authority figures, not just satisfy them.[20] Beach calls this "leading up," and it can be accomplished by learning a superior's preferred communication style and how it changes under stress, paying attention to timing, and using empathy.[21] Kadi Cole calls this "knowing your environment."[22]

Half of the women in this study discussed the importance of female leaders learning to use an authentic Voice. This is very closely tied to the development of emotional intelligence (EI), as it requires both self-awareness and authenticity development. Participants recognized the importance of bringing Voice into leadership conversations, owning their perspectives and opinions, and speaking them clearly, even when they disagree with prevailing opinion. A female executive pastor in a megachurch commented, "I'm very sensitive to what I'm passionate about. I don't feel like I have to squelch that because it's a more feminine way to lead or communicate. If I get passionate, I get passionate. I feel like that's okay. You can see that part of me." Part of using her authentic Voice is not shrinking down her feelings about a topic.

Assertiveness

Men may unintentionally dominate meetings by talking more,[23] and so women leaders need to learn how to assert themselves. Anna Fels claims that women leaders often assume a submissive position and present themselves as less smart, capable, self-confident, or prominent than the men or authorities around them because of fear of rejection or attack. This can be communicated through avoiding eye contact and through body language.[24] Women's leadership programs began training women in assertiveness in the 1970s.[25] Assertiveness is not aggression, however. Aggression is fighting and attacking, whereas assertiveness is stating opinions and ideas. The middle ground between aggression and passivity is being assertive.[26] Women don't have to leap from passivity to hyper-aggression to be heard. Hyper-aggression breeds distrust,[27] whereas effective leadership is assertive.

20. Mohr, *Playing Big*, xiii, 126.
21. Beach, *Gifted to Lead*, 68–69.
22. Cole, *Developing Female Leaders*, 200.
23. Tannen, *You Just Don't Understand*, 95.
24. Fels, *Necessary Dreams*, 153, 157.
25. Baxter, *Language of Female Leadership*, 55–56.
26. Edwards, Matthews, and Rogers, *Mixed Ministry*, locs. 1141–43 of 2590, Kindle; Scott, *Dare Mighty Things*, 116.
27. Lederleitner, *Women in God's Mission*, 97.

Assertiveness involves taking initiative rather than waiting for direction. This can bring social tension, however. Different female leadership coaches have conflicting advice about how to manage this tension. Sheryl Sandberg and Nell Scovell encourage women to be assertive even if it comes with a social cost, but Alice H. Eagly and Linda A. Carli recommend women use niceness and friendliness to ease social tensions when taking initiative.[28] Halee Gray Scott suggests women leaders learn to frame what they want to contribute in a way that it can be received. This means avoiding extremes of aggression and extremes of passivity, which can look like speaking too softly or crying while speaking.[29] Women must walk this tightrope of assertive communication to grow their influence.

LEARNING EFFECTIVE INTERPERSONAL COMMUNICATION

Virtually every participant identified learning to have challenging leadership conversations as important or crucial to their development. Effective interpersonal conversations require women to adapt their communication style to the person receiving their communication. They have to find the right amount of warmth while still being direct in their requests. They need negotiation skills, particularly in confrontation. They also have to learn to describe a vision for a better way forward.

Adaptation of Communication Style

Three-fourths of the female leaders in this study recognized the importance of adapting their communication style in interpersonal conversations. Adapting communication style to the preferences of the other person causes the message to be better received. Sometimes these style preferences are gender based, but most frequently they are just personality based. Participants noted that women have to work harder at adapting their communication than men do. Male leader communication is more often received in its natural style. As Baxter observes, women leaders are concerned about connecting with the people they lead, and so they adapt their style to be able to stay connected while challenging or confronting someone. Men don't experience the same social expectation for connection, so they don't adapt.[30]

Learning people's communication preferences requires a good deal of self-awareness and social awareness, or empathy. Adaptation does not result in

28. Sandberg and Scovell, *Lean In*, 17, 35; Eagly and Carli, *Through the Labyrinth*, 245.
29. Scott, *Dare Mighty Things*, 116.
30. Baxter, *Language of Female Leadership*, 169.

a lack of authenticity, however. Holly Wagner described this adaptation to me: "I'm not denying my femaleness or my femininity but communicating and managing myself in a way that I don't isolate people in the room or cause people to reject what I'm saying." The focus is on a positive outcome for conversations.

Warmth

A female leader deals with many double-bind expectations. She is required to be warm and kind as well as competent and tough. She is also expected to be demanding yet caring. She must advocate for herself but serve others. She must maintain distance while being approachable.[31] These tensions are a juggle for women leaders, requiring them to constantly assess the leadership needs of the moment. When a woman brings warmth into her communication, her words generate energy. Warmth encourages inclusion and engagement and builds group motivation. However, leader toughness requires cool communication. Coolness communicates hierarchy, command, and control. Cool communication is unilateral decision-making. Baxter encourages female leaders to use both warm and cool linguistic strategies.[32] While it is socially acceptable for a man to be either coolly authoritative or warmly inclusive, studies show that authoritative women are resented. Executive coach Jean Hollands calls competent, strong female leaders "bully broads."[33]

The women in this study described having to "dial back" the intensity of their emotions when they speak their opinions so as not to be perceived as overbearing or disrespectful. A female pastor said, "Some of our strong women who are fine with conflict and confrontation—I hate to say this, but—they come off as a bitch instead of a strong leader." Another female pastor noted the different standard for female leaders: "I just think sometimes men can be seen as direct whereas a woman is seen as pushy. That's just a reality. Is it fair? Nope. But it's just a reality." Black women leaders described having to tamp down their intensity when discussing passionate issues to avoid being dismissed or labeled the "angry black woman." Successful female leaders have figured out how to deliver difficult communication without losing control. Those leaders with strong, direct personalities had to learn patience and how to add warmth and descriptors to their communication to successfully connect with the women and men they lead who prefer a more relational, less task-oriented approach.

31. Zheng, Kark, and Meister, "How Women Manage the Gendered Norms."
32. Baxter, *Language of Female Leadership*, 150–53.
33. Hollands, *Same Game, Different Rules*, xii.

Female church leaders face an extra measure of expectation to use warmth in communicating. Expressing warmth when asserting leadership helps women avoid being perceived as harsh or self-serving and allows them to be more likeable to both women and men, reducing resistance.[34] Female leader coaches provide strategies for bringing warmth to communication. Fels encourages smiling while giving directives as an important component of "niceness."[35] Tami Heim, CEO of the Christian Leadership Alliance, recommends "the velvet brick approach," which blends strong decisiveness with compassion.[36] For warmth to be authentic, it must come from a positive outlook. Beach encourages female leaders to keep a sense of humor, and Scott encourages female leaders to train themselves to become optimists, viewing challenges as opportunities.[37]

When female leaders let love for the people entrusted to their care be the fuel for their passion for fulfilling the purposes of God, warmth infuses the way they communicate as leaders.

Direct Communication

Women leaders need to learn the skill of direct communication, which is relationally risky but brings clarity. Women often feel social pressure to be accommodating rather than direct. Sue Edwards, Kelley Matthews, and Henry J. Rogers claim that women are taught that "it is more feminine to be quiet and indirect—to stay in the background," resulting in indirect or manipulative communication that frustrates many men. They recommend women learn to use direct, concise communication styles for leadership conversations.[38] Two-thirds of the women leaders in this study had to adjust their communication to use a more terse, direct style to accommodate the direct style of the male leaders and men around them. Women leaders feel required to adopt more masculine styles to communicate with men.

The women in this study noted that leadership conversations between leaders require brief, bottom-line communication, but when communicating to team members and church family entrusted to their care, they need to adapt their approach. Instead of simply providing a concise to-do list, a woman leader must explain the project's purpose. This inspires people to action by giving a task meaning through connecting it to the church's mission. A female

---

34. Eagly and Carli, *Through the Labyrinth*, 153, 240, 242.
35. Fels, *Necessary Dreams*, 153.
36. Scott, *Dare Mighty Things*, 116.
37. Beach, *Gifted to Lead*, 40; Scott, *Dare Mighty Things*, 102–3, 135.
38. Edwards, Matthews, and Rogers, *Mixed Ministry*, locs. 1107–27 of 2871, Kindle.

campus pastor described how she adapts, warming her communication toward those entrusted to her care: "If I'm sitting around a table in conversation with campus pastors, I would just get to the point. But if I'm sitting with my team, then I would be warm and passive and hoping that they catch this, not drill it in." For the people this woman leads, she uses gentler communication, but for her peers and leaders, she uses a more direct style.

Negotiating

Adapting communication to the needs of others is an essential part of negotiating. Negotiating is the give-and-take required to convince someone to do or give something. Women leaders still learning to negotiate may default to a mothering style of negotiation. Nagging or obliging people to do their duty comes off like a mom getting after her teenage children to do their chores. This approach, even if it is a woman's natural communication style, will have limited success in motivating any person who ever rolled their eyes as a teenager at their nagging mother. "Do this because you should" is not a great negotiation strategy. The verbal skill of negotiation is an essential one for church leaders who rely on volunteer support. Leaders are constantly asking people to give their time, talents, or money to support the work of ministry. Financial compensation is not part of this exchange. The negotiation is based on a shared vision, a relationship, eternal rewards, or a sense of responsibility. When a female leader has less or equal power compared to the person she is attempting to influence, the skill of negotiation becomes particularly important. The use of EI and empathy is also important. Pastor Karolina Gunsser Grant stated, "I try to diagnose a person so that I can relate to them in a really effective way. I'm not just limited to how I prefer to communicate and how I prefer to receive information. This awareness helps me lead in a way that is received by the person that I'm leading." One male pastor claimed that the female leaders on his team are better negotiators than the men because they have better EI. It is not clear if women leaders are better because of their gender, or if they are better because only women with high EI are in leadership.[39]

Power can be spent as capital for executing leadership decisions without consensus; it allows a leader to make unequal leadership transactions.

---

39. Researchers debate whether women are worse negotiators than men. More recent findings suggest that women are good negotiators but care about different things and so do not negotiate for higher pay (Ely, Ibarra, and Kolb, "Taking Gender into Account," 483). This study's findings seem to suggest that women are good negotiators, particularly since maintaining a volunteer work force requires high-level negotiation.

Power enables a woman to ask for something without offering something in return or offering something of lesser value. One participant described her struggle to recognize and use the power she has to make leadership decisions that require others to get on board quickly. If women have less power than men, struggle to recognize or leverage their power, or are hardwired to be more consensus-oriented, their leadership will rely heavily on developing negotiation skills.

Women leaders in this study lean on a variety of negotiation strategies. The most commonly used strategy is relationship building. This requires getting to know people before asking for anything and making relational deposits before making leadership withdrawals. One woman pastor said, "Ask for a heart before you ask for a hand. You have to get to know someone before you can get them to do a job that gets you to the vision." Women leaders in this study also use diplomacy and sensitivity in their negotiation, working to create win-wins, with clear asks for help. Other women use a common female leadership style, a collaborative approach, to create buy-in.[40] This requires some women to rein in their natural instinct to aggressively power through a conversation and bulldoze others. Gifted communicators use convincing rhetoric to persuade others rather than dominate them. Proficiency in these negotiation strategies makes women great managers.

Confrontation

Almost every woman leader in this study described her struggle to manage challenging leadership conversations in which she needs to address a needed change or improvement in a supervisee. Heightened emotion and personality differences make this kind of dialogue particularly difficult to navigate. Some women leaders struggle to rein in their tempers. Others, like me, struggle with fear that these conversations will fail to produce a positive outcome. Over half of the women explained that staying focused on a positive outcome helps keep them calm and leads them through difficult conversations. They are unwilling to live with unresolved conflict and recognize tough conversations as helpful for supporting the growth of others. They want to have these challenging conversations from loving, positive perspectives.

The women in this study reported five strategies for approaching difficult conversations. In the first strategy, a woman leader requests a discussion about the topic at hand a few days ahead of time. Then she has the challenging conversation without ambushing the person entrusted to her care. She then

40. Eagly and Johannesen-Schmidt, "Leadership Styles of Women and Men," 787–88.

checks in a day or two later with the individual after the tough interaction, showing care for their emotional well-being and anxiety level.

A second strategy the women leaders described is to disarm the intensity of confrontation by having the conversation in a relaxed and casual setting. They create intimacy and connection by bringing the person into their home or meeting in a coffee shop rather than having the discussion in a formal setting with a desk between them. A comfortable environment relaxes the hearer so their defenses are down.

Other women leaders use a third strategy, adopting a humble, caring, vulnerable approach and acknowledging partial responsibility for failures.[41] As a leader, I am responsible for the actions of those I lead. So when someone else fails, it is also my failure. Perhaps I didn't communicate goals or strategy clearly enough or give enough time or resources to solving an issue. This strategy prevents the hearer from feeling attacked and isolated, sending the message of "We're in this together."

A fourth strategy is what some call "the love sandwich" and others call "fairy dust—truth—fairy dust." This strategy sandwiches hard truth between affirmations to make the truth easier to receive. The leader opens with an affirmation to build trust, briefly and clearly delivers the hard truth, and then follows up with affirmation to rebuild confidence.

The fifth strategy is asking good questions so that the hearer can self-discover the learning opportunity rather than the leader directly addressing it. This is an incredibly effective teaching method and requires the skill of crafting the right questions. When someone self-discovers a correction, their defenses are down and they are far more likely to adopt the change.

These strategies are designed to make confrontation easier and soften the delivery with love and care.

Vision Casting

Women's leadership experts Herminia Ibarra and Otilia Obodaru found that while women leaders outperform male leaders in many areas, they fall behind in envisioning. This skill involves recognizing emerging trends and opportunities and developing strategies for engaging them. Without envisioning a new future, a leader cannot move an organization forward. Women get stuck in middle-management roles if they do not learn this skill.[42] Once

41. One of the male pastors in this study observed a female tendency to apologize or soften confrontation. He considers this weak or insecure leadership and corrects it in his female leaders, asking them to speak with a stronger Voice.
42. Ibarra and Obodaru, "Women and the Vision Thing."

a woman can see a new future, then she must describe the vision to bring others with her.

Nearly half of the women in this study discussed the importance of learning to cast a vision for a desired future. Only women at leadership level 3, 4, or 5 discussed vision casting, however, indicating this is a more advanced leadership skill, learned later in development. It is also essential for progressing to greater levels of influence.

Vision casting looks different in different kinds of leadership roles. Women leading from the middle of a church have to learn how to contextualize the larger vision of the church in their specific areas of responsibility. Women leading at the top have to learn how to communicate a compelling vision that will inspire people to take risks with them. A woman leader has to become comfortable with the risk she is selling to others before she can communicate the vision effectively. People don't always immediately accept a new vision. The women described learning to be patient and not being discouraged by how slowly people buy in to a vision. Several participants recognized that vision casting is an important first step in negotiation.

Women leaders use story sharing as a strategy for vision casting. They inspire people by presenting an overarching vision or a narrative of the organization and helping people see their individual places inside that story. A kingdom vision realized is the result of engaging with the mission that Jesus gave us. As the women in this study learned effective interpersonal communication, they influenced those around them for kingdom purposes by using empathy to deeply connect and negotiate for win-wins.

LEARNING EFFECTIVE PUBLIC SPEAKING

A woman leader needs to learn effective interpersonal communication, but she also needs to learn skills for communicating to a larger audience. Participants in this study described the importance of female leaders learning effective public-speaking skills. They include preaching and teaching skills and developing ideas and content. Many women prefer to avoid public speaking. It requires them to formulate clear ideas that extend from their true selves, and this vulnerability is risky. But preaching and teaching opportunities publicly validate a woman's leadership and build her influence with people. Public speaking is an essential skill that communicates leadership and authority.[43] Baxter notes that "women enact authority effectively by developing a public

43. Cole, *Developing Female Leaders*, 45.

voice, public speaking."[44] Public speaking empowers large-scale leadership influence, even for those without a teaching or preaching gift.

Elocution skills are developed through practice and through seeking out feedback and coaching. When feedback is not available, a woman can watch videos of her own public speaking to gain self-awareness and self-correct. Nancy Lammers Gross offers various preparation tools for public speaking: using vocal warm-ups (including practicing belly breathing), avoiding heavy drink and smoking, engaging in physical exercise, and practicing stances, gestures, and vocal inflections. She encourages female leaders to think about matching content to vocal tone and style.[45] Rhonda Harrington Kelley and Monica Rose Brennan encourage women to cultivate "audience intelligence" in public speaking, which is the ability to read the responses of a crowd and adapt content and style accordingly, building a connection with the audience.[46] Executive leadership coach Carol Kinsey Goman says that clear, compelling, and brief communication is best for public speaking.[47]

Vocal Control and Presenting Style

Developing presentation skills is an important piece of developing as a public communicator. Almost every male and female study participant discussed the practical elements of becoming more effective speakers.

Women struggle to express opinions if they feel they do not have permission. Gross observes that when a woman speaker is trying not to be offensive or when she is feeling insecure, she constrains her posture and vocal tone by cocking her head to the side and using a sweet, high tone or laughing instead of speaking with intensity despite feeling passionately. "The loss of a woman's Voice leads to the loss of a woman's voice."[48] This leads to women preachers and teachers with "tiny, apologetic, breathy, little-girl voices, or ever-present smiles, or nervous, compromising, inappropriate laughter, or the all-pervasive upward inflection at the end of sentences."[49] Gross describes this as the "disembodied voice." Other markers of a loss of Voice are glottal fry (tension in the vocal cords that produces a raspy voice), low energy, body tension, softness, and too-high pitch.[50] Goman asserts that public speakers with high-pitched voices are perceived as weaker and less confident than those

---

44. Baxter, *Language of Female Leadership*, 150.
45. Gross, *Women's Voices*, locs. 1690, 1765, 1985, 2042, 2131, 2235 of 3081, Kindle.
46. Kelley and Brennan, *Talking Is a Gift*, 66, 73.
47. Goman, "Leadership Presence," 17.
48. Gross, *Women's Voices*, loc. 1278 of 3081, Kindle.
49. Gross, *Women's Voices*, loc. 214 of 3081, Kindle.
50. Gross, *Women's Voices*, locs. 1038, 1247, 1278, 1343 of 3081, Kindle.

with lower-pitched voices, and she encourages women to project confidence by being aware of and avoiding feminine habits of body compacting (hunching, leg crossing, self-hugging), which communicate insecurity.[51] Women preachers in this study had to learn to control their bodies and their voices.

Over half of the female participants described their journey of learning how to control their voices, which tend to get higher and faster when they are nervous or particularly emotional. Roese notes that women are more descriptive, and their voices have greater range than men's, making women sound more emotional. Some men have a difficult time listening to the pitch of female voices or may shut down when a woman preacher sounds emotional.[52] This means that to connect with men, women may need to adjust their vocal tone lower. This study also found that women have to adjust their rhetoric so that even their appeals for action are rooted not in emotion but in practical rationality. The male pastors in this study agreed with the importance of women learning to control their voices. For some of the women in this study, however, a woman lowering her voice to make it more palatable for an audience (particularly a male audience) seemed less authentic and therefore unhelpful.

Other women viewed this differently. One female pastor described a low voice as naturally feminine and a high voice as a culturally influenced variation of what is natural: "Actually, our natural voice, our comfortable voice range, is a lot lower than what we're often socialized to speak at." A third of the survey participants recognized that they had to train their physical voice away from its natural style as they developed communication skills. Other women leaders did not find this to be an issue at all. Frequently, the women leaders who did not describe having to learn to adjust their physical voice also did not report extensive experience in preaching.

As women grow in their preaching skills, they face new hurdles. Over half of the women pastors in this study described adapting their content and style according to their audience. Rather than owning and settling in on a single preaching style, they use social awareness to read the room and adapt to keep their listeners engaged. This kind of dynamic style adjustment is a marker of a skilled communicator. The women identified the importance of female communicators adapting their communication when speaking to men, using less emotion, more boldness, and more strength.

Other participants talked about the importance of authenticity in presenting, which contrasts with adapting one's style to an audience. This is another

51. Goman, "Leadership Presence," 14–16.
52. Roese, *She Can Teach*, 42.

double bind for women, but the best communicators have learned how to live into and manage this tension.

A woman's ability to influence others' perceptions of her leadership has become a focus for leadership coaches who help leaders develop leadership (or executive) presence.[53] Coaching in vocal control and body awareness helps counteract the impact of female leadership insecurities. A significant part of public speaking is communicating leadership presence through body language. This is confidence that people can see. Women described how being free to express their personal fashion preferences—particularly while preaching— was an important part of demonstrating self-confidence and leadership presence. Eye contact, formal and strong body language, physically occupying more space and making the body larger through wide arm movements, and interacting with an audience were also ways to establish leadership presence.

Preaching and Teaching

God-gifted preachers and teachers have a responsibility to be obedient to developing their spiritual gifts in pursuit of their kingdom calling. Preaching and ministry leadership go hand in hand. Preaching and teaching create influence for leadership, and strong leadership creates authority in preaching and teaching. Regional cultures, organizational cultures, and theological environments may make it very difficult for women to develop their gifts, however. The lack of affirmation so many receive in their public ministry gifts robs them of confidence. As Roese notes, a communicator's confidence makes or breaks their effectiveness. She encourages women to rely on effective use of the Bible to overcome this lack of confidence.[54] Gross says that by shrinking their bodies and voices down, even women leaders with highly developed preaching and teaching gifts tend to apologize for stepping into pulpit space where they may not feel welcome.[55] Low confidence may cause women to rely too heavily on other Voices for developing their content or teaching style, making it harder to find their own unique Voice.

As participants developed their public speaking, preaching, and teaching skills, their influence expanded. Level 5 leaders were more critical of their own preaching and teaching skills but recognized the significant importance of developing them.

Women need various types of supports and training to develop their preaching and teaching gifts. Over half of the women shared their ongoing need for

53. Ibarra, Ely, and Kolb, "Women Rising."
54. Roese, *She Can Teach*, 93, 22.
55. Gross, *Women's Voices*, loc. 169 of 3081, Kindle.

training in public speaking, and some felt undertrained. Others were more aggressive and pursued their own training rather than waiting for it to come. Half of the women identified the importance of pursuing formal theological training, studying other preachers, and seeking feedback about their preaching. Some watched videos of themselves preaching to gain self-awareness and correct bad habits. Two-thirds of the women leaders in this study recognized having opportunities to preach as essential for their development. They would not have become good preachers without the opportunity to practice their skills. Being encouraged to preach by the men and leaders in their world was particularly important.

Women preachers often have to overcome insecurity in public speaking. Preaching can bring anxiety, and just a third of the women leaders said they enjoy preaching. Some found that because of their insecurity about preaching and content development, they spend many hours preparing too much material for a sermon, making it harder to commit to preaching opportunities.

Learning to develop content and ideas is another part of preaching and teaching. The goal is not just to provide information but to inspire transformation. When preaching to a mixed-gender audience, the women pastors said they often prioritize sermon content that connects with the men. This involves using bottom-line language, male illustrations, and outcome-oriented content. The best communicators think about connecting with every person in the room, whether male or female, and recognize they need to be intentional about overcoming their natural bias for preaching to audience members who are similar to themselves. One participant, a world-renowned communicator, said she views preaching to men as a cross-cultural exercise. She adapts language the same way she would if she were preaching in a Spanish-speaking context. For her, adaptation is not about earning validation or acceptance from men in the audience but is a missionary effort. She recognizes that men need to hear her message to grow and thrive. As a communicator, she adopts a male paradigm as a loving act so men can encounter Jesus.

The women preachers described using Voice not just to communicate a message but to communicate leader identity. This means a woman owns her female uniqueness and her individual gifts and brings them into her preaching and teaching. A level 5 female pastor said bluntly, "Bring your distinctiveness. Don't be homogenous. Blah." If a woman has a business background, this should come through in her preaching. If she has an academic background, this should come through. If she is a special-needs mother, this should come out in her preaching. People hear not just what she says but who she is. Copying other preachers and communicators or simply performing a rehearsed act leads to a diminished Voice and less-effective ministry. Another level 5 female senior pastor said, "I want to be sharpened by Joyce Meyer, but I don't want to be a second-best version of her. The minute you become somebody else, you've lost something significant." The longer a woman leader has been preaching, the more passionate she is about using her authentic Voice.

While public speaking is an important skill for both men and women leaders to develop, male "report-talk" advantages male public-speaking skill development. Men may not have to adapt to female audiences in the same way that female public speakers need to adapt to include male audience members. Even in egalitarian environments, more men than women preach and teach, which means that women are required to work harder to earn the opportunities to develop their public-speaking skills.

LEARNING TO USE SOCIAL MEDIA AS A LEADERSHIP PLATFORM

Social media does not feature in secular female leadership development studies, but it clearly has significant impact in local church settings on a variety of levels. Well over half of the women leaders in this study shared that engaging social media in healthy and effective ways is a significant challenge for female leaders today. They hesitate to engage because of the negative factors of self-promotion and pride. Social media makes them more likely to hide the truth behind a filter, or it tempts them to value fame over ministry. Social media also reinforces popular cultural values and easily leads to comparison and insecurity. One boomer leader said she has compassion for young female leaders dealing with social media comparison and insecurity: "I didn't have to deal with watching four million others succeeding while I was still sitting in a cubicle."

A third of the women still wrestle with how to use social media well. They rated their ability to effectively use social media as not very well developed or average. Even the three women with the most social media followers described their abilities as average. The skills behind using social media well seem to be somewhat mysterious, and female interview and focus group participants struggled with feeling a tension between promoting God and the church and promoting themselves. The survey participants rated their own abilities to brand or market themselves as low or average. Women leaders' strong desire not to be perceived as self-promoting causes them to hesitate to put their own content on social media.

Emotional intelligence in social media engagement is essential. This means using self-awareness and self-regulation to realign one's personal motivations to represent Jesus and love others well. A female senior pastor with more than four thousand Instagram followers said, "I've had to resolve that I need to be a good steward of the people who are following me on social media as well as create opportunities to gather more followers, not so that I have a large number attached to my name but so that I can share the message God's given me." She focuses her social media engagement on her message and being an ambassador of the gospel rather than on herself. Survey participants viewed social media as helpful to ministry, but only a fifth of the study participants viewed social media as very important to ministry leadership development. Table 4 shows the various social media uses survey participants identified. The most common use was encouraging others and spreading hope.

TABLE 4. Social Media Uses among Survey Participants

Social Media Purpose	Participant N = 47 Using for This Purpose
Encouraging others and spreading hope	30
Keeping in touch with extended family or friends	28
Viewing other people's lives	25
Giving others a glimpse of daily life	21
Networking with other leaders	20

Despite the challenges of social media, it has had a positive role in developing female leaders. Women leaders described the power of social media for broadening worldviews and exposing women to more role models for female leadership. Before social media, a woman could find role models only locally or at a conference. Now women can observe the lives of many kinds of female leaders online. A millennial female leader said, "Accessibility and the depth or the breadth of examples that the girls have to look to today have definitely changed for the better since I was growing up, because of social media." These role models become virtual mentors through online relationships. Social media has also created cross-pollination of different Christian traditions and thought, creating global conversations that have caused historically complementarian churches to invite egalitarian churches to clarify their theology.

Study participants recognized the power of social media as a ministry tool and leadership platform. Few had clearly defined how they choose to interact with social media, but those with the greatest number of followers had the most well-defined strategies. These women use social media for evangelism, for preaching and bringing encouragement and hope to followers, and to connect relationally with people who are widely dispersed, letting themselves be known. Social media provides a window into the lives of church members that pastors might not get otherwise.

Having many followers and "likes" is a very quantitative measurement of leadership influence, and this is something leaders wrestle with. This quantification of influence validates a leader and brings credibility, leading to even more influence for the leader who has figured out the mysteries of leveraging social media.

INFLUENCE EXPANSION THROUGH COMMUNICATION

Leadership is grounded in the connections between individuals, but it is carried through the interactions of conversations and the exchange of ideas. This happens on various levels. The larger the group, the wider the spread of influence. The smaller the group, the deeper the level of influence. Figure 10.1 shows how influence expands from smaller communication platforms to larger ones.

Influence begins in one-on-one or one-on-two mentoring. This is a narrow focus for influence development, but the deeply personal nature of it allows for a great depth of influence. This is how leaders replicate themselves. Influence expands into facilitating conversations in small groups that learn together. This is less-personal and less-vulnerable work, so the depth of influence becomes shallower while the breadth of influence expands. The breadth of influence increases for a leader who steps into boardroom-level strategic conversations and is part of high-level decision-making for an organization. Though her leadership reaches more people, she cannot maintain

DEPTH OF INFLUENCE

Fig. 10.1. Leadership Communication and Influence Progression

relational intimacy with every individual in her church or organization. As a leader reaches more and more people, the nature of her influence changes, shifting from personal accountability to influencing through ideas and setting an example.

SUMMARY

Women are socialized to communicate differently than men. Women tend to communicate to connect, while men tend to communicate to present ideas. A woman must find her unique Voice and learn how to present her ideas and assert herself. Assertiveness is not aggression but stating one's own ideas clearly. Women leaders must learn effective interpersonal communication to produce transformation in those entrusted to their care. They must adapt their communication to the other person, bringing warmth as needed. They must learn direct communication to be able to effectively negotiate and confront when needed. Women must also learn how to cast a compelling vision to those they lead to move out of middle-management roles and into more advanced leadership authority. A woman called to preach and teach sees her influence expand as she learns effective public-speaking skills. These include training her voice and her body. Finally, women who have significant influence have learned to strategically leverage social media as a ministry tool.

THE LIFELONG PROCESS OF
LEADERSHIP DEVELOPMENT

When I was a young girl dreaming about my future, I never anticipated my reality today. God has formed me and my leadership slowly and carefully over my entire life. I'm in my midlife now, and I can look back over the past thirty years and recognize how God shaped me in every season.

In the early years of my childhood, I was cocooned in a protected spiritual nursery with loving and faith-filled Christian parents. I went to a healthy Pentecostal church and a thriving Christian school. I had so many encouragements to my budding faith. I witnessed my brother miraculously and instantaneously healed from life-threatening asthma and my father healed of a terrible back injury. I was sheltered and loved.

Something shifted when I started high school. My faith began to be challenged to grow by my youth pastors and worship pastors, who invited me to serve God in the small things and be faithful in obedience to him. I committed my life to Jesus. I began to learn some simple ministry skills, which opened doors of opportunity for ministry and relationships with mentors. My secular high school environment forced me to think more deeply about parts of my Christianity that I had taken for granted. I began to hunger for God and to love his church in that season. I wanted to be at church every day, and most days I was.

My life shifted again when I got married and two weeks later, my husband and I were in full-time youth ministry. My ministry skills began to grow with each new opportunity, and I learned how to administrate a ministry. My role was largely a support role to my husband, Rich, until it abruptly changed when he died two years later. I was thrust into the front seat of leadership and began to find my way in leading a worship ministry in a megachurch focused on creative ministry. This opportunity accelerated the development of my leadership skills, and after a few years, I was promoted to the executive leadership team of our church. I knew how to make a church hum, and I was good at keeping all the parts moving. In that season, I married my Aussie husband, John, who was another youth pastor and evangelist.

My life transitioned again in my early thirties. After twelve years in the same place, I felt restless and knew God was calling me to step out. I left my comfortable ministry role and began to travel with my husband. Soon after, I began studying at Fuller Theological Seminary and was startled and overjoyed to discover that God used that experience for deep spiritual formation. During the next decade, I learned how to minister out of who I am rather than just what I can do. I became ministries director of City Church Chicago and then executive pastor of ministries. I was responsible for the spiritual development and health of our church family. This season finished as I graduated with my doctorate, having completed my research in female leadership development in local churches.

In 2021 my husband and I accepted new ministry roles as senior pastors of Word of Life Church in metropolitan Washington, DC. This coincided with new opportunities for me to teach at Fuller Seminary and to lead the academics of Ascent College, an Assemblies of God regional Bible college. My ministry focus has shifted again, this time to leadership development, writing, teaching, and preaching.

My journey has never felt rushed. God shaped me slowly, giving me opportunities as I was ready. I share my story to show how leadership can develop. Each new season has brought new opportunities and expanded my influence and responsibility for those entrusted to my care.

TRACKING LEADERSHIP DEVELOPMENT ON A TIMELINE

Leadership researcher J. Robert Clinton calls the slow process of leadership formation "leadership emergence." After studying the lives of thousands of Christian leaders, he developed a theory to explain this process of divinely directed development. Clinton's theory of leadership emergence is that "God develops a leader over a lifetime . . . [using] events and people to impress leadership lessons upon a leader (processing), time, and leader response. Processing is central to the theory."[1] God forms Christian leaders not merely to

1. Clinton, *Making of a Leader*, 21.

exercise power or even for humanitarian causes but to be stewards of God's purposes in the world. Leadership emergence theory explains the increasing leadership capacity of a Christian leader as a divinely guided process over a lifetime influenced by both psychological and sociological shaping.[2]

As God shapes a leader, he increases their leadership capacity in a divinely guided process. The challenging psychological and sociological experiences I faced in my life and ministry were "process items."[3] These process items shaped who I am as a leader and how I lead.[4] The lifelong process of leadership development can be traced by mapping these key events and transitions on a timeline. There are discernible patterns of development consistent among Christian leaders. These patterns provide insight into the kinds of tools God frequently uses to shape leaders. A leadership development timeline allows a leader to trace God's past formation in their life, locate themselves today, and predict where God might be taking them in the future.

Six stages of leadership development along this journey are common to most Christian leaders. Not every Christian leader passes through every stage, and stages vary in length. The first stage begins after birth. In the sovereign foundations stage, God laid a foundation in my life through my childhood experiences, family, and education. In this stage, God sheltered me and showed his love for me. During the second stage, inner life growth, I developed my relationship with God during my teenage years. My faith was tested by challenging experiences, and God began to form my character as I was faithful in the small things. My pastors also identified leadership potential in me. In the third stage, ministry maturing, I said yes to my first ministry leadership opportunity in youth and worship ministry, began to develop ministry skills, discovered my giftedness in ministry administration, and developed leadership relationships with others. The focus of this third stage is doing ministry. In these first three stages, God works more within a leader than through a leader. What a leader learns is more significant than their ministry output or influence.

Development focus shifts in the fourth stage, called life maturing. The theme of this stage is *beingness*. A leader transitions from having influence that comes from what they can successfully do to having influence that comes

---

2. Clinton, *Leadership Emergence Theory*, 27.

3. Clinton defines process items technically: "The actual occurrences from a given life of those providential events, people, circumstances, special divine interventions, inner-life lessons, and/or other like items which God uses to develop that person by shaping leadership character, leadership skills, and leadership values so as to indicate leadership capacity (such as inner integrity, influence potential), expand potential, confirm appointment to roles or responsibilities using that leadership capacity, and direct that leader along to God's appointed ministry level for realized potential." Clinton, *Leadership Emergence Theory*, 81.

4. Clinton, *Leadership Emergence Theory*, 81.

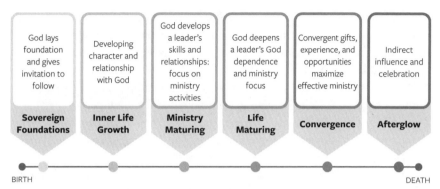

Fig. 11.1. General Timeline of Christian Leadership Development

from who they are. During this stage, I knew my giftedness, but I had to learn to lead differently, to develop a deeper dependence on Jesus and a greater focus. In my fifth and current stage, convergence, God has given me the ideal ministry leadership opportunities that bring together my unique giftedness and ministry experience. The convergence season produces the greatest fruitfulness of a leader's entire ministry.

During the sixth and final stage, afterglow, a retired Christian leader still has indirect influence because of a lifetime of building relationships and ministry, but they no longer carry the responsibilities of day-to-day ministry tasks. This leader is celebrated, and God gets the glory. This final stage ends with death. Not every leader reaches these last few stages. Figure 11.1 shows these six stages plotted on a timeline of a leader's life.[5] While every leader's development journey is unique, these stages are useful for recognizing the ways a leader's journey follows (or diverges from) the general leadership development pattern. Clinton's research largely focuses on men, but it can apply to women leaders as well.

THE LEADERSHIP DEVELOPMENT OF WOMEN

This study builds on Clinton's leadership emergence theory by adapting it to reflect a woman's leadership emergence, tracing her influence growth. Women leaders navigate three distinct phases of development over a lifetime: the budding female leader phase of early leadership, the emerging female leader phase, and the influential female leader phase of advanced leadership influence. Within each phase, a woman leader works through specific aspects of the seven development processes (see fig. 11.2). A female leader may or may

5. Clinton, *Making of a Leader*, 37–39.

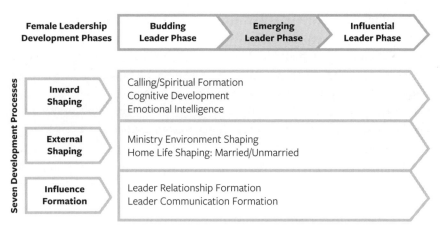

Fig. 11.2. Female Leadership Development Phases and the Seven Development Processes

not become an emerging leader or an influential leader, depending on her calling, gifting, responses to God, and environmental shaping. But those who do become influential leaders pass through these phases.

As each of these seven development processes work, a woman leader develops increasing ministry leadership influence. (Married or unmarried social base formation are interchangeable depending on a female leader's marital status.) Secular researchers and a few Christian researchers have identified various environmental and inner-shaping female leader development process items, and this study found more.[6] The following sections expand on and unpack each phase of development (divided into two or three subphases), explaining the processes associated with each phase. As a woman successfully navigates aspects of her development, she progresses to the next phase and increases in influence.

In each of the following three tables, the first column names the leadership development domain corresponding to each row. Each phase is divided into two or three subphases, which are distinct shifts forward that happen as women progress within a development phase. Each development domain has aspects of processing that are associated with early, middle, or late leadership emergence.

Budding Female Leader Phase

In the budding female leader phase (see table 5), a female leader is in a season of discovery. Most of her leadership is still just potential. She has some of the raw materials for leadership—talent, innate gifts of influence, a relationship with Jesus, an encouraging environment—but she has never led in the church before. It will be some time before her leadership blooms, but the bud is observable.

6. See Clinton's definition of "process items" above in footnote 3.

A budding female leader is discovering her own divine calling and the theological foundations for this calling, and she is discovering her own motivation for kingdom leadership and looking to role models as inspiration. She is in ministry leadership environments that value budding female leaders and see untapped leadership potential to be cultivated in women. If she is married, her husband encourages her calling and recognizes the emerging giftedness in her. He is willing to help around the home to support her. She takes her first wobbling steps in leadership in volunteer roles in her local church.

The budding female leader phase has two subphases. In the first subphase, a woman forms her inner "yes" to the calling of God. This is often catalyzed by an invitation into a ministry role. It might also be catalyzed by an important relationship, perhaps with a spouse or a pastor who identifies giftedness in her and encourages her to consider what God might be asking of her.

In the second subphase of the budding female leader phase, a woman leader takes her first steps of obedience. She receives her first opportunity to lead at a beginner level, perhaps as a small group leader, and processes the theological implications of what she is sensing from the Lord. She recognizes role models she admires and respects, and she begins to emulate them.

TABLE 5. Budding Female Leader Phase

	Process	Subphase 1	Subphase 2
Internal Shaping	Spiritual Calling and Formation	Hears and accepts a divine call to ministry	Processes egalitarian theology, establishes spiritual disciplines, trusts Jesus and obeys him
	Leadership Cognition Formation	Shows wide-eyed interest in church and Christian service	Identifies relatable female leader role models
	Emotional Intelligence Formation	Develops others-focused motivation for ministry	Develops others-focused motivation for ministry
External Shaping	Ministry Environment	Witnesses existing local church pipeline of female leadership development	Receives formal or informal training
	Home Life (Married)	Receives affirmation from her husband of ministry leadership calling	Is empowered by egalitarian marriage as her husband shares home and children management
	Home Life (Unmarried)	Focuses time and attention and prioritizes church	Focuses time and attention and prioritizes church over home and relationships
Influence Formation	Leadership Relationships	Has a leader identify leadership potential in her	Has a male (or female) leader sponsor
	Communication	Has latent leadership talents and gifts	Receives first leadership opportunity in a volunteer role

Emerging Female Leader Phase

In the emerging female leader phase (see table 6), a female leader begins to learn leadership skills, and the bloom of her leadership opens. She says yes to God's call into vocational ministry, accepting the greater demands. As she becomes self-aware of her strengths, leadership style, and unique design, her confidence grows.

The emerging female leader phase has three subphases. In the first subphase, a woman leader accepts her first significant leadership opportunity, often as a part-time or full-time church staff member in a support role or a departmental lead role. She receives training in the practical skills of her responsibilities and becomes aware of what she is good at and not good at through coaching by her leaders. She starts to develop her leader identity. If she is married, she struggles to find the balance of home and work and wrestles with mom guilt. If she is not married, she often overworks and struggles to keep up with her friendships and extended family relationships.

In the second subphase of the emerging female leader phase, a woman becomes more confident in her leadership after seeing success. She develops a clear leadership style. She learns to manage her emotions in many kinds of interactions and stresses and is aware of how her emotions impact those around her. She has figured out how to get the supports she needs at home to be able to manage her family life well while doing ministry, and she has flexibility in her work schedule and location to accommodate her family's needs. Her church provides opportunities and a safe environment for leading alongside men. She has coaches for her leadership in her church and is beginning to connect with advanced leaders beyond her local church.

In the third subphase of the emerging female leader phase, a woman's opportunities to lead expand and she is busy. She may receive an invitation to join the executive ministry team of her church. As she immerses herself in ministry and falls in love with the church, she navigates seasons of neglecting her inner spiritual life. God brings her back into balance as she matures, refocusing her on loving Jesus first. She finds her central identity in being a daughter of God rather than in the ministry role she occupies. She becomes a skilled empathizer, gauging the needs of those she leads. She learns skills for interpersonal communication that empower her leadership and develop her leadership Voice, casting vision and clearly articulating her perspectives. She toughens up, and criticism does not devastate her anymore. She is comfortable receiving the help she needs at home, recognizing it is a win for her family and her ministry. She begins to develop relationships with coaches and mentors outside her local church. She recognizes her need for help and begins to invest in potential leaders who can take on aspects of her ministry responsibilities.

TABLE 6. Emerging Female Leader Phase

	Process	Subphase 1	Subphase 2	Subphase 3
Internal Shaping	Spiritual Calling and Formation	Accepts a divine call to vocational ministry	Learns to steward the church	Refocuses on loving Jesus more than the church
	Leadership Cognition Formation	Develops a unique leader identity and becomes aware of gifts and design	Becomes more confident and develops a leadership style	Puts Christ-centered identity before leader identity
	Emotional Intelligence Formation	Develops self-awareness	Learns to self-regulate and manage emotions	Develops empathy and processes criticism well
External Shaping	Ministry Environment	Has a local church culture that values female leadership and provides skills training	Has a local church staff that provides positive and negative feedback; office space designed to facilitate safe, effective mixed-gender ministry; and flexible work hours and location	Has a local church culture that permits male-female mentoring relationships and provides healthy frameworks for these relationships
	Home Life (Married)	Learns to manage the stress of juggling ministry and home needs and processes mom guilt	Has childcare and/or home management and cleaning support	Gets comfortable with having and using home and childcare support
	Home Life (Unmarried)	Overworks and struggles to maintain personal relationships	Forms a group to provide support for personal, financial, and home needs	Gets comfortable having home management support
Influence Formation	Leadership Relationships	Receives coaching in unique gifts	Has coaches and mentors for leadership internal to her local church	Has coaches and mentors for leadership beyond her local church
	Communication	Learns to lead others and develops practical skills	Learns healthy social media habits	Learns to lead through effective interpersonal communication, starts to develop her Voice, casts vision, and develops others

Influential Female Leader Phase

In the influential female leader phase (see table 7), a female leader becomes increasingly sensitive to the leading of the Holy Spirit and reliant on his direction. She can articulate egalitarian theology and grows in her preaching and teaching skills and her ability to persuade others. She grows in confidence and authenticity and is increasingly focused on developing other leaders. Her environments value female executive team members and want to hear from women leaders.

The influential leader phase has two subphases. In the first subphase, a woman leader knows who she is and what she is called to do, and she does it well. She gains confidence in her leadership and decision-making, although promotions to new roles requiring new skills or new environments that require her to build new relationships cause her to lose some confidence she must rebuild. The stakes are higher, and she must step out in faith and take risks. As she does and those risks pay off in success, her confidence grows again. She learns how to follow the Holy Spirit and depend on Spirit empowerment more than her own ability to lead. She has opportunities for teaching and preaching in her church, and her skills grow. Her role is providing not only church management but also spiritual leadership. She is a full member of her church's executive team. Her husband (if she is married) is secure in his own calling and not threatened by her, and they have figured out their leadership relationship. She has the respect and public support of other pastors and leaders inside and outside her church, both male and female. She is focused on developing emerging leaders in her church community.

In the second subphase of the influential female leader phase, a woman leader maximizes her leadership influence and authority. She leads authentically and is aware of and confident and comfortable with who she is as a leader, her style and strengths. She can clearly articulate egalitarian theology and teaches it to her church and others outside her church. She trains other leaders. This subphase comes with greater opportunities for her to influence others through preaching and writing. She understands the purpose and power of social media and uses it for ministry. In this subphase, her children are typically older and have gained independence, which provides her with greater freedom from the demands of home and more time for ministry. This opportunity for increased ministry focus produces greater ministry fruitfulness. She actively develops peer networks beyond her local church to expand her ministry context. She might be in a traveling preaching ministry or a denominational leadership role.

TABLE 7. Influential Female Leader Phase

	Process	Subphase 1	Subphase 2
Internal Shaping	Spiritual Calling and Formation	Follows the Holy Spirit's leading	Articulates egalitarian theology
	Leadership Cognition Formation	Gains confidence in decision-making and risk-taking	Has confidence in her leadership style and strengths
	Emotional Intelligence Formation	Increases resilience in processing criticism	Develops authenticity
External Shaping	Ministry Environment	Works with local church leaders who value female Voices in executive leadership conversations and provide women opportunities to preach to and teach the entire church	Has opportunities to preach and teach regularly
	Home Life (Married)	Has a husband who is secure in his own calling and not threatened by her leadership	Has greater freedom to focus on ministry, resulting in fruitfulness
	Home Life (Unmarried)	Identifies and establishes reliable support team for home life	Has a strong support team in place, both relationally and at home
Influence Formation	Leadership Relationships	Has influential male and female leaders who publicly validate her leadership inside and outside her local church	Develops peer networks outside her local church
	Communication	Has the opportunity to preach and teach and develops emerging leaders in her local church	Speaks publicly, writes, and uses social media for public ministry

FEMALE LEADERSHIP DEVELOPMENT PHASES AND EXPANDING INFLUENCE AND AUTHORITY

As a female leader is being formed in local church ministry, her influence and authority are expanding. This expansion is most often driven by opportunities that open for her leadership through the sponsorship and validation of a more influential leader. The more powerful a sponsor is, the more rapidly a female leader's influence can expand. An opportunity to lead might present itself before she is ready, and she grows into it. Or she may be waiting for an opportunity that she is already prepared for. Authority comes because a church or organization gives her institutional power attached to a leadership role.

Because of these dynamics, there is some variability in the extent of a woman's authority within each development phase. But typically a woman in the budding leader phase will be at leadership level 1 or 2, an emerging leader will be at level 2 or 3, and an influential leader will be at level 4 or 5 (see fig. 11.3, and see fig. 8.1 for detailed descriptions of the types of roles women have at each leadership level).

Assessing a female leader's leadership level might feel wrong. In truth, this kind of evaluation means comparing a woman's leadership level to men's and women's levels of leadership. Most female leaders are level 1, 2, or maybe 3. Ranking leadership can seem to devalue or demean a woman's leadership. Women leaders reading this have undoubtedly already ranked themselves and started thinking about other more influential leaders with more power. This train of thought is a slippery slide into discouragement. We need to redirect our thoughts about this. No woman's development or calling is comparable to another's. Measuring leadership influence should not be a value judgment. Pop culture's harsh physical beauty measurement gives people a number between 1 and 10 and places greater value on people with higher numbers. This is wrong. A female leader's value is not based on her leadership level but on her posture and faithful obedience to Jesus.

Despite the awkwardness of ranking leadership influence, it is a helpful mirror. Some women have the potential to become highly influential leaders. Those women who are called and gifted for ministry leadership have a spiritual responsibility to steward their calling well. Leadership is a weighty responsibility for which we are accountable to God (Heb. 13:17). We will answer to God for how well we stewarded the gifts and opportunities he presented us with (1 Pet. 4:10; Matt. 25:29; Luke 12:48). He invites us into his work, and the world desperately needs Jesus and his work of restoration. We must grow our leadership influence to meet this need, even though it requires difficult reflection about ourselves and our ministry context.

Not every woman in local church leadership will or even should rise to level 4 or 5, and less influential women leaders have incredible value and are needed. Women who are responsible for fewer people can engage more deeply on a relational level with those entrusted to their care. Greater authority brings greater pressures, responsibilities, and distance from those a leader ministers to, and not every woman is wired to enjoy the dynamics that come with significant authority. The church needs women leading at *every* level of leadership, and they bring tremendous value and strength in whatever capacity they lead.

If right now you are at level 1 or 2 and God has put a dream for significant ministry impact in your heart, then take a breath and remember that God's plan stretches across your entire life. You are not too late or behind. He has you in the palm of his hand, and he will continue to guide your progress for as long as you say yes to him. Don't worry about anyone else's journey.

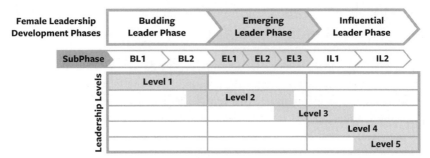

Fig. 11.3. Leadership Levels and Female Leadership Development Phases

God calls and gifts every woman uniquely, and the shape of your leadership development is custom designed for you. What he began in you he will bring to completion, as long as you are faithful to stay the course.

God calls and gifts some women for greater influence, and they must steward their calling well. If we ignore how much influence some women have to preserve other women's feelings, then women will stay stuck in positions with less influence. Only by understanding the conditions that help women expand their influence can we help them rise. This expanding influence gives a female leader ministry impact beyond her local church, where she has formal authority. Her growing influence expands into new environments and brings Jesus to many people. Her unique giftedness shapes the trajectory of her life and the types of roles she occupies.

SUMMARY

Female leadership development is a lifelong process. Clinton's leadership emergence theory provides a useful framework for tracing a woman's leadership development. A woman leader passes through three stages of development. A budding female leader discovers her leadership potential and calling in the first leadership opportunities of her journey. An emerging female leader has local church responsibilities and learns how to do the work of ministry. An influential female leader significantly expands her leadership influence and leads from who she is. As a woman is formed for ministry leadership, her leadership authority and capacity grow.

A FUTURE WHERE WOMEN
LEADERS THRIVE

W omen are shaped uniquely by cultural and social expectations, and they are influenced by female hormones.[1] Egalitarian leaders and feminists typically minimize differences between male and female leaders because complementarians and patriarchists have used gender differences as ammunition to argue that women are innately unsuitable for leadership.[2] Studies largely agree that men and women are far more alike than they are different.[3] As a result, men and women receive identical leadership training and supports in typical egalitarian environments. As mentioned in the introduction, however, this approach has not resulted in equal outcomes for male and female leaders—in numbers or in influence. As Deborah Tannen observes, when we pretend that men and women are the same, and that they must be formed the same way, women lose.[4] The existing learning resources, supports, and training for leaders have largely been designed by men, for men. As a result, even those with the best intentions can miss the key development needs for women leaders. Because their theological position welcomes women

1. Valian, *Why So Slow?*, 80–81; TenElshof, "Psychological Evidence of Gender Differentiation," 233.
2. Eagly and Johannesen-Schmidt, "Leadership Styles of Women and Men," 782; Kay and Shipman, "Confidence Gap"; Tannen, *You Just Don't Understand*, 17.
3. Valian, *Why So Slow?*, 81; Tinsley and Ely, "What Most People Get Wrong about Men and Women," 116.
4. Tannen, *You Just Don't Understand*, 16.

into leadership, egalitarian male leaders often do not recognize the problem revealed by a disparity in outcomes. If approaching male and female leadership development identically has not produced identical results for each gender, then it stands to reason that different approaches are needed.

FEMALE LEADER TRAINING

One reason for the disparity that has been overlooked is a need for female-specific training. This need has been recognized by business leaders but not yet by the church.[5] This is not to say that women are inherently inferior and need additional training that men do not; women often have intuitive strengths for leadership that men may need additional training to develop, such as collaboration and flexibility.[6] Social environments create different expectations for the genders that need to be noted and accommodated for in leadership training.

Because men have been the primary focus of leadership development, women's unique training needs historically have been overlooked. For example, men typically use "report-talk," while women use "rapport-talk," which means that women are less likely to speak up in an executive meeting where men are trying to dominate one another in conversation, and they are less likely to naturally develop public-speaking skills for preaching or other valuable leadership communication skills.[7] Women may need more in-depth public-speaking training than male leaders.

This study found that public communication is a female-specific leadership training need. Existing seminary training for preachers tends to focus on content development and ideas (theology, sermon structure, and exegesis) rather than practical public-speaking skills (projecting, pacing, vocal control). This may well reflect training that has been designed for male leaders. If men are socialized to excel in report-talk, then they may be able to intuitively grasp public-speaking skills more easily than women.

Leadership training for female church leaders also needs to address issues of identity, confidence, and risk-taking. These issues may affect men as well but are not typically focal points in leadership training. Training also needs to deal with emotional intelligence, including self-awareness, self-regulation, motivation, empathy, and social skills. Training should help women process their sense of calling with a theological understanding of the role of women in church leadership. Despite a lifetime in egalitarian churches, I have never

5. Hopkins et al., "Women's Leadership Development," 349.
6. Klenke, *Women and Leadership*, 132.
7. Tannen, *You Just Don't Understand*, 77, 88–89.

heard a sermon explaining egalitarian theology in a Sunday service. Training should cover home life and how to develop egalitarian husband-wife relationships that empower female leaders as well as the importance of and strategies for developing leadership relationships with mentors, mentees, and peers.

A VISION FOR WOMEN LEADERS AS FULL MINISTRY PARTNERS IN THE CHURCH

We need women as full partners with men in spreading the gospel, both as image bearers and as mission bearers. Where men and women partner in ministry leadership, the church is strengthened and grows. The church is how Jesus embodies himself in the world today, and it is the body the Holy Spirit calls us to. We need the ministry leadership and teaching gifts of women focused on building the church. The church loses its strength and reach when women leaders who can't flourish in the church focus their gifts instead on business, academia, nonprofits, or even parachurch ministry. While these are often good causes, they are not the institution that Jesus established for himself.

Despite the resistance to women leaders in the church, this is a time of awakening. We are witnessing important moments, like Saddleback Church's decision to support the pastoral ministry of female teaching pastor Stacie Wood at the cost of being disfellowshipped by their denomination.[8] Increasingly, movements are resourcing women pastors like never before. We need more brave women—like Iresha Hilliard, Tara Beth Leach, Aimee Semple McPherson, and Maria Woodworth-Etter—to pioneer and pastor large churches. We need women in executive roles in denominations, speaking into the patterns of mission and church health, like Ally Cawthorn (Australian Christian Churches), Donna Barrett (Assemblies of God), and Tammy Dunahoo (Foursquare).

Wherever we are located inside the church, we can do something to make this vision a reality. We are standing before not insurmountable barriers but a doorway of opportunity. If we have the prophetic imagination to recognize what God has in mind for male-female partnership in the church and take the strategic steps forward to bring that vision into being, we can see the church thriving in a brand-new way within a generation.

Recommendations for Women Leaders

If you are a woman with leadership gifts and a ministry calling and just starting your leadership journey, you might feel a little bit overwhelmed by

8. Bharath and Smith, "Saddleback Church Doubles Down."

all the factors that affect your leadership progress—especially the things you cannot control. Remember that God is the one sovereignly guiding your development and can be trusted with your future. What is the next faithful step you can take? Start by thinking holistically about your journey.

Which of the seven aspects of development have you paid attention to, and which might need more attention? (The female leadership assessment in chapter 2 will help you think about this.) Don't allow yourself to get frustrated about areas in which you still need to grow. This is the journey of your entire lifetime—you have time! Jesus is not disappointed with your progress; he is cheering you on. Instead of beating yourself up about inadequacies, use the information as a catalyst to develop strategies for focusing on needed development. Asking trusted leaders who know you well about blind spots can also provide you with some growth insights.

This book provides an introduction to egalitarian theology. If you read about egalitarian theology for the first time in this book, keep going! Learning more about egalitarian theology will help you process God's gifts and calling on your life and provide you with confidence in your ministry. Authors like Scot McKnight, Lucy Peppiatt, Kevin Giles, and Craig Keener and many articles at Christian Biblical Equality can provide valuable ideas to think and pray about.[9] It's so important to take time to ask God about these theological questions. Our desire to lead in the church must flow out of our love for Jesus. We love Jesus, and Jesus loves the church. To love Jesus is to love those whom he loves—the church.

The big question for some of you will be this: My church is complementarian, so what should I do now? The answer is, it depends. Many women have been able to create flourishing ministry to other women. Tara Beth Leach, who spent years as a female megachurch pastor, notes that often women's ministry thrives in churches where women are not released into leadership or teaching and preaching ministry.[10] If you feel fully released into your unique gifts and calling, then maybe you are where you need to be. But if you feel suffocated and limited or ignored and shut down, maybe you need to think deeply about the future. Are you able where you are to be faithful to what Jesus is asking you to do and what he put you on the planet to do? If the answer is no, then, as Jesus said, shake the dust off your feet and move on. Go to where your message and your leadership are received (Matt. 10:14).

If you are married, before you take any steps forward, have a series of vulnerable conversations with your husband. Have you thought together about

---

9. See https://www.cbeinternational.org.
10. Leach, *Emboldened*, 99.

your partnership in ministry and how it might differ from your partnership in life? What would the implications be for your spouse if your leadership leveled up? Having these conversations early on can prevent resentment and surprises later if your spouse's marital expectations are not met. Tell him the dreams in your heart for ministry leadership. As you both consider your gifts and callings in the church, explore what model for leadership partnership might best support you both as you walk in obedience to Jesus.

Have a conversation with your pastor about what kinds of leadership are needed in your church. Then put up your hand and volunteer for these opportunities. Or if your pastor asks you to volunteer, say yes. It's so easy to talk ourselves out of any opportunity that comes our way. There are a million reasons why saying yes is a bad idea: it's not the right timing, we don't have the right skill set, we are afraid we will fail at something that matters so much. Don't overthink it. Just say yes and figure out the details later. Instead of thinking about all the ways you could fail, think about what you can do to succeed.

If you want to be hired by your church, make sure you are volunteering in a significant way. The pathway to local church ministry is often not through more seminary education. Don't get me wrong—seminary education is an incredibly valuable way to grow in knowledge and spiritual formation and develop ministry skills. But seminary degrees don't open doors for church leadership opportunity—relationships do. Don't wait to be hired; build your connections and influence within your church before you have an official position. Your pastors will find it easier to promote you if they know you already have the support of the people in the church you will be leading.

If you are on a church staff and feeling stuck, it might be time for a check-in with your pastor about what's next for you. Think ahead about how to approach important conversations with your supervisor about the kinds of support you need to keep going, whether that be financial help, more flexibility, or childcare help. How can you make this a win-win for your leaders? If you are granted flexibility, then you can integrate family with ministry, making both stronger.

To move from the emerging leader phase into the influential leader phase, you will need to do some key things that might make you feel uncomfortable at first. You will need to expand your relationships beyond your church. Push through the awkwardness of engaging unfamiliar networks. These relationships might feel a little bit transactional at first, but some will deepen into friendships that provide authentic emotional support. Relationships that are built around a shared mission for Jesus are just as valuable as friendships, but they will feel different, and that's okay. Don't be afraid to reach out to someone you haven't talked to in six months or a year to get their insights on a new ministry strategy.

If you aren't sure how to begin networking, here are a few strategies that can be helpful. Ask your pastor to introduce you to people. Take initiative at events that gather people in your movement and introduce yourself to people. To connect with women who are doing what you do, consider joining some of the following emerging female ministry leader networks:

- Propel (led by Christine Caine and Tara Beth Leach) offers Propel Ecclesia learning cohorts, which bring women leaders together for five months.[11] This experience is not free but can initiate relationships.
- Women Executive Pastors, or WXP, offers connection for female executive pastors for free, with an optional annual retreat to connect with other women leaders.[12]
- She Rises Circle of 12 provides a seven-month mentoring group of twelve female pastors beginning with a four-day retreat.
- Denominations and church planting networks like Stadia are increasingly offering opportunities to bring women leaders together through ministries and programs like She Starts Churches and Network of Women Ministers in the Assemblies of God.[13]

Just ten years ago, these kinds of opportunities did not exist, but today new networks and learning cohorts are popping up for female leaders and are far more accessible.

For women pastors, continuing to develop public communication skills is essential to becoming an influential leader. If you never went to Bible college or seminary, pursuing formal training can be an excellent way to deepen and improve your teaching and preaching. As painful as it is, watching videos of yourself will help you become aware of and correct bad habits in public speaking. Ask for coaching from gifted communicators. You might be more of a writer than a speaker or be more gifted at social media. Lean into that giftedness and do what you can to make it even stronger.

We need you and Jesus needs you to keep going and keep growing. Keep your heart open and free of resentments. Let go of past experiences in the church that were painful. If you have experienced trauma, get counseling, and do the hard work. The one who called you will be faithful to help you and heal you.

11. https://www.ecclesia.propelwomen.org/.
12. https://wxpastors.com/.
13. https://stadia.org/shestartschurches/; https://www.womenministers.ag.org/.

Recommendations for Learning Institutions Training Women Leaders

Christian ministry learning institutions have a responsibility to shape and steward the ministry future of the women who come for training. Regardless of a university's or seminary's official position about women in ministry leadership or what roles an institution considers women to be suitable for, these schools are responsible for cultivating the unique gifts of each woman.

Women leaders need courses to learn about the development issues faced by women in ministry, and so do men. Every male pastor has women entrusted to his care, and some of those women will be gifted for leadership. Men need to understand how to build environments where women leaders flourish and how to personally support women's leadership emergence. These courses should focus on more than just women's rights and issues of justice in the church; they should focus on giftedness.[14] Justice is important, but this issue is not about fairness, and it should not be relegated to women's studies. This is an issue dealing with the mission of God, egalitarian missiology, and vocational formation for women, which are aspects of practical theology. When women thrive in their leadership calling as full partners in ministry, the kingdom of God thrives, and male leaders are healthier.

Women preachers have unique issues to navigate, and these should be addressed in homiletics course content. We need to train gifted women preachers and teachers, bearing in mind their unique bodies, experiences, and voices. Male pastors need to understand these issues as well so that they can help the women preachers and teachers developing in their ministries.

Practical theology courses should teach egalitarian theology and explain complementarian theology. They should not be electives. Men and women need to wrestle with aspects of these theologies in safe learning environments. Pastors, whether they are male or female, need to be equipped for conversations about women in leadership, a hot-button issue that has become polarized and politicized in a way that it should not be.

Recommendations for Local Churches Raising Women Leaders

If you are a local church leader and you want women leaders in your church but haven't been able to make any significant progress in this regard, I hope you are encouraged and hopeful after reading this book. It is possible to build leadership environments where women leaders thrive, and not only is it possible, but it has happened. Sharing the following ideas with the pastors

14. Leach, *Emboldened*, 131.

and leaders on your team could be a catalyst for moving things forward in your church.

Reflecting on several aspects of your church culture is an important first step. The first consideration is your theology. How well has your team shaped and articulated theological ideas about women in ministry leadership? Does your denomination have a position paper about this topic? So often in egalitarian church environments, women are leading not because the church has a theological conviction about women leaders. They are leading because the church has practical needs and women leaders are the most efficient and available solution. For women leaders to emerge and grow in your church, they need a spiritual reason to use their leadership gifts in their church. Regularly teaching egalitarian theology to your church plants the seeds of vision in young women, presenting the good news that God wants to partner with them in his mission and that he has put the gifts he needs in each of them. Egalitarian theology gives women confidence. Even when they feel rejected or the weight of failure, they know that God himself cheers on their leadership.

Consider next how you identify potential leaders in your context. What reveals potential? Instead of writing off young women who might leave your church to get married or leave a ministry position when they have a baby, consider how you can cultivate them right now. Honor women for their potential, not just for their achievements. Look for women who have been in leadership environments, hearing conversations about leadership decisions and strategy. They are probably not in the places you typically start looking for potential leaders. They aren't in Bible college, they are probably not your youth pastor, and they aren't shadowing your assistant pastor. Does one of your male pastors have a wife who carries more than her fair share of the ministry load? Is your female personal assistant or administrative assistant capable of leading? Are you willing to be inconvenienced by training a new assistant so that she can step into a leadership calling? Do you have a female children's pastor who happens to be an excellent preacher and should move into an executive leadership role? Also consider women who are leading in the corporate world. Is God calling a woman out of business and into ministry leadership? Instead of assuming that she will not abandon her career, perhaps have a conversation and ask her. You might not be able to offer the same kind of money she is receiving now, but you can offer her a life of purpose and perhaps flexible hours and location. She might just be waiting for you to ask.

Now consider your culture around male-female partnership and training. Does your church have well-defined male-female boundaries? Without a clear framework and encouragement, male pastors will hesitate to mentor women. Consider how the leaders connect relationally and design relationship-building activities women can participate in. Instead of heading for the golf course or the football game, have lunch together or take a team walk. One male pastor with many women leaders on his team told me that he goes to the nail spa with these women and gets a pedicure to connect with them. Don't insist on spouses coming along but invite them.

Women are increasingly stepping into administrative and management roles in local churches, but God also calls women to pastor. Give women spiritual leadership roles, not just coordinating roles. Look for women leaders who are well respected and start developing their preaching and teaching gifts. Small opportunities are not insignificant and can be valuable training ground. These small opportunities might be leading a staff chapel or a volunteer training. They might be leading a prayer in a worship service or closing a service. Receiving feedback and opportunities at regular intervals is how women grow. Then consider the preaching roster. If women leaders do not have consistent opportunities to preach, their latent skills will not emerge. Preaching is like a muscle—it must be exercised to grow.

Growing leaders is slow work. You can't rush it because it's not your work—it's God's. All you can do is tend the soil, water it, and adjust the growing conditions. We cultivate, but God grows. So be patient and ask the Holy Spirit to help you see where he is growing women for leadership.

Recommendations for Denominations Empowering Women Leaders

In 2019 the Foursquare Church bypassed its leader-heir-apparent, general superintendent Tammy Dunahoo, and instead elected another man as president.[15] A denomination founded by a woman rejected the natural order, which would have given it the second woman leader in its history. The Assemblies of God USA elected the first woman in its history, Donna Barrett, to the executive leadership team in 2018. And yet these denominations have been perhaps the most overtly egalitarian in the history of the church.

Most efforts within denominations to cultivate women leaders are focused on ordination. The problem with this is that ordination doesn't necessarily create opportunity to lead. In the Assemblies of God, far more women are ordained (validated) to do ministry than are occupying leadership positions. Duke University maintains an ongoing study of 5,333 US churches, regularly surveying them since 1998.[16] In 2019 the study unsurprisingly found that among participating churches, women senior clergy are a significant minority in most denominations (see table 8).

15. Payne, "Why Foursquare's Female Leaders Have It Harder Today."
16. National Congregations Study, "Congregations in 21st Century America," 2.

The number of women pastoring churches has been rising slowly but steadily in all movements during the past twenty years. However, women are pastoring smaller churches, and so the percentage of individuals that women are pastoring relative to their male colleagues is much smaller.[17] A recent study by Lifeway surveyed one thousand Protestant pastors and found that the smaller a congregation is, the more likely it is to be open to a female senior pastor. Sixty-six percent of congregations smaller than 50 members were open to a female senior pastor, while just 41 percent of congregations larger than 250 members were open to a female senior pastor.[18] There are likely multiple reasons for this, but women tend to be given higher-risk leadership assignments in congregations with fewer people and financial resources—the glass cliff syndrome.[19] The opportunities women have to pastor tend to be in small, struggling, rural churches. In these places, salaries and budgets are very low, which may require bivocational ministry. Rural culture adds an additional degree of difficulty for a woman pastoring because these places tend to be conservative areas with traditional views about gender roles. If the locals do not view women as leaders, then a woman will have a much more difficult time earning their trust and respect.

TABLE 8. Percentages of Women as Senior Clergy in Denominations in 2019

Denomination	Percentage of Women as Senior Clergy
Baptist	0.4%
Methodist	19.4%
Lutheran	17%
Presbyterian/Reformed	33.7%
Pentecostal	16.7%
Episcopal	43.8%

Episcopalians and Presbyterians reported the largest percentages of female senior pastors in the Lifeway study. Notably, even denominations with a theologically egalitarian view of women pastors do not come close to a full representation of women, which would be women occupying half of the senior leadership roles. Other studies paint an even bleaker picture for women leaders. In 2017 Barna reported that just 9 percent of pastors were women.[20]

Denominations looking to grow their corpus of female pastors should consider a few key initiatives. Foursquare made the decision a few years ago to end their denominational women's ministry. They realized that their most

17. Association of Religion Data Archives, "Explore the National Congregations Study Data."
18. Earls, "Leadership Roles of Women Divide Protestant Denominations."
19. Cole, *Developing Female Leaders*, 52–53.
20. Barna Group, *State of Pastors*, 12.

capable female leaders were expending their energy and giftedness in women's ministry rather than the whole church. Ending women's ministry resulted in more Foursquare women getting ordained. This is an interesting step, but it is just a step.

Beyond ordination, women pastors need opportunity. Many more women are credentialed as ministers than are active in pastoral ministry roles. Egalitarian denominations have focused on ordination of women over initiatives that create opportunities for them to lead. Denominations have well-established traditions and policies that govern local church autonomy. But denominations with more centralized authority can be more intentional about sharing leadership opportunities with women. If your movement has a centralized authority structure, then this hierarchy can be a trellis on which women can grow. If authority is decentralized, then this is trickier. Denominational leaders can encourage local churches to consider ordained women for their open pastorates. Often churches with no pastors are looking to be led by their denomination in their search for a new pastor. In the Assemblies of God, district leaders can appoint female pastors to district-affiliated churches.

Creating and funding a church planting initiative for women church planters can be an excellent way to create new opportunity. Women pastors who plant churches can build a culture where women and men thrive in ministry from the very beginning. The church planting group Stadia established an initiative to support women in church planting called She Starts Churches.[21] Sending women planters to places where local culture is going to be more favorable toward women leaders is one of the keys to this kind of initiative's success.

Consider how women leaders connect with others in your movement. Do you have networks of female leaders? This may be low-hanging fruit for change. What would an initiative to connect ordained women with women working toward ordination look like? If you consider creating cohorts of women, then organizing them by their phase of development will make this a much richer experience. Budding female leaders may find themselves out of their depth in conversations with influential leaders. Influential female leaders will experience a gathering with emerging leaders as an output of energy and involuntary mentoring rather than a life-giving meeting with women "who just get me." Needs assessments are critical for grouping women leaders appropriately. Women leaders at each phase of development have different learning needs, and curriculum content should be matched to those needs to maximize effectiveness. Having cohorts of women pastors who work together to grow

---

21. https://stadia.org/shestartschurches/.

their churches could be incredibly valuable. This cohort model reflects Debra Meyerson's "tempered radical" approach, which looks first to address change that can be done easily without significant, confrontational disruption.[22]

Women pastors need more than opportunity; they also need resources and strategies for growing their churches. If a woman pastor is given a rural church or one in need of revitalization, her denomination should consider providing financial support for the first three years. Women pastors often need a way to fund their pastoral ministry in order for it to survive. Women leaders are increasingly pursuing nonprofit work and other types of parachurch home missions efforts so that they can fundraise for their ministry. But if they have to work a job while they pastor, their church will stay small. Intentionally putting church planting, home missions, leadership development, or church revitalization budget percentages toward women can help empower growth. Financial support can look like a denominational program that funds childcare needs for female pastors. Often, local churches are financially underequipped to support childcare needs. Denominations can also fund and provide leadership coaches, formal and nonformal ministry training, and mentorship programs for women pastors. Denominations need defined strategies to grow women pastors' churches from small churches to midsize churches to large churches.

Denominational involvement doesn't have to begin at ordination. Denominations can cultivate pipelines of female leaders within their local churches by providing programs and patterns for female leadership development. This begins with training male pastors to look for potential female pastors and to cultivate them. The capacity of female leaders being ordained is shaped by their local church experiences. A female pastor who grew up in a small church will likely lead a small church, unless she is provided an apprenticeship opportunity in a larger church environment. Exposure to new environments is one of the most valuable learning experiences a movement can provide to a female leader.

TELLING THE STORY OF WOMEN PASTORS

We need to tell the stories of women leading to inspire our collective imagination. This requires looking for women leading and their unique fruit and then elevating their stories—in publications, in social media, on screens, and on platforms at national conferences. Remarkable women *are* doing remarkable things in ministry leadership, and by placing value on these stories and

---

22. Meyerson, "Radical Change, the Quiet Way."

spreading them far and wide, we can change cultural biases and assumptions about women leaders in local churches.

In no way am I diminishing the value of small churches or small-church pastors. But the fact is that church leaders who pastor more people can make a broader impact. More people resources means that the church can do more to help others. More financial resources change how a female leader can engage and serve her local community. More people sharing the gospel means that more people hear the gospel. I'm also not glorifying small churches as a superior type of ministry because that's where we most commonly find women pastoring. We don't have to devalue any existing model of Christian ministry to place value on women leaders. We need women in all types of pastoral ministries. We need women pastoring micro-churches, small traditional churches, rural churches with steeples, urban storefront churches, suburban sprawling megachurches, international multilingual churches, church plants, nontraditional churches that meet in bars, churches focused on justice, and churches focused on evangelism—churches of all worship styles, races, ethnicities, passions, and ages! We need women in church multiplication and mission. We need women pastoring in all types of churches, and we can be guaranteed that when they are, they will break the old molds and innovate new ways of doing and being the body of Christ.

Soli deo gloria.

BIBLIOGRAPHY

Adeney, Frances S. *Women and Christian Mission: Ways of Knowing and Doing Theology.* Eugene, OR: Pickwick, 2015.

"Assemblies of God 16 Fundamental Truths." Assemblies of God. Accessed August 11, 2023. https://ag.org/Beliefs/Statement-of-Fundamental-Truths.

Association of Religious Data Archives. "Explore the National Congregations Study Data: Denominational Affiliation by Gender of Head or Senior Clergyperson." Accessed January 13, 2023. https://www.thearda.com/ncs/ncs2018/dencode3_clergsex.asp.

Backes, Beth. "#ChurchToo." *Influence Magazine*, May 30, 2018. https://influencemagazine.com/practice/churchtoo.

Barna Group. *The State of Pastors: How Today's Faith Leaders Are Navigating Life and Leadership in an Age of Complexity.* Ventura, CA: Barna Group and Pepperdine University, 2017.

Barrett, Donna. "Healthy Workplace Boundaries in a #MeToo Era." *Influence Magazine*, August 15, 2018. https://influencemagazine.com/Practice/Healthy-Workplace-Boundaries-in-a--MeToo-Era.

Barsh, Joanna, and Lareina Lee. "Unlocking the Full Potential of Women in the US Economy." Genius. Accessed March 30, 2019. https://genius.com/Joanna-barsh-unlocking-the-full-potential-of-women-in-the-us-economy-annotated.

Bartchy, S. Scott. "Undermining Ancient Patriarchy: The Apostle Paul's Vision of a Society of Siblings." *Biblical Theology Bulletin: Journal of Bible and Culture* 29, no. 2 (May 1999): 68–78. https://doi.org/10.1177/014610799902900203.

Barton, Ruth Haley. *Equal to the Task: Men and Women in Partnership.* Downers Grove, IL: InterVarsity, 1998. Kindle.

Baxter, Judith. *The Language of Female Leadership.* New York: Palgrave Macmillan, 2010.

Beach, Nancy. *Gifted to Lead: The Art of Leading as a Woman in the Church.* Grand Rapids: Zondervan, 2008.

Beaty, Katelyn. *Celebrities for Jesus: How Personas, Platforms, and Profits Are Hurting the Church*. Grand Rapids: Brazos, 2022.

Bennhold, Katrin. "Another Side of #MeToo: Male Managers Fearful of Mentoring Women." *New York Times*, January 27, 2019, sec. World. https://www.nytimes.com /2019/01/27/world/europe/metoo-backlash-gender-equality-davos-men.html.

Bergvall, Victoria L. "Toward a Comprehensive Theory of Language and Gender." *Language in Society* 28, no. 2 (1999): 273–93.

Bharath, Deepa, and Peter Smith. "Saddleback Church Doubles Down on Support for Female Pastors." *Religion News Service*, March 1, 2023. http://religionnews.com/2023 /03/01/saddleback-church-doubles-down-on-support-for-female-pastors/.

Bonem, Mike, and Roger Patterson. *Leading from the Second Chair: Serving Your Church, Fulfilling Your Role, and Realizing Your Dreams*. Minneapolis: Fortress, 2005.

Bosch, David J. *Transforming Mission: Paradigm Shifts in Theology of Mission*. American Society of Missiology Series. Maryknoll, NY: Orbis Books, 2011.

Bradberry, Travis, and Jean Greaves. *Emotional Intelligence 2.0*. San Diego: TalentSmart, 2009.

Briggs, Megan. "Barna Study: 3 Times More Female Pastors Compared to 25 Years Ago." *ChurchLeaders*, February 28, 2017. https://churchleaders.com/news/299915-barna -study-3-times-female-pastors-compared-25-years-ago.html.

Brubaker, Timothy. "Spirit-Led Followers: Rethinking Transformational Leadership Theory." *Evangelical Missions Quarterly* 49, no. 2 (April 2013): 138–45.

Byrnes, James P., David C. Miller, and William D. Schafer. "Gender Differences in Risk Taking: A Meta-Analysis." *Psychological Bulletin* 125, no. 3 (May 1999): 367–83. https:// doi.org/10.1037/0033-2909.125.3.367.

Cadsby, C. Bram, and Elizabeth Maynes. "Gender, Risk Aversion and the Drawing Power of Equilibrium in an Experimental Corporate Takeover Game." *Journal of Economic Behavior & Organization* 56 (2005): 39–59.

Catalyst. "The Double-Bind Dilemma for Women in Leadership: Damned If You Do, Doomed If You Don't." New York: Catalyst, 2007.

Catford, Cheryl. "Women's Experiences: Challenges for Female Leaders in Pentecostal Contexts." In *Raising Women Leaders: Perspectives on Liberating Women in Pentecostal and Charismatic Contexts*, edited by Shane Clifton and Jacqueline Grey, loc. 442–1049 of 8092. Australasian Pentecostal Studies Supplementary Series Book 3. Parramatta, NSW: Australasian Pentecostal Studies, 2009. Kindle.

Clinton, J. Robert. *Leadership Emergence Theory: A Self-Study Manual for Analyzing the Development of a Christian Leader*. Altadena, CA: Barnabas Publishers, 1989.

———. *Leadership Training Models*. Altadena, CA: Barnabas Publishers, 1984.

———. *The Making of a Leader: Recognizing the Lessons and Stages of Leadership Development*. Colorado Springs: NavPress, 2012.

———. "Social Base Processing: Environments Out of Which a Leader Works." The Research and Resources of Bobby Clinton. Updated 2019. https://bobbyclinton.com /store/clinton-gold/social-base-processing/.

Clinton, J. Robert, and Richard W. Clinton. *Unlocking Your Giftedness: What Leaders Need to Know to Develop Themselves and Others.* Altadena, CA: Barnabas Publishers, 1993.

Cole, Kadi. *Developing Female Leaders: Navigate the Minefields and Release the Potential of Women in Your Church.* Nashville: Thomas Nelson, 2019.

Cormode, Scott. *The Innovative Church: How Leaders and Their Congregations Can Adapt in an Ever-Changing World.* Grand Rapids: Baker Academic, 2020.

Crabtree, Loralie. "Women Ministers in the Assemblies of God." PowerPoint presentation, Northpoint Bible College and Seminary, Haverhill, MA, March 2021. https://northpoint.edu/wp-content/uploads/2021/03/3.24.21-Rev.-Loralie-Crabtree-Presentation.pdf.

Crouch, Andy. *Playing God: Redeeming the Gift of Power.* Downers Grove, IL: IVP Books, 2013.

Cuss, Steve. *Managing Leadership Anxiety: Yours and Theirs.* Nashville: Thomas Nelson, 2019.

Dixon, Rob. *Together in Ministry: Women and Men in Flourishing Partnerships.* Downers Grove, IL: IVP Academic, 2021.

Du Mez, Kristin Kobes. *Jesus and John Wayne: How White Evangelicals Corrupted a Faith and Fractured a Nation.* New York: Liveright, 2020.

Eagly, Alice H., and Linda A. Carli. *Through the Labyrinth: The Truth about How Women Become Leaders.* Boston: Harvard Business School Press, 2007.

Eagly, Alice H., and Mary C. Johannesen-Schmidt. "The Leadership Styles of Women and Men." *Journal of Social Issues* 57, no. 4 (December 2001): 781–97.

Eagly, Alice H., and Blair T. Johnson. "Gender and Leadership Style: A Meta-Analysis." *Psychological Bulletin* 108, no. 2 (September 1990): 233–56. https://doi.org/10.1037/0033-2909.108.2.233.

Earls, Aaron. "Leadership Roles of Women Divide Protestant Denominations." Lifeway Research, August 23, 2022. https://research.lifeway.com/2022/08/23/leadership-roles-of-women-divide-protestant-denominations/.

Edwards, Sue, Kelley Matthews, and Henry J. Rogers. *Mixed Ministry: Working Together as Brothers and Sisters in an Oversexed Society.* Grand Rapids: Kregel, 2008. Kindle.

Ely, Robin J., Herminia Ibarra, and Deborah M. Kolb. "Taking Gender into Account: Theory and Design for Women's Leadership Development Programs." *Academy of Management Learning & Education* 10, no. 3 (September 2011): 474–93.

Emmert, Ashley. "The State of Female Pastors." WomenLeaders.com, October 15, 2015. https://www.christianitytoday.com/women-leaders/2015/october/state-of-female-pastors.html.

Equal Measures 2030. *Harnessing the Power of Data for Gender Equality: Introducing the 2019 EM2030 SDG Gender Index.* https://equalmeasures2030.org/2019-sdg-gender-index-report/.

Fels, Anna. *Necessary Dreams: Ambition in Women's Changing Lives.* New York: Anchor Books, 2004.

Glanville, Elizabeth Loutrel. "Leadership Development for Women in Christian Ministry." PhD diss., Fuller Theological Seminary, 2000.

Glasser, Arthur F., Charles E. Van Engen, and Shawn B. Redford. *Announcing the Kingdom: The Story of God's Mission in the Bible*. Grand Rapids: Baker Academic, 2003.

Goleman, Daniel, Richard E. Boyatzis, and Annie McKee. *Primal Leadership: Unleashing the Power of Emotional Intelligence*. Boston: Harvard Business Review Press, 2013.

Goman, Carol Kinsey. "Leadership Presence: What Women Can and Cannot Control." *Leadership Excellence* (April 2018): 14–18.

Grenz, Stanley J., and Denise Muir Kjesbo. *Women in the Church: A Biblical Theology of Women in Ministry*. Downers Grove, IL: InterVarsity, 1995. Kindle.

Gross, Nancy Lammers. *Women's Voices and the Practice of Preaching*. Grand Rapids: Eerdmans, 2017. Kindle.

Haddad, Mimi. "Tracking Errors in Bible Translation." *CBE International*, December 5, 2017. https://www.cbeinternational.org/resource/tracking-errors-bible-translation/.

Hammond, Sue Annis. *The Thin Book of Appreciative Inquiry*. 3rd ed. Bend, OR: Thin Book Publishing, 2013.

Hollands, Jean. *Same Game, Different Rules: How to Get Ahead without Being a Bully Broad, Ice Queen, or "Ms. Understood."* New York: McGraw Hill, 2002.

Hollywood, Kathryn Grace. "A Comparative Study of Feminine Dimensions of Religious Leadership Development." PhD diss., Fordham University, 1990.

Holmes, Janet. "Women's Talk in Public Contexts." *Discourse and Society* 3, no. 2 (1992): 131–50.

Holstein, James A., and Jaber F. Gubrium. *The Active Interview*. Vol. 37. Qualitative Research Methods. Thousand Oaks, CA: SAGE Publications, 1995.

Hopkins, Margaret M., Deborah A. O'Neil, Angela Passarelli, and Diana Bilimoria. "Women's Leadership Development Strategic Practices for Women and Organizations." *Consulting Psychology Journal: Practice and Research* 60, no. 4 (December 2008): 348–65. https://doi.org/10.1037/a0014093.

Howell, Susan Harris. *Buried Talents: Overcoming Gendered Socialization to Answer God's Call*. Downers Grove, IL: InterVarsity, 2022.

"How Women & Men Are Feeling After #MeToo | #MentorHer." Lean In, 2018. https://leanin.org/sexual-harassment-backlash-survey-results.

Hull, Gretchen Gaebelein. *Equal to Serve: Women and Men Working Together Revealing the Gospel*. Grand Rapids: Baker, 1998.

Ibarra, Herminia, Robin J. Ely, and Deborah M. Kolb. "Women Rising: The Unseen Barriers." *Harvard Business Review*, September 1, 2013. https://hbr.org/2013/09/women-rising-the-unseen-barriers.

Ibarra, Herminia, and Otilia Obodaru. "Women and the Vision Thing." *Harvard Business Review*, January 1, 2009. https://hbr.org/2009/01/women-and-the-vision-thing.

James, Carolyn Custis. *Half the Church: Recapturing God's Global Vision for Women*. Grand Rapids: Zondervan, 2010.

———. *Malestrom: Manhood Swept into the Currents of a Changing World*. Grand Rapids: Zondervan, 2015.

Kay, Katty, and Claire Shipman. "The Confidence Gap: Evidence Shows That Women Are Less Self-Assured Than Men—and That to Succeed, Confidence Matters as Much as Competence. Here's Why, and What to Do about It." *The Atlantic*, May 2014. https://www.theatlantic.com/magazine/archive/2014/05/the-confidence-gap/359815/.

Kelley, Rhonda Harrington, and Monica Rose Brennan. *Talking Is a Gift: Communication Skills for Women*. Nashville: B&H, 2014.

Klenke, Karin. *Women and Leadership: A Contextual Perspective*. New York: Springer Publishing, 1996.

Krivkovich, Alexis, Irina Starikova, Kelsey Robinson, Rachel Valentino, and Lareina Yee. "Women in the Workplace 2022." McKinsey & Company and Lean In. October 18, 2022. https://www.mckinsey.com/featured-insights/diversity-and-inclusion/women-in-the-workplace-archive#section-header-2022.

Leach, Tara Beth. *Emboldened: A Vision for Empowering Women in Ministry*. Downers Grove, IL: IVP Books, 2017.

Ledbetter, Bernice, and Michael Kinsman. "Ensuring #MeToo Movement Advances Diversity in Leadership." *Workforce*, February 28, 2019. https://www.workforce.com/2019/02/28/ensuring-metoo-movement-advances-diversity-in-leadership/.

Lederleitner, Mary. *Women in God's Mission: Accepting the Invitation to Serve and Lead*. Downers Grove, IL: InterVarsity, 2018.

Lee-Barnewall, Michelle. *Neither Complementarian nor Egalitarian: A Kingdom Corrective to the Evangelical Gender Debate*. Grand Rapids: Baker Academic, 2016.

Lingenfelter, Sherwood G. *Transforming Culture: A Challenge for Christian Mission*. 2nd ed. Grand Rapids: Baker Academic, 1998.

Maddox, Marion. "Rise Up Warrior Princess Daughters: Is Evangelical Women's Submission a Mere Fairy Tale?" *Journal of Feminist Studies in Religion* 29, no. 1 (2013): 9–26.

Majola, Aloo. "The Power of Bible Translation." *Priscilla Papers* 33, no. 2 (April 26, 2019). https://www.cbeinternational.org/resource/power-bible-translation/.

Maros, Susan L. *Calling in Context: Social Location and Vocational Formation*. Downers Grove, IL: IVP Academic, 2022.

Martin, Bernice. "The Pentecostal Gender Paradox: A Cautionary Tale for the Sociology of Religion." In *The Blackwell Companion to Sociology of Religion*, edited by Richard K. Fenn, 52–66. Malden, MA: Blackwell, 2003.

McClellan, Hannah. "Assemblies of God Ordains Record Number of Women." *Christianity Today*, August 5, 2022. https://www.christianitytoday.com/news/2022/august/assemblies-god-ordain-women-record.html.

McConnell, Douglas. *Cultural Insights for Christian Leaders: New Directions for Organizations Serving God's Mission*. Grand Rapids: Baker Academic, 2018. Kindle.

McKinney, Lois. "Leadership: Key to the Growth of the Church." In *Discipling through Theological Education by Extension: A Fresh Approach to Theological Education in the 1980s*, edited by Virgil Gerber, 179–91. Chicago: Moody, 1980.

McKnight, Scot. "Women Ministering." *E-Quality, a Publication of Christians for Biblical Equality International* 7, no. 3 (Autumn 2008): 5–7.

McLachlan, Stacey. "Instagram Demographics in 2022: Most Important User Stats for Marketers." *Social Media Marketing & Management Dashboard*, March 24, 2022. https://blog.hootsuite.com/instagram-demographics/.

Meyerson, Debra. "Radical Change, the Quiet Way." *Harvard Business Review*, October 1, 2001. https://hbr.org/2001/10/radical-change-the-quiet-way.

Mickelsen, Alvera, ed. "Empowering Women and Men to Use Their Gifts Together in Advancing the Gospel." Paper presented at the 2004 Forum for World Evangelization hosted by the Lausanne Committee for World Evangelization, Pattaya, Thailand, October 2004. https://lausanne.org/occasional-paper/empowering-women-and-men-to-use-their-gifts-together-in-advancing-the-gospel-lop-53.

Miller, Becky Castle. "Misinterpreting 'Head' Can Perpetuate Abuse." *CBE International*, December 5, 2017. https://www.cbeinternational.org/resource/misinterpreting-head-can-perpetuate-abuse/.

Miller, Elizabeth. "Women in Australian Pentecostalism: Leadership, Submission, and Feminism in Hillsong Church." *Journal for the Academic Study of Religion* 29, no. 1 (2016): 52–76. https://doi.org/10.1558/jasr.v29i1.26869.

Moe, Jennifer. "Discerning an Uphill Calling: Women's Journeys to Ministry." Master's thesis, Wheaton College Graduate School, 2009. http://www.tren.com/search.cfm?p088-0204.

Mohr, Tara Sophia. *Playing Big: Practical Wisdom for Women Who Want to Speak Up, Create, and Lead*. New York: Penguin Group, 2014.

Morgan, Anna. "Female Leaders in Egalitarian Churches: A Model for Female Ministry Leadership Development." PhD diss., Fuller Theological Seminary, 2022.

Murnen, Sarah K., Carrie Wright, and Gretchen Kaluzny. "If 'Boys Will Be Boys,' Then Girls Will Be Victims? A Meta-Analytic Review of the Research That Relates Masculine Ideology to Sexual Aggression." *Sex Roles* 46, nos. 11/12 (June 2002): 359–75.

National Congregations Study. "Congregations in 21st Century America: A Report from the National Congregations Study." Durham, NC: Duke University, 2021.

Nee, Watchman. *Spiritual Authority*. New York: Christian Fellowship Publishers, 2014.

Northouse, Peter G. *Leadership: Theory and Practice*. 7th ed. Los Angeles: SAGE Publications, 2016.

Ovans, Andrea. "How Emotional Intelligence Became a Key Leadership Skill." *Harvard Business Review*, April 28, 2015. https://hbr.org/2015/04/how-emotional-intelligence-became-a-key-leadership-skill.

Payne, Leah. *Gender and Pentecostal Revivalism: Making a Female Ministry in the Early Twentieth Century*. Edited by Amos Yong and Wolfgang Vondey. Charis: Christianity & Renewal—Interdisciplinary Studies. New York: Palgrave MacMillan, 2015.

———. "Why Foursquare's Female Leaders Have It Harder Today." *Christianity Today*, May 29, 2019. https://www.christianitytoday.com/ct/2019/may-web-only/foursquare-church-aimee-semple-mcpherson-tammy-dunahoo.html.

Peppiatt, Lucy. *Rediscovering Scripture's Vision for Women: Fresh Perspectives on Disputed Texts*. Downers Grove, IL: IVP Academic, 2019.

Prime, Jeanine. *Women "Take Care," Men "Take Charge": Stereotyping of U.S. Business Leaders Exposed*. New York: Catalyst, 2005.

Raelin, Joseph A., ed. *Leadership-as-Practice: Theory and Application*. New York: Routledge, 2016.

Raven, Bertram H. "The Bases of Power and the Power/Interaction Model of Interpersonal Influence: Bases of Power." *Analyses of Social Issues and Public Policy* 8, no. 1 (September 15, 2008): 1–22. https://doi.org/10.1111/j.1530-2415.2008.00159.x.

Reeves, Richard. "Toxic Masculinity Is a Harmful Myth. Society Is in Denial about the Problems of Boys and Men." *Big Think*, October 17, 2022. https://bigthink.com/the-present/toxic-masculinity-myth/.

Roese, Jackie. *She Can Teach: Empowering Women to Teach the Scriptures Effectively*. Eugene, OR: Wipf & Stock, 2013.

"The Role of Women in Ministry." Assemblies of God. Accessed August 11, 2023. https://ag.org/Beliefs/Position-Papers/The-Role-of-Women-in-Ministry.

Rolls, Judith A. "The Influence of Language Style and Gender on Perceptions of Leadership Potential: A Review of Relevant Literature." Paper presented at the 79th Annual Meeting of the Speech Communication Association, Miami Beach, FL, November 1993.

Roncone, Gene, and Assemblies of God District/Network Superintendents. *Female Lead Pastors: A Discussion Worth Having*. September 2021. https://penndel.org/wp-content/uploads/2021/09/Female-Lead-Pastors.pdf.

Sandberg, Sheryl, and Nell Scovell. *Lean In: Women, Work and the Will to Lead*. New York: Knopf, 2013.

Schmitt, David P. "The Truth about Sex Differences." *Psychology Today*, November 7, 2017. https://www.psychologytoday.com/articles/201711/the-truth-about-sex-differences.

Scott, Halee Gray. *Dare Mighty Things: Mapping the Challenges of Leadership for Christian Women*. Grand Rapids: Zondervan, 2014.

Shambaugh, Rebecca. *It's Not a Glass Ceiling, It's a Sticky Floor*. New York: McGraw Hill, 2008. Kindle.

Stackhouse, John G., Jr. *Partners in Christ: A Conservative Case for Egalitarianism*. Downers Grove, IL: InterVarsity, 2015.

Statham, Anne. "The Gender Model Revisited: Differences in the Management Styles of Men and Women." *Sex Roles* 16, nos. 7/8 (1987): 409–29.

Strauss, Anselm, and Juliet Corbin. *Basics of Qualitative Research: Grounded Theory Procedures and Techniques*. Newbury Park, CA: SAGE Publications, 1990.

Suby-Long, Sallie. "The Role of Transformational Learning in Women's Leadership Development." PhD diss., Capella University, 2012.

Tannen, Deborah. *You Just Don't Understand: Women and Men in Conversation*. New York: HarperCollins, 2013.

Tarr-Whelan, Linda. *Women Lead the Way: Your Guide to Stepping Up to Leadership and Changing the World*. San Francisco: Berrett-Koehler Publishers, 2009. Kindle.

TenElshof, Judith K. "Psychological Evidence of Gender Differentiation." In *Women and Men in Ministry: A Complementary Perspective*, edited by Robert L. Saucy and Judith K. TenElshof, 229–46. Chicago: Moody, 2001.

Tinsley, Catherine H., and Robin J. Ely. "What Most People Get Wrong about Men and Women: Research Shows the Sexes Aren't So Different." *Harvard Business Review*, June 2018, 114–21.

Turner, Mary Donovan, and Mary Lin Hudson. *Saved from Silence: Finding Women's Voice in Preaching*. St. Louis: Lucas Park Books, 2014.

University of Michigan Institute for Social Research. "Exactly How Much Housework Does a Husband Create?" EurekAlert! The Global Source for Science News, April 4, 2008. http://www.eurekalert.org/pub_releases/2008-04/uom-ehm040408.php.

Valian, Virginia. *Why So Slow? The Advancement of Women*. Cambridge, MA: MIT Press, 1998.

Van Leeuwen, Mary Stewart. "Opposite Sexes or Neighboring Sexes? What Do the Social Sciences Really Tell Us?" In *Women, Ministry, and the Gospel: Exploring New Paradigms*, edited by Mark Husbands and Timothy Larsen, 171–96. Downers Grove, IL: IVP Academic, 2007.

Villacorta, Wilmer G. *Tug of War: The Downward Ascent of Power*. Eugene, OR: Wipf & Stock, 2017.

Vinnicombe, Susan, and Val Singh. "Women-Only Management Training: An Essential Part of Women's Leadership Development." *Journal of Change Management* 3, no. 4 (January 31, 2003): 294–306.

Wilkerson, Robyn. *Shattering the Stained Glass Ceiling: A Coaching Strategy for Women Leaders in Ministry*. Springfield, MO: Influence Resources, 2017. Kindle.

Willard, Dallas. Foreword to *How I Changed My Mind about Women in Leadership: Compelling Stories from Prominent Evangelicals*, edited by Alan F. Johnson, 9–11. Grand Rapids: Zondervan, 2010.

———. *Renovation of the Heart: Putting on the Character of Christ*. Colorado Springs: NavPress, 2002.

Wingard, Jason. "#MeToo, Fear, and the Future of Women's Leadership." *Forbes*, March 11, 2019. https://www.forbes.com/sites/jasonwingard/2019/03/11/metoo-fear-and-the-future-of-womens-leadership/.

Yeh, Allen. "The Future of Mission Is from Everyone to Everywhere: A Look at Polycentric Missiology." *Lausanne Global Analysis* 7, no. 1 (January 2018). https://lausanne.org/content/lga/2018-01/future-mission-everyone-everywhere.

Zheng, Wei, Ronit Kark, and Alyson Meister. "How Women Manage the Gendered Norms of Leadership." *Harvard Business Review*, November 28, 2018. https://hbr.org/2018/11/how-women-manage-the-gendered-norms-of-leadership.

APPENDIX A

DISCUSSION QUESTIONS

CHAPTER 1

1. What kinds of ministry leadership roles have you seen women occupy in your context?
2. How does egalitarian theology affect your ministry environment?
3. What is your theology of marriage?
4. What kinds of opportunities for missional engagement does egalitarian theology empower?
5. What opportunities does the church have to engage within the feminist movement?

CHAPTER 2

1. Who carries responsibility for developing the potential in a female leader?
2. How does the model of female leadership development presented in this chapter impact male church leaders?
3. What kinds of challenges would a local church leadership team looking to develop women navigate?
4. How might a ministry environment that only partially limits women's leadership impede a female leader's development?
5. How much control can a woman exert over her own leadership development?

6. How might generational or cultural attitudes support or impede female leadership development and in which of the seven processes?

7. What kinds of leadership relationships might be more challenging for women to develop?

8. What are biblical examples of these seven processes at work?

CHAPTER 3

1. What has been your experience of discerning God's calling for your life?

2. What makes you hesitate to fully obey what you sense God asking?

3. What are your natural abilities, acquired skills, and spiritual gifts?

4. How have you observed spiritual authority in action?

5. What is your experience with a theology of women's roles in the church?

CHAPTER 4

1. What kinds of female leader role models have you observed in your ministry context?

2. How does your regional culture view the intersection between women and leadership?

3. What kinds of leadership risks are worth taking, and what kinds should be avoided?

4. What is the line between confidence and pride?

5. What qualities are shared by the most effective visionaries you have encountered?

CHAPTER 5

1. How can you cultivate safety in relationships that enables the kind of feedback that can bring awareness to blind spots?

2. What do you do to regulate your emotions when you are flooded by feelings?

3. How do you balance empathizing with the difficulties faced by those entrusted to your care and challenging them to grow?

4. What kinds of social cues do you watch to tune into what people around you aren't saying?

5. What is the relationship between anxiety and your ability to manage leadership relationships well?

6. What have you observed about the most authentic, emotionally intelligent leaders you know?

CHAPTER 6

1. How can you better support single women leading in your context?
2. If you are married, do you consider your marriage to be egalitarian?
3. What kinds of domestic supports are reasonable for churches to provide to a female leader as a fringe benefit?
4. What are some ethical considerations surrounding different methods of providing childcare support?
5. What are the strengths/opportunities and weaknesses/challenges of the different types of husband-wife leadership partnerships?
6. What are biblical examples of each type of husband-wife leadership partnership?

CHAPTER 7

1. What aspects of your church culture have been hindrances to women leading?
2. What aspects of your church culture are a support to women leading?
3. Are women represented at every level of leadership in your church?
4. How might you go about addressing gender discrimination in a ministry setting?
5. What are ways to facilitate sponsorship of female leaders?

CHAPTER 8

1. What are barriers women leaders face to increasing their personal and organizational power?
2. Have you observed female leaders in each of the five levels of leadership?
3. What are the benefits of women receiving leadership mentoring?
4. What are ways that you can mentor women leaders?
5. What difficulties have you observed or experienced for women leaders developing peer networks?
6. What benefits come from having a strong network of leadership peers?
7. What can you do to cultivate these important female leader relationships?

CHAPTER 9

1. What is your leadership team's culture around male-female boundaries?
2. What are your observations of Bible passages about men and women in leadership together?
3. What has been your personal experience with male-female boundaries?
4. What do you think about Matt's story? What might you do differently or adopt yourself?
5. What is your personal ethic about boundaries with people on your ministry team and in your church?

CHAPTER 10

1. Do you agree that men and women have gender-based use of language, or do you think language itself is gendered? How have you noticed these dynamics play out in your own life?
2. What aspects of interpersonal leadership conversations do you find the most challenging?
3. In what ways are women using public communication in your church?
4. What is the greatest challenge for women in public communication?
5. How do you think social media is best leveraged for ministry?

CHAPTER 11

1. In which phase of development are you?
2. What aspects of that phase do you recognize in your daily life?
3. What are the next steps for your development?
4. How can you best support the budding female leaders around you?
5. How can you best support the emerging female leaders around you?

CHAPTER 12

1. In the recommendations for female leadership training, what stood out to you as a personal need or a need of the women on your team?
2. What human flourishing do you envision being possible if the women in your church were released as full partners in ministry leadership?
3. Which recommendations resonated with you as a step you can take?

APPENDIX B

STUDY INSTRUMENTS

FEMALE INTERVIEW GUIDE

Review informed consent.

1. Please describe yourself
   - What is your full name?
   - What year were you born, and what is your age?
   - What is your current marital status?
   - Do you have children? How old are they?
   - Can you briefly describe your leadership role and your leadership influence?
2. How were these formational factors important in your leadership development? Which were most important?
   - Accepting a divine calling to ministry
   - Discovering your unique God-given giftedness and design
   - Developing your gifts and abilities
   - Receiving training and coaching from other leaders, either male or female
   - Learning how to process positive and negative feedback you received about your leadership
   - Maturing spiritually

Can you correlate any of these factors with your early leadership development or more recent development? Can you associate different factors with different seasons of influence?

3. How were these factors important for learning how to think like a leader? Which were most important?

   • Developing a leader identity (viewing yourself as a leader)

   • Understanding the need to take risks and developing the courage to take those risks

   • Gaining confidence in your own leadership abilities and decision-making skills

   • Growing in emotional intelligence (self-awareness, self-regulation, motivation, empathy, and social skills)

   Can you correlate any of these factors with your early leadership development or more recent development? Can you associate different factors with different seasons of influence?

4. How were these factors important for learning to relate to other people as a leader? Which were most important?

   • Discovering your own leadership style and being comfortable in it

   • Developing leadership presence as you relate to others

   • Learning how to negotiate with others for what you need from them

   • Developing strategic (intentional and purposeful, not just default or preferential) relationships

   • Learning to market or brand yourself and social media

   Can you correlate any of these factors with your early leadership development or more recent development? Can you associate different factors with different seasons of influence?

5. How were these factors important for learning to communicate as a leader? Which were most important?

   • Learning to use more "masculine" communication styles when communicating to men in leadership conversations (getting to the point quicker, etc.)

   • Training your physical voice to sound different from its natural style for leadership purposes (avoiding uptalking, lowering pitch)

   • Developing public speaking skills

   • Developing preaching and teaching gifts (including learning to study the Bible and theology)

- Learning how to present a compelling vision and persuading people to adopt it
- Learning how to have challenging leadership conversations (using direct vs. indirect, aggression vs. passivity, warmth/embracing vs. cool/distancing words)

    Can you correlate any of these factors with your early leadership development or more recent development? Can you associate different factors with different seasons of influence?

6. What was the role of egalitarian theology in your leadership development?

    Egalitarian theology can be applied both in the home (husbands and wives are equal in status) and in ministry (men and women are equally gifted and called by God to any kind of ministry leadership).

    - How has your understanding of egalitarian theology and 1 Tim. 2:11–15 influenced your leadership journey?

        "A woman should learn in quietness and full submission. I do not permit a woman to teach or to assume authority over a man; she must be quiet. For Adam was formed first, then Eve. And Adam was not the one deceived; it was the woman who was deceived and became a sinner. But women will be saved through childbearing—if they continue in faith, love and holiness with propriety" (1 Tim. 2:11–15).

    - How has your understanding of egalitarian theology and Ephesians 5:21–23 influenced your marriage?

        "Submit to one another out of reverence for Christ. Wives, submit yourselves to your own husbands as you do to the Lord. For the husband is the head of the wife as Christ is the head of the church, his body, of which he is the Savior" (Eph. 5:21–23).

7. How have any of these family and home dynamics affected your leadership journey? Which were most important?

    - Marrying a husband who celebrates and supports your leadership
    - Having a husband who carries equal responsibilities with your children and home and makes decisions with you instead of for you
    - Needing extra support with child-rearing (from nannies, daycare, grandparents, etc.)
    - Managing home responsibilities in addition to ministry
    - Caring for the needs of parents, adult children, and other family members

        Can you correlate any of these factors with your early leadership development or more recent development? Can you associate different factors with different seasons of influence?

8. How have these ministry expectations affected your leadership journey? Which were most important?

- Your, your family's, your pastor's, or your church's theological understanding of the role of female leadership in the church
- Expectations from others or yourself that female ministry and leadership should be for other women in a women's ministry context
- Expectations from others or yourself about what a female ministry leader should look like or dress like

   Can you correlate any of these factors with your early leadership development or more recent development? Can you associate different factors with different seasons of influence?

9. How did these relational factors affect your leadership journey? Which were most important?

- Having another leader identify leadership potential in you
- Developing strategic relational networks with other female pastors and ministry leaders both inside and outside your church
- Having mentors who spoke into your personal or leadership journey
- Having sponsors who opened doors for you
- Having role models who were examples for you
- Developing a leadership relationship with your husband (how does yours work?)
- Developing leadership partnerships or mentoring relationships with other men not your husband

   Can you correlate any of these factors with your early leadership development or more recent development? Can you associate different factors with different seasons of influence?

10. How have professional/office environmental factors affected your leadership journey? Which were most important?

- Having flexibility in office hours to be able to take care of family and children's needs
- Having the freedom to have a nonlinear ministry leadership journey that may have taken seasons off from work for childbirth or other responsibilities
- Receiving clear and direct feedback about your work and leadership from supervisors
- Receiving access to leadership opportunities within your organization or outside

- Receiving recognition for accomplishments within your organization that led to trust in your leadership
Can you correlate any of these factors with your early leadership development or more recent development? Can you associate different factors with different seasons of influence?

11. How have you handled boundaries with men?
    - What do you view as healthy leadership boundaries, and what have you implemented? Do you follow or agree with the Billy Graham rule?
    - How do you deal with sexual attraction?
    - How have you and your team navigated cross-gendered mentoring or coaching?

12. How have any of these factors been hindrances or important to your leadership journey?
    - The impact of #MeToo or #ChurchToo movement—have you been positively or negatively impacted by this?
    - Gender discrimination in ministry settings
    - Wage inequality
    - Sexual harassment or abuse from other ministry leaders
    - Difficulties obtaining cross-gendered mentoring or sponsorship
    - Difficulties developing networking relationships with male pastors
    - Theological opposition
    - Need for frequent travel or rigid ministry work environments
    - Regional cultural opposition
    Can you correlate any of these factors with your early leadership development or more recent development? Can you associate different factors with different seasons of influence?

13. What are your observations from investing in female ministry leaders?
    - What developmental factors have you noticed female leaders navigating that male leaders don't seem to deal with? What issues are unique to a female leader's developmental journey?
    - Which factors have you already processed that a younger female ministry leader probably has not yet faced?
    - How have the possibilities and expectations for developing female ministry leaders changed since your early formation years?

MALE INTERVIEW GUIDE

Review informed consent.

1. Please describe yourself
   - What is your full name?
   - What year were you born, and what is your age?
   - What is your current marital status?
   - Do you have children? How old are they?
   - Can you briefly describe your leadership role in your church and your leadership influence beyond your church? This includes your title and what and who you are responsible for leading.

2. How has your view of egalitarian theology influenced how you approach leadership development for women in your church?
   - How has your understanding of 1 Timothy 2:11–15 influenced how you position and develop women leaders in your church?
     "A woman should learn in quietness and full submission. I do not permit a woman to teach or to assume authority over a man; she must be quiet. For Adam was formed first, then Eve. And Adam was not the one deceived; it was the woman who was deceived and became a sinner. But women will be saved through childbearing—if they continue in faith, love and holiness with propriety" (1 Tim. 2:11–15).
   - How has your understanding of Ephesians 5:21–23 influenced your marriage?
     "Submit to one another out of reverence for Christ. Wives, submit yourselves to your own husbands as you do to the Lord. For the husband is the head of the wife as Christ is the head of the church, his body, of which he is the Savior" (Eph. 5:21–23).

3. Which of these factors have you observed to be important in the development of female church leaders?
   - Accepting a divine calling to ministry
   - Discovering and developing her unique God-given giftedness and design
   - Being able to receive training and coaching from other leaders, either male or female
   - Learning how to process positive and negative feedback she received about her leadership
   - Maturing spiritually

4. In what ways has learning to think like a leader been important in leadership development for women on your team?

- Developing a leader identity (viewing herself as a leader)
- Understanding the need to take risks and developing the courage to take those risks
- Gaining confidence in her own leadership abilities and decision-making skills
- Growing in emotional intelligence (self-awareness, self-regulation, motivation, empathy, and social skills)

5. In what ways has learning to relate to others as a leader been important in leadership development for women on your team?

- Discovering her leadership style and being comfortable in it
- Developing leadership presence as she relates to others
- Learning how to negotiate with others for what she needs from them
- Developing strategic (intentional and purposeful, not just default or preferential) relationships
- Learning to market or brand herself and using social media

6. In what ways has learning to communicate as a leader been important in leadership development for women on your team? Which have been the most important?

- Learning to use more stereotypically "masculine" communication styles when communicating to men in leadership conversations (getting to the point quicker, etc.)
- Training her physical voice to sound different from its natural style for leadership purposes (avoiding uptalking, lowering pitch)
- Developing public speaking skills
- Developing preaching and teaching gifts (including learning to study the Bible and theology)
- Learning how to present a compelling vision and persuading people to adopt it
- Learning how to have challenging leadership conversations (using direct vs. indirect, aggression vs. passivity, warmth/embracing vs. cool/distancing words)

7. How do family and home dynamics affect a woman's ministry leadership journey? Which are most important?

- Marrying a husband who celebrates and supports her leadership

- Having a husband who carries equal responsibilities with her children and home and makes decisions with her instead of for her
- Needing or having extra support with child-rearing (from nannies, daycare, grandparents, etc.)
- Managing home responsibilities in addition to ministry
- Caring for the needs of parents, adult children, and other family members

8. How do these types of relationships affect a female ministry leader's development? Which are most important?
   - Having another leader help her identify her leadership potential
   - Developing strategic relational networks with other female pastors and ministry leaders both inside and outside her church
   - Having mentors who spoke into her personal or leadership journey
   - Having sponsors who opened doors for her
   - Having role models who were examples for her
   - Developing a leadership relationship with her husband
   - Developing leadership partnerships or mentoring relationships with other men not her husband
   - How does your leadership partnership with your wife work?

9. How do these ministry expectations affect a female leader's development? Which are most important?
   - Her own, her family's, her pastor's, or her church's theological understanding of the role of female leadership in the church
   - Expectations that female ministry and leadership should be for other women in a women's ministry context
   - Cultural expectations about gender roles
   - Expectations about what a female ministry leader should look like or dress like

10. What values or culture does a leadership team or church staff need to embrace for female leaders to flourish? Are any of these environmental factors important?
    - Having the freedom to have a nonlinear ministry leadership journey to take seasons off from work/ministry for childbirth or other responsibilities
    - Receiving clear and direct feedback about her work and leadership from supervisors

- Having flexibility in office hours to be able to take care of family and children's needs
- Receiving access to leadership opportunities within her organization or outside
- Receiving recognition for accomplishments within her organization that led to trust in her leadership

11. How do you build healthy male-female ministry leadership relationships? What do you view as healthy cross-gender leadership boundaries and which have you implemented? Do you follow or agree with the Billy Graham rule?
    - What is your team culture around handling issues of sexual attraction?
    - How have you and your team navigated cross-gendered mentoring or coaching?
    - Has #MeToo or #ChurchToo affected the way that you and your team approach male-female leadership relationships?

12. What developmental supports or training does a female leader need that a male leader might not need? What types of challenges do women leaders deal with that men don't seem to face? Would female leaders benefit from female-specific leadership training?

FOCUS GROUP GUIDE

Review informed consent.
Things to consider:

- Feel free to respond to what others have said—agree or disagree. But be honoring of other women's experiences. Everyone's experiences and perspectives are valuable to this study.
- Don't feel like you are obligated to weigh in on every idea.
- Everyone leads in churches where women are flourishing and growing. But it doesn't mean that was always the case or is perfectly true. I am trying to understand what is working more than to understand what isn't, however.
- Think about different points of your leadership development. Were some things more important in different seasons? Are some things more important now that didn't used to be?

1. Please describe yourself
   - What is your first name?
   - What year were you born, and what is your age?
   - What is your current marital status?
   - Do you have children? How old are they?
   - Can you briefly describe your leadership role in your church and your leadership influence beyond your church? This includes your title and what and who you are responsible for leading.
2. How have these developmental factors been important in your leadership formation? Which were most important?
   - Accepting a divine calling to ministry
   - Discovering your unique God-given giftedness and design
   - Developing your gifts and abilities
   - Receiving training and coaching from other leaders, either male or female
   - Learning how to process positive and negative feedback you received about your leadership
   - Maturing spiritually
     Can you correlate any of these factors with your early leadership development or more recent development? Can you associate different factors with different seasons of influence?

3. How have these factors been important for learning how to think like a leader? Which were most important?
   - Developing a leader identity (viewing yourself as a leader)
   - Understanding the need to take risks and developing the courage to take those risks
   - Gaining confidence in your own leadership abilities and decision-making skills
   - Growing in emotional intelligence (self-awareness, self-regulation, motivation, empathy, and social skills)
     Can you correlate any of these factors with your early leadership development or more recent development? Can you associate different factors with different seasons of influence?

4. How have these factors been important for learning to relate to other people as a leader? Which were most important?
   - Discovering your own leadership style and being comfortable in it
   - Developing leadership presence as you relate to others
   - Learning how to negotiate with others for what you need from them
   - Developing strategic (intentional and purposeful, not just default or preferential) relationships
   - Learning to market or brand yourself and social media
     Can you correlate any of these factors with your early leadership development or more recent development? Can you associate different factors with different seasons of influence?

5. How has developing these communication skills affected your leadership development? Which were most important?
   - Learning to use more "masculine" communication styles when communicating to men in leadership conversations (getting to the point quicker, etc.)
   - Training your physical voice to sound different from its natural style for leadership purposes (avoiding uptalking, lowering pitch)
   - Developing public speaking skills
   - Developing preaching and teaching gifts (including learning to study the Bible and theology)
   - Learning how to present a compelling vision and persuading people to adopt it
   - Learning how to have challenging leadership conversations (using direct vs. indirect, aggression vs. passivity, warmth/embracing vs. cool/distancing words)

Can you correlate any of these factors with your early leadership development or more recent development? Can you associate different factors with different seasons of influence?

6. What was the role of egalitarian theology in your leadership development?

   Egalitarian theology can be applied both in the home (husbands and wives are equal in status) and in ministry (men and women are equally gifted and called by God to any kind of ministry leadership).

   • How has your understanding of egalitarian theology and 1 Timothy 2:11–15 influenced your leadership journey?

   "A woman should learn in quietness and full submission. I do not permit a woman to teach or to assume authority over a man; she must be quiet. For Adam was formed first, then Eve. And Adam was not the one deceived; it was the woman who was deceived and became a sinner. But women will be saved through childbearing—if they continue in faith, love and holiness with propriety" (1 Tim. 2:11–15).

   • How has your understanding of egalitarian theology and Ephesians 5:21–23 influenced your marriage?

   "Submit to one another out of reverence for Christ. Wives, submit yourselves to your own husbands as you do to the Lord. For the husband is the head of the wife as Christ is the head of the church, his body, of which he is the Savior" (Eph. 5:21–23).

7. How have these family and home dynamics (or their absence) affected your leadership journey? Which were most important?

   • Marrying a husband who celebrates and supports your leadership, or not marrying

   • Having a husband who carries equal responsibilities with your children and home and makes decisions with you instead of for you

   • Needing extra support with child-rearing (from nannies, daycare, grandparents, etc.)

   • Managing home responsibilities in addition to ministry

   • Caring for the needs of parents, adult children, and other family members

   • Being single

   Can you correlate any of these factors with your early leadership development or more recent development? Can you associate different factors with different seasons of influence?

8. How did these relational factors affect your leadership journey? Which were most important?

   • Having another leader identify leadership potential in you

- Developing strategic relational networks with other female pastors and ministry leaders both inside and outside your church
- Having mentors who spoke into your personal or leadership journey
- Having sponsors who opened doors for you
- Having role models who were examples for you
- Developing a leadership relationship with your husband
- Developing leadership partnerships or mentoring relationships with other men not your husband

  Can you correlate any of these factors with your early leadership development or more recent development? Can you associate different factors with different seasons of influence?

9. How have these ministry expectations affected your leadership journey? Which were most important?

   - Your, your family's, your pastor's, or your church's theological understanding of the role of female leadership in the church
   - Expectations from others or yourself that female ministry and leadership should be for other women in a women's ministry context
   - Expectations from others or yourself about what a female ministry leader should look like or dress like

     Can you correlate any of these factors with your early leadership development or more recent development? Can you associate different factors with different seasons of influence?

10. How have professional/office environmental factors affected your leadership journey? Which were most important?

    - Having flexibility in office hours to be able to take care of family and children's needs
    - Having the freedom to have a nonlinear ministry leadership journey that may have taken seasons off from work for childbirth or other responsibilities
    - Receiving clear and direct feedback about your work and leadership from supervisors
    - Receiving access to leadership opportunities within your organization or outside
    - Receiving recognition for accomplishments within your organization that led to trust in your leadership

      Can you correlate any of these factors with your early leadership development or more recent development? Can you associate different factors with different seasons of influence?

11. How have you handled boundaries with men?

- What do you view as healthy leadership boundaries, and what have you implemented? Do you follow or agree with the Billy Graham rule?
- How do you deal with sexual attraction?
- How have you and your team navigated cross-gendered mentoring or coaching?
- What are your observations from investing in other female ministry leaders?
- What developmental factors have you noticed female leaders navigating that male leaders don't seem to deal with? What issues are unique to a female leader's developmental journey?
- Which factors have you already processed that a young female ministry leader probably has not yet faced?
- How have the possibilities and expectations for developing female ministry leaders changed since your early formation years?

SURVEY QUESTIONS (completed by female leaders of local churches)

1. Are you employed by your local church?
   a. No, volunteer
   b. Yes, part-time
   c. Yes, full-time

2. Which best describes your leadership role in your local church?
   a. Volunteer small group leader
   b. Volunteer team/departmental leader
   c. Paid support/administrative staff
   d. Paid staff departmental leader/director
   e. Staff pastor
   f. Campus or teaching pastor in a multisite church
   g. Executive team member or pastor in a single-site church
   h. Executive team member or pastor in a multisite church
   i. Senior/lead pastor in a single-site church
   j. Senior/lead pastor in a multisite church
   k. Denomination/movement oversight of multiple churches

3. How many social media followers do you have on the platform you are most active on?
   a. Do not use social media
   b. 0–99
   c. 100–299
   d. 300–499
   e. 500–999
   f. 1000–1,999
   g. 2000–2,999
   h. 3,000–4,999
   i. 5,000–9,999
   j. 10,000–14,999
   k. 15,000–24,999
   l. 25,000–39,999
   m. 40,000–74,999
   n. 75,000–99,999
   o. 100,000–499,999
   p. 500,000 or more

4. Is any of the following true?

    a. I have planted a church.

    b. I have planted more than one church.

    c. I have published a book(s).

    d. I have hosted a large conference.

    e. I have preached/taught in churches beyond my local church.

    f. I have influence in churches or organizations in other states or nations.

    g. I carry a leadership role in my denomination or movement.

5. Does your church embrace egalitarian theology by releasing women to preach, teach, pastor, and lead other men and women?

    a. Yes

    b. No

6. Has your church empowered women into high-level decision-making leadership roles (for example, the board, eldership, or executive team)?

    a. Yes

    b. No

7. What is your age?

    a. Under 18 (end of survey)

    b. 18–24

    c. 25–34

    d. 35–44

    e. 45–54

    f. 55–64

    g. 65+

8. What is your current marital status?

    a. Single, never married

    b. Single, previously married

    c. Married

    d. Widowed

Section for Married Participants

1. Select the statements that most closely describe your marriage. If you were previously married, please select the statement that best describes how your marriage worked in the past. If none of these fit, please select "other" and indicate how it differs from these descriptions.

a. I do not consider my marriage to be egalitarian. My husband is the leader of our family, and he sets the course and makes major decisions. My role is to support his leadership inside and outside the home by managing our home and children well. My ministry is secondary to this responsibility.

b. I consider my marriage to be mostly egalitarian, but when we come to a stalemate, I defer to my husband. My husband makes the final call in major decisions, but he values and seeks out my opinions and considers them very important factors in his decision.

c. My marriage is egalitarian. We carry equal authority and responsibility in our home, and we make decisions together, leaning on each other's expertise, gifting, and passions for making decisions. We don't move forward on things until we come to agreement.

d. Other (please specify)

2. How important has it been to develop a leadership relationship with your husband (figuring out how you will partner together in ministry leadership)? (Answer using a sliding scale of 0–100: 0 = not relevant, 50 = helpful, 100 = crucial.)

3. Are you still working to define your leadership partnership with your husband? (Answer using a sliding scale of 0–100: 0 = we don't know how to work together in leadership, 50 = we have made progress but are still figuring out our leadership partnership, 100 = we understand and respect each other's leadership roles well.)

4. Which statement best describes your local church ministry leadership partnership with your spouse? Select all that have applied in various seasons.

a. I am unmarried and lead alone.

b. I am unmarried but lead in equal partnership with another man or woman I am not married to.

c. I lead in my local church, but my husband is more of a behind-the-scenes guy or not directly involved in ministry leadership. He is not connected to my leadership role.

d. I carry a mutual leadership role with my husband—we have the same title and share mutual responsibilities with equal authority.

e. I lead in my local church, and my husband is also in ministry, but we do not lead in the same areas or share responsibilities.

f. I'm not sure. My husband and I are trying to figure this out still.

g. Other (please specify)

5. How important has it been in your leadership development to have a husband who celebrates and supports your ministry and leadership? (Answer using a sliding scale of 0–100: 0 = not relevant, 50 = helpful, 100 = crucial.)

Section for Single Participants

1. How important has it been to your leadership journey as a single female local church leader to create a personal support system? (Answer using a sliding scale of 0–100: 0 = not relevant, 50 = helpful, 100 = crucial.)
2. How important do you consider it to be for you to someday have a husband who celebrates and supports your ministry and leadership? (Answer using a sliding scale of 0–100: 0 = not relevant, 50 = helpful, 100 = crucial.)
3. Which statement best describes your current local church ministry leadership partnership?
   a. I am unmarried and lead alone.
   b. I am unmarried but lead in equal partnership with another man or woman I am not married to.
   c. I am unmarried but lead alongside family members I am not married to.
   d. Other (please specify)
4. Has caring for the needs of parents or other family members affected your leadership journey?
   a. It has not had a measurable effect.
   b. Rarely have I needed to adapt my leadership responsibilities to my extended family.
   c. Sometimes my church responsibilities have had to wait while I take care of family.
   d. I frequently have had to work my leadership around my family's needs and expectations.

Section for Mothers (questions 1-81) and All Participants (questions 8-81)

1. Do you have children?
   a. Yes
   b. No (skip to question 8)

2. In which stages of development are your children?

a. I have very young children not yet in school.

b. I have school-age children.

c. I have preteens or teenagers.

d. I have adult children at home.

e. I have adult children living independently.

3. How important has it been to your leadership journey for you to have extra support with child-rearing from paid support, friends, or family? (Answer using a sliding scale of 0–100: 0 = not relevant, 50 = helpful, 100 = crucial.)

4. How important has it been to your leadership to have freedom to take seasons off from leading (due to family needs) and come back? (Answer using a sliding scale of 0–100: 0 = not relevant, 50 = helpful, 100 = crucial.)

5. How important has it been to your ministry longevity to have flexibility in your office hours to take care of your family and children's needs? (Answer using a sliding scale of 0–100: 0 = not relevant, 50 = helpful, 100 = crucial.)

6. My egalitarian marriage has empowered my ministry because my husband carries equal weight at home and in parenting and supports my ministry.

a. Agree

b. Neither agree nor disagree

c. Disagree

d. Strongly disagree

e. Not applicable

7. Have you felt mom guilt as a result of struggling to meet your own standards for ministry and family balance?

a. Agree

b. Neither agree nor disagree

c. Disagree

d. Strongly disagree

8. How important has it been to your leadership journey to have extra support with home management (from people other than your husband)? (Answer using a sliding scale of 0–100: 0 = not relevant, 50 = helpful, 100 = crucial.)

9. Which statements best describe the ministry leadership mentors you have had?

   a. I have wanted but not had ministry leadership mentors or coaches who have made significant impact on my development.

   b. I have had mostly male ministry leadership mentors and coaches.

   c. I have had mostly female ministry leadership mentors and coaches.

   d. I have had both men and women who mentored or coached me in ministry leadership.

   e. I have not felt like I needed ministry leadership mentors.

   f. I have had a spiritual mentor/pastor(s) but not a leadership coach.

   g. I have had a leadership coach but not a spiritual mentor/pastor.

   h. I have had a therapist but not a ministry leadership mentor or coach.

10. How important have leadership role models been in your development (leaders you could identify with and see yourself becoming like)? (Answer using a sliding scale of 0–100: 0 = not relevant, 50 = helpful, 100 = crucial.)

11. How important has it been to your leadership development to receive clear and direct feedback about your work from supervisors? (Answer using a sliding scale of 0–100: 0 = not relevant, 50 = helpful, 100 = crucial.)

12. How important has it been to your leadership development to have access to leadership opportunities within your organization or outside? (Answer using a sliding scale of 0–100: 0 = not relevant, 50 = helpful, 100 = crucial.)

13. How important has having another leader identify leadership potential in you been in your leadership journey? (Answer using a sliding scale of 0–100: 0 = not relevant, 50 = helpful, 100 = crucial.)

14. How important have sponsors been in your leadership journey (a sponsor opens doors of opportunity for your leadership)? (Answer using a sliding scale of 0–100: 0 = not relevant, 50 = helpful, 100 = crucial.)

15. How important have mentors been in your leadership development? (Answer using a sliding scale of 0–100: 0 = not relevant, 50 = helpful, 100 = crucial.)

16. How important has it been to your influence development to receive public recognition for your accomplishments within your organization? (Answer using a sliding scale of 0–100: 0 = not relevant, 50 = helpful, 100 = crucial.)

17. Does your church leadership team value and encourage you to share your opinions and ideas?

    a. Rarely or never does anyone ask my opinion or for my idea.

    b. My bosses have asked for my opinions and ideas.

    c. My peers have asked for my opinions and ideas.

    d. The team I'm leading has asked for my opinions and ideas.

    e. My ministry partner has asked for my opinions and ideas.

18. Have any of these factors been hindrances or important to your leadership journey?

    a. #MeToo or #ChurchToo movement

    b. Gender discrimination in ministry settings

    c. Wage inequality

    d. Sexual harassment or abuse from other ministry leaders

    e. Difficulties obtaining cross-gendered mentoring or sponsorship

    f. Theological opposition

    g. Need for frequent travel that made family dynamics difficult

    h. Regional cultural opposition

    i. Rigid ministry work environments

    j. Other (please specify)

19. How important has obeying a divine calling to ministry been in your leadership formation? (Answer using a sliding scale of 0–100: 0 = not relevant, 50 = helpful, 100 = crucial.)

20. How important has it been in your leadership formation to develop self-awareness of your unique God-given giftedness and design? (Answer using a sliding scale of 0–100: 0 = not relevant, 50 = helpful, 100 = crucial.)

21. How would you rate your current self-awareness of your God-given giftedness and design? (Answer using a sliding scale of 0–100: 0 = not at all developed, 100 = very well developed.)

22. How important has developing your skills, gifts, and abilities been in your leadership formation? (Answer using a sliding scale of 0–100: 0 = not relevant, 50 = helpful, 100 = crucial.)

23. How would you rate your current progress in developing your leadership skills, gifts, and abilities? (Answer using a sliding scale of 0–100: 0 = not at all developed, 100 = very well developed.)

24. How important has developing a leader identity (viewing yourself as a leader) been in the process of learning to think like a leader?

(Answer using a sliding scale of 0–100: 0 = not relevant, 50 = helpful, 100 = crucial.)

25. How would you rate your progress in developing a leader identity (viewing yourself as a leader)? (Answer using a sliding scale of 0–100: 0 = not at all developed, 100 = very well developed.)

26. To what extent have you been pioneering a new female leadership role or identity that you have never seen or heard of (perhaps before you stepped into your leadership role, you saw only men in this particular type of role)? (Answer using a sliding scale of 0–100: 0 = I've pioneered a leadership role that I've only ever seen a man do, 100 = I am emulating a female leader who I respect.)

27. How important has understanding the need to take risks and developing the courage to take those risks been in the process of learning to think like a leader? (Answer using a sliding scale of 0–100: 0 = not relevant, 50 = helpful, 100 = crucial.)

28. How would you rate your current development of calculated risk-taking in ministry leadership? (Answer using a sliding scale of 0–100: 0 = not at all developed, 100 = very well developed.)

29. How important has gaining confidence in your own leadership and decision-making skills been in the process of learning to think like a leader? (Answer using a sliding scale of 0–100: 0 = not relevant, 50 = helpful, 100 = crucial.)

30. How would you rate your current development of confidence in your own leadership and decision-making skills? (Answer using a sliding scale of 0–100: 0 = not at all developed, 100 = very well developed.)

31. How important has learning to avoid comparison to other leaders been in the process of learning to think like a leader? (Answer using a sliding scale of 0–100: 0 = not relevant, 50 = helpful, 100 = crucial.)

32. How often do you compare yourself to other leaders? (Answer using a sliding scale of 0–100: 0 = I frequently compare myself to other leaders, 50 = I sometimes compare myself to other leaders, 100 = I rarely compare myself to other leaders.)

33. How important has growing in empathy been in the process of learning to think like a leader? (Answer using a sliding scale of 0–100: 0 = not relevant, 50 = helpful, 100 = crucial.)

34. How well developed is your use of empathy in leadership? (Answer using a sliding scale of 0–100: 0 = not at all developed, 100 = very well developed.)

35. How important has growing your social skills been in the process of learning to think like a leader? (Answer using a sliding scale of 0–100: 0 = not relevant, 50 = helpful, 100 = crucial.)

36. How well developed are your social skills in ministry leadership? (Answer using a sliding scale of 0–100: 0 = not at all developed, 100 = very well developed.)

37. How important has it been to learn to self-manage your own emotions and reactions in the process of learning to think like a leader? (Answer using a sliding scale of 0–100: 0 = not relevant, 50 = helpful, 100 = crucial.)

38. How would you rate your self-management of your own emotions and reactions? (Answer using a sliding scale of 0–100: 0 = not at all developed, 100 = very well developed.)

39. How important has it been to learn how to be authentically yourself in learning to think like a leader? (Answer using a sliding scale of 0–100: 0 = not relevant, 50 = helpful, 100 = crucial.)

40. How well aligned is your leadership persona with your authentic self? (Answer using a sliding scale of 0–100: 0 = not aligned, 50 = somewhat aligned, 100 = well aligned.)

41. How important has it been to learn to process criticism well in learning to think like a leader? (Answer using a sliding scale of 0–100: 0 = not relevant, 50 = helpful, 100 = crucial.)

42. How would you rate your ability to process criticism into personal or organizational growth? (Answer using a sliding scale of 0–100: 0 = not at all developed, 100 = very well developed.)

43. How important have discovering your own leadership style and being comfortable with it been for learning to relate to others as a leader? (Answer using a sliding scale of 0–100: 0 = not relevant, 50 = helpful, 100 = crucial.)

44. How well developed are your awareness of and comfort with your own leadership style? (Answer using a sliding scale of 0–100: 0 = not at all developed, 100 = very well developed.)

45. Is your personality naturally more dominant and aggressive or gentle and accommodating? (Answer using a sliding scale of 0–100: 0 = dominant/aggressive, 100 = peaceful/accommodating.)

46. How important has it been to adapt your natural personality style in order to lead others who are different? (Answer using a sliding scale of 0–100: 0 = not relevant, 50 = helpful, 100 = crucial.)

47. How would you rate your ability to adapt your natural personality in order to lead others who are different? (Answer using a sliding scale of 0–100: 0 = not at all developed, 100 = very well developed.)

48. How important has developing observable leadership presence been in learning to relate to others as a leader (leadership presence could be defined as your personal power or charisma or leadership gravitas)? (Answer using a sliding scale of 0–100: 0 = not relevant, 50 = helpful, 100 = crucial.)

49. How well developed is your leadership presence? (Answer using a sliding scale of 0–100: 0 = not at all developed, 100 = very well developed.)

50. Which statement best describes your experience with egalitarian theology (in brief, egalitarian theology is the idea that God calls and gifts women to teach and hold leadership roles without any limits)?

    a. I don't know much about egalitarian theology and haven't needed it to lead in my church context.

    b. I wish I understood egalitarian theology better and sometimes feel hampered or uneasy that I can't articulate it to others when they ask me about what the Bible says about women leading.

    c. I had to learn egalitarian theology to feel an inner release to do ministry. I learned it before I started leading in my local church.

    d. I learned egalitarian theology because I had to reconcile my sense of calling and leadership gifting to ministry leadership with my theology. I learned it in the early years of leading.

    e. My learning and teaching egalitarian theology have been important in helping others accept my teaching ministry. I did not learn it until later in my ministry journey when I was challenged by people who could not receive ministry from a female.

    f. I was raised by parents and/or a church that taught me egalitarian theology.

    g. Other (please specify)

51. What do you believe God wants from female leaders in the church? How does egalitarian theology empower your female leadership? (open-ended response)

52. How important has learning to negotiate with others for what you need from them been in learning to relate to others as a leader? (Answer using a sliding scale of 0–100: 0 = not relevant, 50 = helpful, 100 = crucial.)

53. How would you rate your ability to negotiate with others for what you need from them? (Answer using a sliding scale of 0–100: 0 = not at all developed, 100 = very well developed.)

54. How important has learning to market yourself or personal branding been in learning to relate to others as a leader? (Answer using a sliding scale of 0–100: 0 = not relevant, 50 = helpful, 100 = crucial.)

55. How well would you rate your ability to market yourself or communicate your personal brand? (Answer using a sliding scale of 0–100: 0 = not at all developed, 100 = very well developed.)

56. How important has learning to use social media for ministry and influence been in learning to relate to others as a leader? (Answer using a sliding scale of 0–100: 0 = not relevant, 50 = helpful, 100 = crucial.)

57. How would you rate your ability to use social media for ministry and influence? (Answer using a sliding scale of 0–100: 0 = not at all developed, 100 = very well developed.)

58. What are your primary social media uses?

   a. Viewing other people's lives

   b. Giving people a glimpse of my daily life

   c. Encouraging others and spreading hope

   d. Spreading a message/platform for my Voice

   e. Teaching the Bible/education

   f. Networking with other leaders

   g. Keeping in touch with extended family and friends

   h. Engaging in conversations about hot topics

   i. Monetizing through sponsorships and paid ads

   j. Creating beauty and art

   k. Reading/viewing news

   l. Other (please specify)

59. As you have developed communication skills for leading, how important has it been to use more stereotypically "feminine" communication styles when communicating to women in leadership conversations (checking in about feelings and family first, softening language and tone, using indirect, gentler approaches)? (Answer using a sliding scale of 0–100: 0 = not relevant, 50 = helpful, 100 = crucial.)

60. As you have developed communication skills for leading, how important has it been to use more stereotypically "masculine" communication styles when communicating to men in leadership conversations (getting to the point quicker, etc.)? (Answer using a sliding scale of 0–100: 0 = not relevant, 50 = helpful, 100 = crucial.)

61. As you have developed communication skills for leading, how important has it been to train your physical voice to sound different from its natural style (avoiding uptalking, slowing down, lowering the pitch of your voice)? (Answer using a sliding scale of 0–100: 0 = not relevant, 50 = helpful, 100 = crucial.)

62. Have you found communication style preferences to be more an issue of gender or personality? (Answer using a sliding scale of 0–100: 0 = gender, 100 = personality.)

63. How important has developing public speaking skills been in learning to communicate to others as a leader in the church? (Answer using a sliding scale of 0–100: 0 = not relevant, 50 = helpful, 100 = crucial.)

64. How well developed are your public speaking skills in ministry leadership? (Answer using a sliding scale of 0–100: 0 = not at all developed, 100 = very well developed.)

65. How important has it been to developing leadership influence to cultivate preaching and teaching gifts, including learning to study the Bible and theology? (Answer using a sliding scale of 0–100: 0 = not relevant, 50 = helpful, 100 = crucial.)

66. How well developed are your preaching and teaching gifts? (Answer using a sliding scale of 0–100: 0 = not at all developed, 100 = very well developed.)

67. How well developed is your Bible and theology knowledge? (Answer using a sliding scale of 0–100: 0 = not at all developed, 100 = very well developed.)

68. How important has it been to developing leadership influence to learn how to present a compelling vision and persuade people to adopt it? (Answer using a sliding scale of 0–100: 0 = not relevant, 50 = helpful, 100 = crucial.)

69. How well developed are your skills for presenting a compelling vision and persuading people to adopt it? (Answer using a sliding scale of 0–100: 0 = not at all developed, 100 = very well developed.)

70. How important has it been to learn how to have challenging leadership conversations (balancing indirect vs. direct communication, aggression vs. passivity, warmth vs. coolness)? (Answer using a sliding scale of 0–100: 0 = not relevant, 50 = helpful, 100 = crucial.)

71. How would you rate your ability to have challenging leadership interpersonal conversations? (Answer using a sliding scale of 0–100: 0 = not at all developed, 100 = very well developed.)

72. How important to developing your leadership influence has it been to learn to verbalize and defend your perspectives? (Answer using a sliding scale of 0–100: 0 = not relevant, 50 = helpful, 100 = crucial.)

73. How comfortable are you with verbalizing and defending your leadership perspectives? (Answer using a sliding scale of 0–100: 0 = not at all comfortable, 100 = very comfortable.)

74. In developing your leadership influence, how important has it been to cultivate strategic relationships with stakeholders (intentional and purposeful, not just default or preferential)? (Answer using a sliding scale of 0–100: 0 = not relevant, 50 = helpful, 100 = crucial.)

75. How would you rate your ability to cultivate strategic relationships with stakeholders (intentional and purposeful, not just default or preferential)? (Answer using a sliding scale of 0–100: 0 = not at all developed, 100 = very well developed.)

76. How well developed are your strategic relational networks with other female pastors and ministry leaders both inside and outside your church? (Answer using a sliding scale of 0–100: 0 = not at all developed, 100 = very well developed.)

77. How important has it been to develop ministry leadership relationships with men who are not your husband (this might include men who mentored you or partnered with you in leadership or men you mentored)? (Answer using a sliding scale of 0–100: 0 = not relevant, 50 = helpful, 100 = crucial.)

78. As a leader, how do you approach boundaries with men?

   a. I follow the Billy Graham rule: unmarried men and women should never be alone together. I do not have personal relationships with men I'm not married or related to.

   b. I set clear boundaries in relationships with all men, or with women with same-sex attraction (for example, I do not ride alone in cars with men I'm not married to).

   c. I use self-awareness and set boundaries in relationships with people I am attracted to, particularly when I am vulnerable.

   d. I do not have set boundaries and don't often think about them. Preset boundaries can be too limiting and restrictive.

   e. Men in my world set boundaries that I have to respect. I don't feel as if I choose these boundaries.

   f. Other (please specify)

79. How important has it been to your leadership development to learn how to develop and empower other leaders inside your organization? (Answer using a sliding scale of 0–100: 0 = not relevant, 50 = helpful, 100 = crucial.)

80. What developmental factors have you noticed female leaders navigating that male leaders don't seem to deal with? Which issues are unique to a female leader's developmental journey? (open-ended response)

81. Are there any issues that were important to your leadership development that this survey did not ask about? If so, what are they? (open-ended response)

STUDY INTERVIEW AND FOCUS GROUP PARTICIPANT DESCRIPTORS

Participant descriptors are coded in the chart below. Each participant received a series of tags indicating the data collection methodology, church, marital status, McKinney leadership level (see page 39 in chap. 2), and marriage leadership partnership (see page 87 and following in chap. 6).

Codes for the chart below:
FI = female interview
FG = female focus group
MI = male interview
C = church
M = married
S = single

I have grouped generations as baby boomer: 1955–1964, Gen X: 1965–1974, xennial: 1975–1984, millennial: 1985–1994.

Participant Code	Church Code	Number of Campuses in Church	Title	Marital Status	McKinney Level of Leadership	Birth Year / Age / Generation	Marriage Type
FEMALE PARTICIPANTS							
FI1	C1	1	Senior Pastor / Founder	M	5	1960 / 60 / Baby Boomer	3
FI2	C2	6	Lead Pastor / Founder	M	5	1978 / 41 / Xennial	3
FI3	C3	5	Senior Pastor / Founder	M	5	1975 / 45 / Xennial	2
FI4	C4	37	Executive Pastor	M	5	1961 / 59 / Baby Boomer	4
FI5	C5	5	Senior Pastor / Founder	M	5	1972 / 47 / Gen X	2
FI6	C6	2	Senior Pastor / Founder	M	4	1959 / 60 / Baby Boomer	3
FI7	C7	7	Senior Pastor / Founder	M	4	1963 / 57 / Baby Boomer	1
FI8	C8	1	Lead Pastor / Founder	M	4	1979 / 40 / Xennial	2
FI13	C15	10	Campus Pastor	M	4	1972 / 47 / Gen X	4
FI12	C12	3	Lead Pastor	M	3	1987 / 32 / Millennial	1
FI11	C11	2	Lead Pastor	M	4	1978 / 41 / Xennial	2
FI10	C10	5	Executive Pastor	M	3	1982 / 37 / Xennial	3
FI9	C4	37	Campus Pastor	M	3	1978 / 41 / Xennial	3
FG2.1	C9	10	Campus Pastor	M	3	1982 / 37 / Xennial	2
FG1.2	C13	2	Lead Pastor / Founder	M	4	1970 / 50 / Gen X	1
FG4.1	C14	1	Executive Pastor	S	4	1971 / 48 / Gen X	n/a
FG1.1	C3	5	Campus Pastor	M	3	1977 / 42 / Xennial	2
FG2.2	C10	5	Executive Assistant	S	2	1991 / 29 / Millennial	n/a
FG2.3	C9	10	Campus Pastor	M	3	1975 / 45 / Xennial	2
FG4.2	C16	5	Executive Pastor	M	3	1968 / 52 / Gen X	4
FG2.4	C17	1	Executive Director	M	3	1978 / 41 / Xennial	4
FG4.3	C18	1	Associate Pastor	M	2	1972 / 47 / Gen X	4
FG4.4	C19	5	Executive Director	M	3	1977 / 42 / Xennial	4
FG3.1	C20	1	Executive Creative Pastor	M	3	1980 / 40 / Xennial	4
FG2.5	C15	10	Campus Pastor	M	3	1987 / 32 / Millennial	4
FG3.2	C21	2	Creative / Youth Pastor	M	2	1986 / 34 / Millennial	4
FG1.3	C22	2	Children's Director	M	2	1985 / 35 / Millennial	4
FG3.3	C12	3	Campus Director	S	3	1974 / 45 / Gen X	n/a
FG4.5	C23	10	Executive Pastor	M	3	1975 / 44 / Xennial	4
FG1.4	C22	2	Personal Assistant	M	2	1990 / 29 / Millennial	4
FG2.6	C12	3	Student Ministries Pastor	M	3	1972 / 48 / Gen X	3
MALE PARTICIPANTS							
MI1	C5	5	Senior Pastor / Founder	M	5	1975 / 45 / Xennial	2
MI2	C10	5	Senior Pastor / Founder	M	5	1959 / 60 / Baby Boomer	1
MI3	C15	10	Senior Pastor	M	5	1971 / 48 / Gen X	1
MI4	C12	3	Senior Pastor	M	4	1987 / 32 / Millennial	1
MI5	C24	2	Senior Pastor / Founder	M	4	1980 / 40 / Xennial	2
MI6	C3	5	Senior Pastor/Founder	M	5	1970 / 50 / Gen X	2

APPENDIX D

STUDY SURVEY PARTICIPANT DESCRIPTORS

Are you employed by your local church? | Which best describes your leadership role in your local church?

#	no, I am a volunteer leader	yes, part-time	yes, full-time	volunteer small group leader	volunteer team / department leader	paid support / administrative staff	paid staff departmental leader/ director	staff pastor	campus or teaching pastor in a multisite church	executive team member or pastor in a single-site church	executive team member or pastor in a multisite church	senior/lead pastor in a single-site church	senior/ lead pastor in a multisite church	denomination/ movement oversight of multiple churches
1	X				X									
2	X			X										
3	X				X									
4	X				X									
5	X		X			X								
6	X									X				
7		X					X							
8			X			X								
9			X			X								
10			X							X				
11			X					X						
12		X					X							
13			X				X							
14			X				X							
15			X				X							
16			X					X						
17			X							X				
18			X					X						
19			X					X						
20			X			X								
21			X					X						
22	X											X		
23			X							X				

	Are you employed by your local church?			Which best describes your leadership role in your local church?										
	no, I am a volunteer leader	yes, part-time	yes, full-time	volunteer small group leader	volunteer team / department leader	paid support / administrative staff	paid staff departmental leader/ director	staff pastor	campus or teaching pastor in a multisite church	executive team member or pastor in a single-site church	executive team member or pastor in a multisite church	senior/lead pastor in a single-site church	senior/ lead pastor in a multisite church	denomination/ movement oversight of multiple churches
24			x					x						
25			x				x							
26			x				x	x						
27			x				x							
28			x					x						
29			x						x					
30			x								x			
31			x						x					
32			x								x			
33			x						x					
34			x								x			
35		x								x				
36			x					x						
37		x								x				
38		x									x			
39			x							x				
40			x							x				
41			x							x				
42			x								x			
43	x							x						
44		x											x	
45			x											x
46	x											x		
47			x										x	

How many social media followers do you have on the platform you are most active on? (Four participants didn't answer this question.)

	Do not use social media	0–99	100–299	300–499	500–999	1,000–1,999	2,000–2,999	3,000–4,999	5,000–9,999	10,000–14,999	15,000–24,999	25,000–39,999	40,000–74,999	75,000–99,999	100,000–499,999	500,000 or more
1					x											
2						x										
3					x											
4					x											
5			x													
6					x											
7		x														
8					x											
9						x										
10					x	x										
11					x											
12			x													
13					x											
14							x									
15						x										
16							x									
17						x										
18		x														
19					x											
20			x													
21					x											
22				x												

How many social media followers do you have on the platform you are most active on? (Four participants didn't answer this question.)

	Do not use social media	0–99	100–299	300–499	500–999	1,000–1,999	2,000–2,999	3,000–4,999	5,000–9,999	10,000–14,999	15,000–24,999	25,000–39,999	40,000–74,999	75,000–99,999	100,000–499,999	500,000 or more
23					x											
24						x										
25						x										
26						x										
27					x											
28						x										
29						x										
30								x								
31					x											
32									x							
33					x											
34							x									
35			x													
36								x								
37						x										
38				x												
39					x											
40							x									
41						x										
42							x									
43													x			

ANALYSIS OF STUDY PARTICIPANTS' LEADERSHIP AUTHORITY

Participant Code	Leads Church Members	Leads Volunteers	On Paid Church Staff	Leads Paid Staff	Speaks on Platform	Preaches in Sunday Church	Executive-Level Pastor / Director	Campus or Senior Pastor of One Location	Campus / Lead Pastor of Multiple Sites
FEMALE PARTICIPANTS									
FI1	x	x	x	x	x	x	x	x	
FI2	x	x	x	x	x	x	x		
FI3	x	x	x	x	x	x	x		x
FI4	x .	x	x	x	x	x	x	x	
FI5	x	x	x	x	x	x	x		x
FI6	x	x	x	x	x	x	x	x	x
FI7	x	x	x	x	x	x	x	x	
FI8	x	x	x	x	x	x	x	x	
FG 1.1	x	x	x	x	x	x	x	x	
FI9	x	x	x	x	x	x	x	x	x
FG 2.1	x	x	x	x	x	x	x	x	
FI10	x	x	x	x	x	x	x	x	
FI11	x	x	x	x	x	x	x	x	x
FI12	x	x		x	x	x		x	x
FG1.2	x	x	x	x	x	x	x	x	x
FG4.1	x	x	x	x	x	x	x		
FI13	x	x	x	x	x	x	x	x	
FG2.2	x	x	x						
FG2.3	x	x	x	x	x	x	x	x	
FG4.2	x	x	x	x	x	x	x		x
FG2.4	x	x	x	x	x		x		
FG4.3	x	x	x		x	x	x		
FG4.4	x	x	x	x			x		
FG3.1	x	x	x	x	x		x		
FG2.5	x	x	x	x	x	x	x	x	
FG3.2	x	x	x		x	x			
FG1.3	x	x	x	x	x	x			
FG3.3	x	x	x	x	x	x			
FG4.5	x	x	x	x	x	x	x		
FG1.4	x	x	x						
FG2.6	x	x	x	x	x		x		
MALE PARTICIPANTS									
MI1	x	x	x	x	x	x	x	x	x
MI2	x	x	x	x	x	x	x	x	x
MI3	x	x	x	x	x	x	x	x	x
MI4	x	x	x	x	x	x	x	x	x
MI5	x	x	x	x	x	x	x	x	x
MI6	x	x	x	x	x	x	x	x	x

Participant Code	Senior Pastor of Multisite	Denominational or Network Leadership Role	Preaching or Consulting Ministry beyond Local Church	International Influence	Published Author or Large Conference Host	Number of Instagram Followers	McKinney Level of Leadership
FEMALE PARTICIPANTS							
FI1		x	x	x	x	42,100	5
FI2	x		x	x	x	23,900	5
FI3	x	x	x	x	x	15,500	5
FI4		x	x	x	x	13,500	5
FI5	x				x	12,900	5
FI6	x			x	x	11,200	4
FI7	x				x	4,564	4
FI8		x	x		x	4,010	4
FG 1.1						3,433	3
FI9						3,036	3
FG 2.1			x			2,694	3
FI10		x	x		x	2,524	3
FI11		x				2,173	4
FI12	x		x			1,858	3
FG1.2	x		x			1,784	4
FG4.1		x				1,373	4
FI13		x	x			1,112	4
FG2.2						1,015	2
FG2.3						904	3
FG4.2			x			890	3
FG2.4						832	3
FG4.3			x			749	2
FG4.4						742	3
FG3.1						575	3
FG2.5						457	3
FG3.2						434	2
FG1.3						388	2
FG3.3						305	3
FG4.5						202	3
FG1.4						199	2
FG2.6						0	3
MALE PARTICIPANTS							
MI1	x	x	x	x		17,700	5
MI2	x	x	x	x	x	19,500	5
MI3	x	x	x			5,471	5
MI4	x		x			2,166	4
MI5	x	x	x			5,269	4
MI6	x	x	x	x	x	13,100	5

APPENDIX F

STUDY ASSUMPTIONS, DELIMITATIONS, LIMITATIONS, RELIABILITY, AND VALIDITY

ASSUMPTIONS

As a researcher, I brought some assumptions into my work. I am a Christian Pentecostal pastor, which means I place a high value on the Bible and use a hermeneutic of trust for a biblical interpretation. I have an egalitarian theological viewpoint of marriage and ministry, which is also a bias I bring to my research. I recognize that God has already raised up women who function as effective leaders in the church, which means I had an existing population that could be studied. However, even though God sovereignly forms leaders, I believe that leadership can and should be cultivated through training, mentoring, and networks. I believe that some churches are effectively training, supporting, and empowering female leaders and that these environments should be explored.

My biggest assumption is that the church will be stronger and the kingdom will advance with more female leadership. This made the years of work on this study worth the personal cost. I love local churches and believe they are the kingdom outposts God has established in the world. They do the hard, slow work of establishing the lordship of Jesus in the lives and communities they touch. I don't believe that women need to leave the church for their leadership to thrive. Churches desperately need women leaders because God's plan for kingdom advancement is centered in the work of local churches.

DELIMITATIONS AND LIMITATIONS

To make this study focused (and doable—I was a solo researcher), I needed to narrow the scope. So while I explored all the theological viewpoints that impact female leadership development in the church, this study does not engage the theological debate about whether women should or shouldn't lead. I researched only churches that hold an egalitarian theological perspective. There are complementarian churches that empower women (to a point) that are effectively developing women leaders, but this study does not examine those environments. Furthermore, I did not study women or men leading in complementarian theological environments. All the participants practice egalitarian theology, so there was no context for debating complementarian theology.

I delimited this study to egalitarian churches in Australia, Canada, and the United States. Because the center and origin of my denominational context is in Australia, I needed to include Australia in my sample. Furthermore, I did not study cross-cultural dynamics in female leadership development, even though these dynamics exist within local churches. Issues of race and ethnicity and female leadership development in the majority world are also beyond the scope of this study. I delimited this study to heterosexual, cisgender female leaders in ministry.

I did not explore best practices for male leadership development that may overlap with women's leadership development needs but delimited the research to issues that are specific to women only.

As a researcher, I was limited by my natural bias. I fit the qualifications for study participants, and I have already formed strong opinions. It would have been nearly impossible for me to keep my bias from affecting the questions I asked and how I asked them. However, I received feedback about my questions before asking them, and I refrained from expressing my opinions in conversations with participants. Even when I agreed with respondents in focus groups, I invited alternate perspectives to attempt to compensate for my bias. In interviews, I repeated respondents' answers to make sure I was correctly understanding them to prevent filtering answers through my bias.

RELIABILITY AND VALIDITY

I needed to be very careful about obtaining reliability and validity. While this study did not achieve complete saturation, I could easily identify significant trends. This increased the reliability and the likelihood that the results could be reproduced. I carefully followed the interview and focus group guides but allowed the follow-up prompts to vary to get at the information I needed. I minimized the impact of bias by getting multiple perspectives about my interview guides and conducting pretest interviews and a focus group. My final statements do not generalize findings to all female church leaders in egalitarian contexts but pertain to the groups in my sample. The additional survey method I conducted should improve the reliability of this study.

Active interviews allowed each respondent to create a narrative as a storyteller in collaboration with the interviewer.[1] Active interviews potentially biased the results to some extent, however, since I introduced ideas that might have been true for participants' development and asked them to respond to them. The participants may have withheld aspects of their leadership development because I did not ask about those issues specifically. I asked open-ended questions to conclude the interviews, inviting participants to bring up new issues. Several new topics came up as vitally important that were not included in my prompts, which makes me hopeful that the format of the questions did not bias the answers significantly. I compared and contrasted data from each of my methods to ensure that I obtained accurate, valid findings.

To prepare for these methods, I pretested my instruments to ensure reliable and valid results. This gave me valuable feedback that I used to refine my questions. The pretest participants are not included in the findings.

I had to be careful with the respondents from my own church because of personal relationships and power differentials and the likelihood of these skewing my data. I used the focus group of my female employees as a pretest, and I used the interview with my female senior pastor as a pretest rather than including it in my sample. I gave them permission to speak freely and confidentially, not saying what they believed I wanted to hear, without risk of a loss of my esteem or favor. This protected the study from being skewed by the power dynamics around me personally, making the findings more reliable and valid.

1. Holstein and Gubrium, *Active Interview*, 28, 37.

INDEX